ROMANS
A Verse-by-Verse Study

ROMANS
The Greatest Treatise Ever Written

A Verse-by-Verse Study

Ellet J. Waggoner

CFI Book Division
Gordonsville, Tennessee

Copyright © 2019 by CFI Book Division

Cover and interior design by CFI Graphic Design

All Rights Reserved. No part of this book may be reproduced in any form or by any electronic or mechanical means including information storage and retrieval systems without permission from its publisher, CFI Book Division.

Published by CFI Book Division
P.O. Box 159, Gordonsville, Tennessee 38563

ISBN-10: 0-9975122-5-3
ISBN-13: 978-0-9975122-5-0

Printed in the United States of America

Typeset in 11.5/13.5 Minion Pro

An appeal from the Apostle Paul—

"Consider what I say, for the Lord shall give thee understanding in all things."

2 Timothy 2:7

CONTENTS

    From the Author 9
1. The Power of God Is In the Gospel 11
2. The Sin of Others Is Our Sin, Too. 39
3. The Free Grace of God 61
4. Believing God's Tremendous Promise 81
5. Grace Which Much More Abounds 95
6. Christ's Yoke Is Easy, His Burden Light. 111
7. Married to the Wrong Man 119
8. Glorious Freedom From a Bad "Marriage". 129
9. Who Are True Israelites?. 153
10. Glad Tidings of Good Things 163
11. All Israel Shall Be Saved 171
12. How Righteousness by Faith Becomes Practical. 179
13. The Believer and the Civil Government 185
14. God Is the Only Judge 193
15. "Praise the Lord, All You Gentiles!". 201
16. Personal Greetings 211
    Appendix A 213

Note to Reader
From the Author

Source for these studies is from: E.J. Waggoner, "Studies in Romans," *The Signs of the Times* 21, 41 (October 17, 1895), pp. 2-4 (642-644).

Under this heading it is proposed to conduct, as nearly as can be done in writing, a class study of the Epistle to the Romans. It is designed to be literally a study, and it is hoped that the "study" will not be all on the part of the writer, but that the readers of the *Signs of the Times* will be encouraged to acquire for themselves an acquaintance with an epistle that is doubtless the greatest treatise ever written.

In each number the text for the week will be quoted, in order to facilitate the study. The reader, however, should use his Bible freely. Read the verses to be studied very frequently, and form the habit of questioning each verse, after the manner indicated below, only more closely. In this way the force of the words, used by the apostle will stand out clearly, and the thought will be fixed in the mind, in the exact words of the Scripture.

Inspiration assures us that in all of the epistles of Paul there are "some things hard to be understood." 2 Peter 3:16. Perhaps this is the case with the Epistle to the Romans in a greater degree than with any other epistle. But they are not impossible to be understood, and it is only the "unlearned and unstable" who wrest them unto their own destruction who thus miss the point of Paul's writings. They who have a desire to understand and who read the simple promises of the Bible with profit, will not be among that number.

In beginning this study it will be an encouragement to the reader if he will remember that it is simply a letter written to the church in Rome. We can not suppose that the congregation in Rome differed from the great body of Christians in general, and of them we read that "not many wise men after the flesh, not many mighty, not many noble, are called." 1 Corinthians 1:26. The truest followers of Jesus have always been among "the common people." So in the church in Rome there were doubtless shopkeepers, artisans, day laborers, carpenters, gardeners, etc., and many servants in the families of wealthy citizens, together with a few who might hold some position of rank. When we consider that it was confidently expected that people of this sort would understand the letter, we may be encouraged to believe that the same class of people can understand it now.

Paul's exhortation and assurance to Timothy form the best guide to the study of all the epistles, and the whole Bible as well. "Consider what I say, for the Lord shall give thee understanding in all things." "God is his own interpreter." The words of the Bible explain the Bible. This is why you should closely question the text so as to get at exactly what is said, in connection with what precedes and follows. Nothing can take the place of prayerful meditation upon the exact words of the Bible. By this means the most unlearned in this world's wisdom may become mighty in the Scriptures. The Lord has said just what he means, and the only way to find out just what he means is to become thoroughly familiar with just what he says, just as he says it.

The notes that accompany the text in this study are designed to fix the student's attention more closely upon the word, and for the benefit of the casual reader. That the study of this epistle may be greatly blessed in those who pursue it, and that the word may become more highly esteemed by all, because of the increased light that the Holy Spirit may cause to flash from it, is the earnest prayer of the writer.

The Salutation—Romans 1:1-17

"Paul, a servant of Jesus Christ, called to be an apostle, separated unto the Gospel of God (which he had promised afore, by his prophets in the Holy Scriptures), concerning his Son Jesus Christ our Lord, which was made of the seed of David according to the flesh; and declared to be the Son of God with power, according to the Spirit of holiness, by the resurrection from the dead; by whom we have received grace and apostleship, for obedience to the faith among all nations, for his name; among whom are ye also the called of Jesus Christ; to all that be in Rome, beloved of God, called to be saints: Grace to you, and peace, from God our Father and the Lord Jesus Christ."

Chapter 1

The Power of God Is In the Gospel

The Salutation—Romans 1:1-7

1 Paul, a servant of Jesus Christ, called to be an apostle, separated unto the gospel of God 2 (which He had promised afore, by His prophets in the Holy Scriptures), 3 concerning His Son Jesus Christ our Lord, which was made of the seed of David according to the flesh; 4 and declared to be the Son of God with power, according to the Spirit of holiness, by the resurrection from the dead; 5 by whom we have received grace and apostleship, for obedience to the faith among all nations, for His name; 6 among whom are ye also the called of Jesus Christ: 7 to all that be in Rome, beloved of God, called to be saints: Grace to you, and peace, from God our Father and the Lord Jesus Christ.

A Bond Servant—"Paul, a servant of Jesus." It is thus that the apostle introduces himself to the Romans. In several other epistles the same expression is used. Some people would be ashamed to acknowledge themselves servants; the apostles were not.

It makes a vast difference whom one serves. The servant derives his importance from the dignity of the one served. Paul served the Lord Jesus Christ. Everybody may serve the same Master. "Know ye not, that to whom ye yield yourselves servants to obey, his servants ye are to whom ye obey?" Romans 6:16. Even the ordinary house servant who yields to the Lord is the servant of the Lord, and not of man. "Servants, obey in all things your masters according to the flesh; not with eyeservice, as menpleasers; but in singleness of heart, fearing God; and whatsoever ye do, do it heartily, as to the Lord, and not unto men; knowing that of the Lord ye shall receive the reward of the inheritance; for ye serve the Lord Jesus Christ." Colossians 3:22-24. Such a consideration as this can not fail to glorify the most menial drudgery.

Our version does not give us the full force of the term which the apostle uses when he calls himself a servant. It is really "bond servant." He used the ordinary Greek word for slave. If we are really the Lord's servants, we are servants bound to Him for life. It is a bondage that is itself freedom, "for he that is called in the Lord, being a servant, is the Lord's freeman; likewise also he that is called, being free, is Christ's servant." 1 Corinthians 7:22.

Separated—The apostle Paul was "separated unto the gospel." So is every one who is really the servant of the Lord. "No man can serve two masters; for either he will hate the one, and love the other; or else he will hold to the one, and despise the other. Ye can not serve God and mammon." Matthew 6:24. No man can serve the Lord and have other service besides that.

"Do you mean to say that a merchant or other business man can not be a Christian?" By no means. What I said was that a man can not serve the Lord and at the same time have other service. "And whatsoever ye do in word or deed, do all in the name of the Lord Jesus, giving thanks to God and the Father by Him." Colossians 3:17. If the man is not serving the Lord in his business, then he is not serving the Lord at all. The true servant of Christ is truly separated.

But this does not mean that he separates himself from personal contact with the world. The Bible gives no countenance to monkery. The most hopeless sinner is he who thinks himself too good to associate with sinners. How then are we to be separated unto the gospel? By the presence of God in the heart. Moses said to the Lord: "If Thy presence go not with me, carry us not up thence. For wherein shall it be known here that I and Thy people have found grace in Thy sight? Is it not in that Thou goest with us? so shall we be separated, I and Thy people, from all the people that are upon the face of the earth." Exodus 33:15, 16.

But the one who is separated to the public ministry of the gospel as the apostle Paul was, is separated in a special sense in that he may not engage in any other business for personal gain. "No man that warreth entangleth himself with the affairs of this life; that he may please him who hath chosen him to be a soldier." 2 Timothy 2:4. He can not take any position, however high under earthly governments. To do so is to dishonor his Master, and to belittle his service. The minister of the gospel is the ambassador of Christ, and there is no other position that can approach it in honor.

The Gospel of God—The apostle declared that he was "separated unto the gospel of God." It is the gospel of God "concerning His Son Jesus Christ." Christ is God and therefore the gospel of God, of which the apostle speaks in the first verse of the chapter, is identical with "the gospel of Christ" of which he speaks in the sixteenth verse.

Too many people separate the Father and the Son in the work of the gospel. Many do so unconsciously. God, the Father, as well as the Son, is our Saviour. "God so loved the world, that He gave His only-begotten son." John 3:16. "God was in Christ, reconciling the world unto Himself." 2 Corinthians 5:19. "The council of peace" is "between them both." Zechariah 6:13. Christ came to the earth only as the representative of the Father. Whoever saw Christ, saw the Father also. John 14:9. The works which Christ did, were the works of the Father, who dwelt in Him. Verse 10.

Even the words which He spoke, were the words of the Father. Verse 24. When we hear Christ saying, "Come unto Me, all ye that labor and are heavy laden, and I will give you rest," we are listening to the gracious invitation of God the Father. When we see Christ taking the little children up in His arms, and blessing them, we are witnessing the tenderness of the Father. When we see Christ receiving sinners, mingling with them, and eating with them, forgiving their sins, and cleansing the hideous lepers with a touch, we are looking upon the condescension and compassion of the Father. Even when we see our Lord upon the cross, with the blood streaming from His side, that blood by which we are reconciled to God, we must not forget that "God was in Christ, reconciling the world unto Himself," so that the apostle Paul said, "the church of God, which He hath purchased with His own blood." Acts 20:28.

The Gospel in the Old Testament—The gospel of God to which the apostle Paul declared himself to be separated, was the gospel "which He had promised afore by His prophets in the Holy Scriptures" (Romans 1:2); literally, the gospel which He had before announced or preached. This shows us that the Old Testament contains the gospel, and also that the gospel in the Old Testament is the same gospel that is in the New. It is the only gospel that the apostle preached. That being the case, it should not be thought strange for people to believe the Old Testament, and to refer to it as of equal authority with the New Testament.

We read that God "preached before the gospel unto Abraham, saying, In thee shall all nations be blessed." Galatians 3:8. The gospel preached to the people when Paul lived was the same gospel that was preached unto the ancient Israelites. See Hebrews 4:2. Moses wrote of Christ, and so much of the gospel is to be found in his writings that a man who does not believe what Moses wrote, can not believe in Christ. John 5:46, 47. "To Him give all the prophets witness, that through His name whosoever believeth in Him shall receive remission of sins." Acts 10:43.

Paul had only the Old Testament when he went to Thessalonica, "and three Sabbath days reasoned with them out of the Scriptures, opening and alleging, that Christ must needs have suffered, and risen again from the dead." Acts 17:2, 3.

Timothy had nothing in his childhood and youth but the Old Testament writings, and the apostle wrote to him: "Continue thou in the things which thou hast learned and hast been assured of, knowing of whom thou hast learned them; and that from a child thou hast known the Holy Scriptures, which are able to make thee wise unto salvation through faith which is in Christ Jesus." 2 Timothy 3:14, 15.

Then go to the Old Testament with the expectation of finding Christ and His righteousness there, and you will be made wiser unto salvation. Do not discriminate between Moses and Paul, between David and Peter, between Jeremiah and James, between Isaiah and John.

The Seed of David—The gospel of God is "concerning His Son Jesus Christ our Lord, which was made of the seed of David according to the flesh." Romans 1:3. Read the history of David, and of the kings who descended from him, and who became the ancestors of Jesus, and you will see that on the human side the Lord was handicapped by His ancestry as badly as anybody can ever be. Many of them were licentious and cruel idolaters. Although Jesus was thus compassed with infirmity, He "did no sin, neither was guile found in His mouth." 1 Peter 2:22. This is to give courage to men in the lowest condition of life. It is to show that the power of the gospel of the grace of God can triumph over heredity.

The fact that Jesus was made of the seed of David means that He is heir to the throne of David. Of David's throne the Lord said, "Thine house and thy kingdom shall be established forever before thee; thy throne shall be established forever." 2 Samuel 7:16. David's kingdom is therefore coextensive with the inheritance promised to Abraham, which is the whole world. See Romans 4:13.

The angel said of Jesus, "The Lord God shall give unto Him the throne of His father David; and He shall reign over the house of Jacob forever; and of His kingdom there shall be no end." Luke 1:32, 33. But all this involved His bearing the curse of the inheritance, and suffering death. "For the joy that was set before Him" He "endured the cross, despising the shame." Hebrews 12:2. "Wherefore God also hath highly exalted Him, and given Him a name which is above every name." Philippians 2:9.

As with Christ, so with us; it is through much tribulation that we enter the kingdom. He who fears reproach, or who makes his lowly birth, or his inherited traits, an excuse for his shortcomings, will fail of the kingdom of heaven. Jesus Christ went to the lowest depths of humiliation in order that all who are in those depths might, if they would, ascend with Him to the utmost heights of exaltation.

Power by the Resurrection—Although Jesus Christ was of lowly birth, He was "declared to be the Son of God with power, according to the Spirit of holiness, by the resurrection from the dead." Romans 1:4. Was He not the Son of God before the resurrection? and was He not so declared to be? Certainly; and the power of the resurrection was manifested in all His life. To speak of nothing else, the power of the resurrection was shown in His raising the dead, which He did by the power dwelling in Him. But it was the resurrection from the dead that settled the matter beyond all doubt for men.

After His resurrection He met the disciples, and said unto them, "All power is given unto Me in heaven and in earth." Matthew 28:18. The death of Christ shattered all the hopes that they had centered in Him; but when He "showed Himself alive after His passion by many infallible proofs, being seen of them forty days" (Acts 1:3), they had ample proof of His power.

Their sole work thenceforth was to be witnesses of His resurrection and of its power. The power of the resurrection is according to the Spirit of holiness, for it was by the Spirit that He was raised. The power given to make men holy is the power that raised Jesus from the dead. "His divine power hath given unto us all things that pertain to life and godliness."

The Obedience of Faith—Paul said that through Christ he had received grace and apostleship for the obedience of faith among all nations. True faith is obedience. "This is the work of God, that ye believe on Him whom He hath sent." John 6:29. Christ said, "Why call ye Me, Lord, Lord, and do not the things which I say?" Luke 6:46. That is, a profession of faith in Christ which is not accompanied by obedience, is worthless. "Faith, if it hath not works, is dead." James 2:17. "For as the body without the spirit is dead, so faith without works is dead also." Verse 26.

A man does not breathe in order to show that he lives, but because he is alive. He lives by breathing. His breath is his life. So a man can not do good works in order to demonstrate that he has faith, but he does good works because the works are the necessary result of faith. Even Abraham was justified by works, because "faith wrought with his works, and by works was faith made perfect. And the scripture was fulfilled which saith, Abraham believed God, and it was imputed unto him for righteousness."

"Beloved of God"—That was a most comforting assurance that was given "to all that are in Rome." How many people have wished that they could hear an angel direct from glory say to them what Gabriel said to Daniel, "Thou art greatly beloved"! The apostle Paul wrote by direct inspiration of the Holy Spirit, and so the message of love came as directly from heaven to the Romans as it did to Daniel. The Lord did not single out a few favorites by name, but declared that all in Rome were beloved of God.

Well, there is no respect of persons with God, and that message of love to the Romans is ours as well. They were "beloved of God" simply because "God so loved the world, that He gave His only-begotten Son, that whosoever believeth in Him should not perish, but have everlasting life." John 3:16. "The Lord hath appeared of old unto me, saying, Yea, I have loved thee with an everlasting love; therefore with loving-kindness have I drawn thee." Jeremiah 31:3. And this everlasting love to men is not shaken, although they forget it; for to those who have turned away, and fallen by their iniquity, He says, "I will heal their backsliding, I will love them freely." Hosea 14:43. "If we believe not, yet He abideth faithful; He can not deny Himself."

"Called Saints"—The reader will notice that the words "to be" in Romans 1:7 are indicated as supplied, so that instead of "called to be saints," we may read literally, "called saints." God calls all men to be saints, but all those who *accept* Him He calls saints. That is their title. When God calls people saints, they are saints.

These words were addressed to the church *in* Rome, and not to the Church *of* Rome. The Church of Rome has always been apostate and pagan. It has abused the word "saint" until in its calendar it is almost a term of reproach. No greater sin has ever been committed by Rome than the distinction it has made between "saints" and ordinary Christians, making practically two standards of goodness. It has led people to think that laboring men and housewives were not and could not be saints, and has thus discounted true, everyday piety, and has put a premium on pious laziness and self-righteous deeds.

But God has not two standards of piety, and all the faithful people in Rome, poor and unknown as many of them were, He called saints. It is the same today with God, although men may reckon differently.

The first seven verses of the first chapter of Romans are the salutation. No uninspired letter ever embraced so much in its greeting as this one. The apostle was so overflowing with the love of God that he could not write a letter without covering almost the whole gospel in the salutation. The next eight verses may well be summarized in the words "debtor to all,"

for they show the completeness of the apostle's devotedness to others. Let us read them carefully, and not be content with one reading:

Debtor to All—Romans 1:8-15

8 First, I thank my God through Jesus Christ for you all, that your faith is spoken of throughout the whole world. 9 For God is my witness, whom I serve with my spirit in the gospel of His Son, that without ceasing I make mention of you always in my prayers; 10 making request, if by any means now at length I might have a prosperous journey by the will of God to come unto you. 11 For I long to see you, that I may impart unto you some spiritual gift, to the end ye may be established; 12 that is, that I may be comforted together with you by the mutual faith both of you and me. 13 Now I would not have you ignorant, brethren, that oftentimes I purposed to come unto you, (but was let [hindered] hitherto,) that I might have some fruit among you also, even as among other Gentiles. 14 I am debtor both to the Greeks, and to the barbarians; both to the wise, and to the unwise. 15 So, as much as in me is, I am ready to preach the gospel to you that are at Rome also.

A Great Contrast—In the days of the apostle Paul the faith of the church in Rome was spoken of throughout all the world. Faith means obedience; for faith is counted for righteousness, and God never counts a thing so unless it is so. Faith "worketh by love." Galatians 5:6. And this work is a "work of faith." 1 Thessalonians 1:3. Faith also means humility, as is shown by the words of the prophet, "Behold, his soul which is lifted up is not upright in him; but the just shall live by his faith." Habakkuk 2:4. The upright man is the just man; the man whose soul is lifted up is not upright or just; but the just man is such because of his faith; therefore only the man whose soul is not lifted up has faith. The Roman brethren, therefore, in the days of Paul, were humble.

But it is far different now. An instance is given by the *Catholic Times* of June 15, 1894. The pope had said, "We gave authority to the bishops of the Syrian rite to meet in synod at Mossul," and had commended the "very faithful submission" of those bishops and had ratified the election of the patriarch by "Our Apostolic authority." An Anglican paper had expressed surprise, saying, "Is this a free union of equal churches, or is it submission to one supreme and monarchical head?" To which the *Catholic Times* replies: "It is not a free union of equal churches, but it is submission to one supreme and monarchical head. ... To our Anglican pleader we say, You

are not really surprised. You know well what Rome claims and always will claim,—obedience. That claim is now, if it ever was, before the world."

But that claim was not before the world in the days of Paul. In those days it was the church *in* Rome; now it is the Church *of* Rome. The church *in* Rome was famous for its humility, and its obedience to God. The Church *of* Rome is famous for its haughty assumption of the power of God, and for its demand for obedience to itself.

Praying Without Ceasing—The apostle exhorted the Thessalonians to "pray without ceasing." 1 Thessalonians 5:17. He did not exhort others to do that which he did not do himself, for he told the Romans that without ceasing he made mention of them always in his prayers. It is not to be supposed that the apostle had the brethren at Rome on his mind every waking hour of the day, for in that case he could not have thought of anything else. No man can be consciously in prayer every moment, but all can continue "instant in prayer," or, as Young translates it, "in the prayer persevering." Romans 12:12.

This is in harmony with what the Saviour said, that "men ought always to pray, and not to faint," or grow weary. Luke 18:1. In the parable that follows, the unjust judge complains of the "continual coming" of the poor widow. That is an illustration of praying without ceasing. It is not that we are to be every moment in conscious prayer, for then important duties would be neglected, but it is that we should not grow weary of praying.

A Man of Prayer—This is what Paul was. He made mention of the Romans in all his prayers. To the Corinthians he wrote, "I thank my God always on your behalf." 1 Corinthians 1:4. To the Colossians, "We give thanks to God and the Father of our Lord Jesus Christ, praying always for you." Colossians 1:3. Still more emphatically he wrote to the Philippians, "I thank my God upon every remembrance of you, always in every prayer of mine for you all making request with joy." Philippians 1:3, 4. Again to the Thessalonians, "We give thanks to God always for you all, making mention of you in our prayers; remembering without ceasing your work of faith," etc. 1 Thessalonians 1:2, 3. And further, "Night and day praying exceedingly that we might see your face, and might perfect that which is lacking in your faith." 1 Thessalonians 3:10. To his beloved son in the faith he wrote, "I thank God, whom I serve from my forefathers with pure conscience, that without ceasing I have remembrance of thee in my prayers night and day." 2 Timothy 1:3.

"Rejoice Evermore"—The secret of this is to "pray without ceasing." See 1 Thessalonians 5:16, 17. The apostle Paul prayed for others so much that he had no time to worry about himself. He had never seen the Romans, yet he prayed for them as earnestly as for the churches that he had raised up. Recounting his labors and sufferings, he adds that they are "beside those things that are without, that which cometh upon me daily, the care of all the churches." 2 Corinthians 11:28.

"As sorrowful, yet always rejoicing." He fulfilled the law of Christ by bearing the burdens of others. Thus it was that he was able to glory in the cross of our Lord Jesus Christ. Christ suffered on the cross for others, but it was "for the joy that was set before Him." They who are wholly devoted to others, share the joy of their Lord, and can rejoice in Him.

"A Prosperous Journey"—Paul prayed earnestly that he might have a prosperous journey by the will of God to visit Rome. Read the twenty-seventh chapter of Acts, and you will learn just what kind of journey he had. Most people would say that it was not a prosperous journey. Yet we do not hear any complaint from Paul; and who can say that he did not have a prosperous trip? "All things work together for good to them that love God," therefore it must have been prosperous. It is well for us to consider these things.

We are apt to look at matters from a wrong side. When we learn to look at them as God looks at them, we shall find that things that we regard as disastrous are prosperous. How much mourning we might save if we always remembered that God knows much better than we do how our prayers should be answered!

Spiritual Gifts—When Christ "ascended up on high, He led captivity captive, and gave gifts unto men." Ephesians 4:8. These gifts were the gifts of the Spirit, for He said, "It is expedient for you that I go away; for if I go not away, the Comforter will not come unto you; but if I depart, I will send Him unto you." John 16:7. And Peter said on the day of Pentecost: "This Jesus hath God raised up, whereof we all are witnesses. Therefore being by the right hand of God exalted, and having received of the Father the promise of the Holy Ghost, He hath shed forth this, which ye now see and hear." Acts 2:32.

These gifts are thus described: "Now there are diversities of gifts, but the same Spirit. And there are differences of administrations, but the same Lord. And there are diversities of operations, but it is the same God which worketh all in all. But the manifestation of the Spirit is given to every man to profit withal. For to one is given by the Spirit the word of wisdom; to another the word of knowledge by the same Spirit; to another faith by the same Spirit; to another the gifts of healing by the same Spirit; to another the working of miracles; to another prophecy; to another discerning of spirits; to another divers kinds of tongues; to another the interpretation of tongues; but all these worketh that one and the selfsame Spirit, dividing to every man severally as he will." 1 Corinthians 12:4-11.

Established by Spiritual Gifts—"But the manifestation of the Spirit is given to every man to profit withal." What is the profit? "For the perfecting of the saints, for the work of the ministry, for the edifying of the body of Christ; till we all come in the unity of the faith, and of the knowledge of the Son of God, unto a perfect man, unto the measure of the stature of the fullness of Christ." Ephesians 4:12, 13.

The gifts of the Spirit must accompany the Spirit. As soon as the early disciples received the Spirit in accordance with the promise, they received the gifts. One of the gifts, speaking with new tongues, was manifested that very day. It follows, therefore, that the absence of the gifts of the Spirit in any marked degree in the church, is evidence of the absence of the Spirit, not entirely, of course, but to the extent that God has promised it.

The Spirit was to abide with the disciples forever, and therefore the gifts of the Spirit must be manifest in the true church until the second coming of the Lord. As before stated, the absence of any very marked manifestation of the gifts of the Spirit is evidence of the absence of the fullness of the Spirit; and that is the secret of the weakness of the church, and the great divisions that exist. Spiritual gifts establish the church; therefore the church that does not have those gifts can not be established.

Who May Have the Spirit?—Whoever asks for it with earnest desire. See Luke 11:13. The Spirit has already been poured out, and God has never withdrawn the gift; it only needs that Christians should ask and accept.

"I Am Debtor"—That was the keynote of Paul's life, and it was the secret of his success. Nowadays we hear of men saying, "The world owes me a living." But Paul considered that he owed himself to the world. And yet he received nothing from the world but stripes and abuse. Even that which he had received before Christ found him was a total loss. But Christ had found him, and given Himself to him, so that he could say, "I am crucified with Christ; nevertheless I live; yet not I, but Christ liveth in me; and the life which I now live in the flesh I live by the faith of the Son of God, who loved me, and gave Himself for me." Galatians 2:20.

As Christ's life was his life, and Christ gave Himself for the world, Paul necessarily became a debtor to the whole world. This has been the case of every man who has been a servant of the Lord. "David, after he had served his own generation by the will of God, fell on sleep." Acts 13:36. "Whosoever will be great among you, let him be your minister; and whosoever will be chief among you, let him be your servant; even as the

Son of man came not to be ministered unto, but to minister, and to give His life a ransom for many." Matthew 20:26-28.

Personal Labor—There is a foolish notion prevalent that ordinary labor is degrading, especially to a minister of the gospel. It is not all the fault of the ministers themselves, but largely the fault of the foolish people about them. They think that a minister must always be faultlessly attired, and that he must never soil his hands with ordinary manual labor. Such ideas were never gained from the Bible. Christ Himself was a carpenter, yet many professed followers of Him would be shocked if they should see their minister sawing and planing boards, or digging in the ground, or carrying parcels.

There is a false dignity altogether too prevalent, which is utterly opposed to the spirit of the gospel. Paul was not ashamed nor afraid to labor. And this he did not merely occasionally, but day after day while he was engaged in preaching. See Acts 18:3, 4. He said, "These hands have ministered unto my necessities, and to them that were with me." Acts 20:34. He was speaking to the leaders of the church when he said, "I have showed you all things, how that so laboring ye ought to support the weak, and to remember the words of the Lord Jesus, how He said, It is more blessed to give than to receive." Verse 35.

Slandering Paul—At the second international convention of the Student Volunteer Movement for Foreign Missions, the main address for one evening was on the subject of "Paul, the Great Missionary." The speaker said that "Paul had a faculty for dividing up the work so that he undertook very little of it himself." It was a foolish and wicked idea to present before young volunteers for missionary service, because it was an utter falsehood, and it was anything but a compliment to the apostle.

In addition to what has been cited above, read the following: "Neither did we eat any man's bread for naught; but wrought with labor and travail night and day, that we might not be chargeable to any of you." 2 Thessalonians 3:8. "I will very gladly spend and be spent for you." 2 Corinthians 12:15. "Are they ministers of Christ? (I speak as a fool) I am more; in labors more abundant, in stripes above measure, in prisons more frequent." 2 Corinthians 11:23. "But by the grace of God I am what I am; and His grace which was bestowed upon me was not in vain; but I labored more abundantly than they all; yet not I, but the grace of God which was with me." 1 Corinthians 15:10.

The grace of God is manifest in service for others. The grace of Christ led Him to give Himself for us, and to take upon Himself the form and condition of a servant. Therefore he who has the most of the grace of Christ will labor the most. He will not shun work, even though it be the most menial service. Christ went to the lowest depths for the sake of man; therefore he who thinks that any service is beneath him, is altogether too high for association with Christ.

Gospel Liberty—Gospel liberty is the liberty that God gives men through the gospel. It expresses His idea of freedom. It is the freedom seen in nature and in all the works of His hands. It is the freedom of the winds, blowing where they list; it is the freedom of the flowers, scattered everywhere through wood and meadow; it is the freedom of the birds, soaring unrestrained through the heavens; the freedom of the sunbeam, shooting from its parent orb and playing on cloud and mountain top; the freedom of the celestial orbs, sweeping ceaselessly on through infinite space. This is the freedom which flows out from the great Creator through all His works.

Tasting Freedom Now—It is sin that has produced what is narrow and contracted and circumscribed, that has erected boundary lines, and made men stingy. But sin is to be removed, and then perfect liberty will be realized once more in every part of creation. Even now this freedom may be tasted, by having sin removed from the heart. To enjoy this freedom through eternity is the glorious privilege now offered in the gospel to all men. Who that claims to love liberty can let this opportunity pass unimproved?

We have covered the introduction to the main body of the epistle. The first seven verses are the salutation; the next eight treat of personal matters concerning the apostle and the brethren in Rome, the fifteenth verse being the link which unites the introduction to the directly doctrinal portion of the epistle.

Let the reader note carefully the verses referred to, and he will readily see that this is not an arbitrary division, but that it plainly appears. If in reading any chapter, one will note the different topics touched upon, and the change from one subject to another, he will be surprised to find how much easier it is to grasp the contents of the chapter, and to hold them in mind. The reason why so many people find it difficult to recall what they read in the Bible, is that they try to remember it in bulk, without giving special thought to the details.

In expressing his desire to meet with the Roman brethren, the apostle declared himself to be debtor to both Greeks and barbarians, both to the wise and to the unwise, and therefore ready to preach the gospel even in Rome, the capital of the world. The fifteenth verse, and the expression, "preach the gospel," give the keynote to the whole of the epistle, for the apostle glides from this naturally into his theme. Accordingly, we have next—

The Gospel Defined—Romans 1:16, 17

> 16 For I am not ashamed of the gospel of Christ; for it is the power of God unto salvation to every one that believeth; to the Jew first, and also to the Greek. 17 For therein is the righteousness of God revealed from faith to faith; as it is written, The just shall live by faith.

"Not Ashamed"—There is no reason why any man should be ashamed of the gospel; nevertheless, many men have been and are ashamed of it. Many people are so ashamed of it that they could not think of lowering themselves so much as to make a profession of it; and many who do make a profession of it are ashamed to let it be known. What is the cause of all this shame? It is that they do not know what the gospel is. No man who really knows what the gospel is, will be ashamed of it, or of any part of it.

Desire for Power—There is nothing that men desire so much as power. It is a desire that God Himself has planted in man. Unfortunately, the devil has deceived the most of mankind, so that they seek for power in the wrong way. They think that it can be found in the possession of wealth or political position, and so they rush to secure those things. But these do not supply the power for which God has created the desire. This is shown by the fact that they do not satisfy.

No man was ever yet satisfied with the power that he obtained by wealth or position. However much they have, they desire more. No man finds in them just what he thought he would; and so he grasps after more, thinking that he will find his heart's desire farther on; but all in vain. Christ is "the desire of all nations" (Haggai 2:7), the only Source of complete satisfaction, because He is the embodiment of all the real power there is in the universe—the power of God—"Christ the power of God" (l Corinthians 1:24).

Power and Knowledge—It is commonly said that knowledge is power. That depends. If we take the statement of the poet, that "the proper study of mankind is man," then certainly knowledge is anything but power. Man is nothing but weakness and sin. All men know that they are sinners, that they do things that are not right, but that knowledge gives them no power to change their course. You may tell a man all his faults, and if you tell him nothing more, you have weakened rather that strengthened him.

But he who with the apostle Paul determines to know nothing "save Jesus Christ and Him crucified," has knowledge that is power. "And this is life eternal, that they might know Thee the only true God, and Jesus Christ, whom Thou hast sent." John 17:3. To know Christ is to know the power of His endless life. It is for lack of this knowledge that men are destroyed. Hosea 4:6. But since Christ is the power of God, it is quite correct to say that power is the one thing that men need; and the only real power, the power of God, is revealed in the gospel.

The Glory of Power—All men honor power. Wherever power is manifested, there will always be found men to admire. There is no one who does not admire and applaud power in some form. Powerful muscles are admired and boasted of, whether they be those of man or of beast. A mighty engine that moves vast weights with ease always attracts attention, and men honor the one who constructed it. The man of wealth, whose money can command the service of thousands, always has admirers, no matter how his money is obtained. The man of noble birth and position, or the monarch of a great nation, has multitudes of followers who applaud his power. Men desire to be connected with such an one, because they derive a certain dignity from the connection, although the power is not transferable.

But all the power of earth is frail and but for a moment, while the power of God is eternal. The gospel is the power, and if men would but recognize it for what it is, there would not be any who would be ashamed of it. Paul said, "God forbid that I should glory, save in the cross of our Lord Jesus Christ." Galatians 6:14. The reason for this was that the cross is the power of God. 1 Corinthians 1:18. The power of God, in whatever form manifested, is glory, and not for shame.

Christ Not Ashamed—Concerning Christ we read, "For both He that sanctifieth and they who are sanctified are all of one; for which cause He is not ashamed to call them brethren." Hebrews 2:11. "God is not ashamed to be called their God; for He hath prepared for them a city." Hebrews 11:16. Surely if the Lord is not ashamed to be called the brother of poor, weak, sinful mortals, man has no reason to be ashamed of him. "Behold, what manner of love the Father hath bestowed upon us, that we should be called the sons of God." 1 John 3:1. Ashamed of the gospel of Christ! Could there possibly be a worse case of the exaltation of self above God? For to be ashamed of the gospel of Christ, which is the power of God, is an evidence that the man who feels thus ashamed really thinks himself superior to God, and that it is a lowering of his dignity to be associated with the Lord.

"Ashamed of Jesus! sooner far
　　Let evening blush to own a star;
He sheds the beams of light divine
　　O'er this benighted soul of mine.

"Ashamed of Jesus! just as soon
　　Let midnight be ashamed of noon;
'Twas midnight with my soul till He,
　　Bright Morning Star, bade darkness flee."

Saved by Faith—The gospel is the power of God unto salvation to every one that believes. "By grace are ye saved through faith; and that not of yourselves; it is the gift of God." Ephesians 2:8. "He that believeth and is baptized shall be saved." Mark 16:16. "As many as received Him, to them gave He power to become the sons of God, even to them that believe on His name." John 1:12. "With the heart man believeth unto righteousness." Romans 10:10. "This is the work of God, that ye believe on Him whom He hath sent." John 6:29. Faith works.

Time would fail to tell of those "who through faith subdued kingdoms, wrought righteousness, obtained promises, … out of weakness were made strong," etc. Hebrews 11:33, 34. Men may say, "I can not see how it is possible for one to be made righteous simply by believing." It makes no difference what you can see; you are not saved by sight, but by faith. You do not need to see how it is done, because it is the Lord who does the work of saving. Christ dwells in the heart by faith (Ephesians 3:17), and because He is our righteousness, "He also is become my salvation" (Isaiah 12:2). We shall have salvation by faith illustrated more fully as we proceed in our study, because the book of Romans is devoted wholly to this one thing.

"To the Jew First"—When Peter, at the request of Cornelius, the Roman centurion, and the command of the Lord, went to Caesarea to preach the gospel to the Gentiles, his first words when he heard the story of Cornelius were, "Of a truth I perceive that God is no respecter of persons; but in every nation he that feareth Him, and worketh righteousness, is accepted with Him." Acts 10:34, 35.

This was the first time that Peter had ever perceived that truth, but it was not the first time that that thing was true. It had been a truth as long as God had existed. God never chose anybody to the exclusion of anybody else. The wisdom that comes from above is "without partiality." James 3:17. It is true that the Jews as a nation were wonderfully favored by the Lord: but they lost all their privileges simply because they assumed

that God loved them better than He did anybody else, and were exclusive. All through their history God was trying to make them see that what He gave them was for the whole world, and that they were to pass on to others the light and privileges which they shared.

The cases of Naaman, the Syrian, and of the Ninevites to whom Jonah was sent, are among the many instances by which God sought to show the Jews that He was no respecter of persons.

Then why was the gospel preached "to the Jew first"? Simply because the Jews were nearest. Christ was crucified at Jerusalem. It was from there that He commissioned His disciples to preach the gospel. At His ascension He said, "Ye shall be witnesses unto Me both in Jerusalem, and in all Judea, and in Samaria, and unto the uttermost part of the earth." Acts 1:8. It was most natural that they should begin to preach the gospel in the place and to the people nearest them. This is the secret of all missionary work. He who does not labor in the gospel in his home, will not do any gospel work although he goes to a foreign country.

The Righteousness of God—The Lord says: "Lift up your eyes to the heavens, and look upon the earth beneath; for the heavens shall vanish away like smoke, and the earth shall wax old like a garment; and they that dwell therein shall die in like manner; but My salvation shall be forever and My righteousness shall not be abolished. Hearken unto Me, ye that know righteousness, the people in whose heart is My law." Isaiah 51:6, 7. "My tongue shall speak of Thy work; for all Thy commandments are righteousness." Psalm 119:172.

The righteousness of God, therefore, is His law. Let this not be forgotten. The term "the righteousness of God" occurs frequently in the book of Romans, and much confusion has resulted from giving it arbitrary and varying definitions. If we accept the definition given in the Bible, and do not abandon it in any instance, it will simplify matters very much. The righteousness of God is His perfect law.

Righteousness and Life—But the Ten Commandments, whether engraved on tables of stone or written in a book, are only the statement of the righteousness of God. Righteousness means right doing. It is active. The righteousness of God is God's right doing, His way. And since all His ways are right, it follows that the righteousness of God is nothing less than the life of God. The written law is not action, but is only a description of the action. It is a picture of the character of God.

The very life and character of God are seen in Jesus Christ, in whose heart was the law of God. There can be no righteousness without action. And as there is none good but God, it follows that there is no righteousness except in the life of God. Righteousness and the life of God are one and the same thing.

Righteousness in the Gospel—"For therein is the righteousness of God revealed." Wherein? In the gospel. Bear in mind that the righteousness of God is His perfect law, a statement of which is found in the Ten Commandments. There is no such thing as a conflict between the law and the gospel. Indeed, there are not in reality two such things as the law and the gospel. The true law of God is the gospel; for the law is the life of God, and we are "saved by His life." The gospel reveals the righteous law of God, because the gospel has the law in itself. There can be no gospel without law. Whoever ignores or rejects the law of God, has no knowledge whatever of the gospel.

The First View—Jesus said that the Holy Spirit should convince the world of sin and of righteousness. John 16:8. This is the revelation of the righteousness of God in the gospel. "Where no law is, there is no transgression." Romans 4:15. Sin can not be known except by the law. Romans 7:7. Therefore it follows that the Spirit convicts of sin by making known the law of God. The first view of the righteousness of God has the effect of making a man feel his sinfulness, just as we feel our littleness when gazing upon a lofty mountain. And as the grandeur of the great mountains grows upon us, so God's righteousness which is "like the great mountains" (Psalm 36:6) appears greater the more we look at it. Therefore he who looks continually at the righteousness of God, must continually acknowledge his own sinfulness.

The Second, Deeper View—Jesus Christ is the righteousness of God. And "God sent not His Son into the world to condemn the world; but that the world through Him might be saved." John 3:17. God does not reveal His righteousness in the gospel in order to cause us to cower before Him because of our unrighteousness, but that we may take it and live by it. We are unrighteous, and God wishes us to realize it, in order that we may be willing to receive His perfect righteousness. It is a revelation of love; for His righteousness is His law, and His law is love. 1 John 5:3.

So "if we confess our sins, He is faithful and righteous to forgive us our sins, and to cleanse us from all unrighteousness." 1 John 1:9. If when the preaching of the gospel reveals to us the law of God, we reject it and find fault with it because it condemns our course, we are simply saying that we do not desire that God should put His own righteousness upon us.

Living by Faith—"As it is written, The just shall live by faith." Christ is "our life." Colossians 3:4. We are "saved by His life." Romans 5:10. It is by faith that we receive Christ Jesus, for He dwells in our hearts by faith.

Ephesians 3:17. Dwelling in our hearts, He is life, for out of the heart are the issues of life. Proverbs 4:23.

Now the word comes, "As ye have therefore received Christ Jesus the Lord, so walk ye in Him; rooted and built up in Him, and stablished in the faith." Colossians 2:6, 7. As we receive Him by faith, and we walk in Him as we have received Him, we shall "walk by faith, and not by sight."

"From Faith to Faith"—This seemingly difficult expression, which has been the subject of so much controversy, is very simple when we allow the Scripture to explain itself. In the gospel "the righteousness of God" is "revealed from faith to faith; as it is written, The just shall live by faith." Note that "from faith to faith" is said to be parallel with "the just shall live by faith." Just means righteous.

The reader has noticed that some versions have "righteous" in 1 John 1:9 where the King James Version has "just." Both are the same. God's life is righteousness; He desires that our lives shall be righteousness also, and therefore He gave us His own life. This life becomes ours by faith. That is, just as we live naturally by breathing, so we are to live spiritually by faith, and our whole life is to be spiritual. Faith is the breath of life to the Christian. So just as we naturally live from breath to breath, we are to live spiritually from faith to faith.

We can live but one breath at a time; so we can not live spiritually except by present faith. If we live a life of conscious dependence upon God, His righteousness will be ours, for we shall breathe it in continually. Faith gives us strength, for those who have exercised it "out of weakness were made strong." Hebrews 11:34.

So of those who accept the revelation of God's righteousness "from faith to faith," it is said, "They go from strength to strength; every one of them in Zion appeareth before God." Psalm 84:7.

Let us not forget that it is from the very words of the Bible that one is to learn. All the real help that any teacher can be to any one in the study of the Bible is to show him how to fix his mind more clearly upon the exact words of the sacred text. Therefore, first of all, read the text over many times. Do not do this hastily, but carefully, paying particular attention to every statement. Do not waste one moment in speculating as to the possible meaning of the text. There is nothing worse than guessing the meaning of a text of Scripture, unless it is the acceptance of somebody else's guess. Nobody can know any more of the Bible than the Bible itself tells; and the Bible is just as ready to tell its story to one person as to another.

Question the text closely. Probe it again and again, always in a reverent, prayerful spirit, to make it reveal itself. Do not be discouraged if you do not at once see all that there is in the text. Remember that it is the word of God, and that it is infinite in its depth, and that you can never exhaust it. When you come across a difficult statement, go back and consider it in connection with what precedes. Do not think that you can ever get at the full meaning of any text apart from its connection. By constant application to the words of the text, in order to be sure that you know exactly what it says, you will soon have them constantly in your mind; and it is then that you will begin to reap some of the rich fruits of Bible study; for at unexpected times new light will flash from them, and through them from other scriptures as you read.

The Justice of Judgment—Romans 1:18-20

18 For the wrath of God is revealed from heaven against all ungodliness and unrighteousness of men, who hold the truth in unrighteousness; 19 because that which may be known of God is manifest in them; for God hath showed it unto them. 20 For the invisible things of Him from the creation of the world are clearly seen, being understood by the things that are made, even His external power and Godhead; so that they are without excuse.

How Men Lost Knowledge—Romans 1:21-23

21 Because that, when they knew God, they glorified Him not as God, neither were thankful; but became vain in their imaginations, and their foolish heart was darkened. 22 Professing themselves to be wise, they became fools, 23 and changed the glory of the uncorruptible God into an image made like to corruptible man, and to birds, and fourfooted beasts, and creeping things.

Result of Ignoring God—Romans 1:24-32

24 Wherefore God also gave them up to uncleanness, through the lusts of their own hearts, to dishonor their own bodies between themselves; 25 who changed the truth of God into a lie, and worshipped and served the creature more than the Creator, who is blessed forever. Amen. 26 For this cause God gave them up unto vile affections; for even their women did change the natural use into that which is against nature; 27 and likewise also the men, leaving the natural use of the woman, burned in their lust one toward another; men with men working that which is

unseemly, and receiving in themselves that recompense of their error which was meet. 28 And even as they did not like to retain God in their knowledge, God gave them over to a reprobate mind, to do those things which are not convenient; 29 being filled with all unrighteousness, fornication, wickedness, covetousness, maliciousness; full of envy, murder, debate, deceit, malignity; whisperers, 30 backbiters, haters of God, despiteful, proud, boasters, inventors of evil things, disobedient to parents, 31 without understanding, covenant breakers, without natural affection, implacable, unmerciful; 32 who knowing the judgment of God, that they which commit such things are worthy of death, not only do the same, but have pleasure in them that do them.

All Unrighteousness Condemned—The wrath of God is revealed from heaven against all ungodliness and unrighteousness of men. "All unrighteousness is sin." 1 John 5:17. "But sin is not imputed when there is no law." Romans 5:13. Therefore enough of the law of God is known in all the world to deprive all people of any excuse for sin. The statement in this verse is equal to that in the next chapter, that "there is no respect of persons with God." His wrath is manifested against all unrighteousness. No person in the world is so great that he can sin with impunity, and no person is so insignificant that his sin will be overlooked. There is strict impartiality with God. He "without respect of persons judgeth according to every man's work." 1 Peter 1:17.

Restraining the Truth—The statement is that men "hold down the truth in unrighteousness." Some people have superficially read Romans 1:18 as though it said that men may possess the truth while they themselves are unrighteous. It does not say so. Sufficient evidence that such a thing is not meant is found in the fact that the apostle is speaking in this chapter especially of those who did not possess the truth, but had exchanged it for a lie. Although they had lost all knowledge of the truth, they were in condemnation for their sin.

The statement is that people restrain the truth by unrighteousness. We might note the fact that when Jesus went into His own country "He did not many mighty works there because of their unbelief." Matthew 13:58. But the apostle in the text before us means much more than this. He means, as the context plainly shows, that people by their perverseness restrain the working of the truth of God in their own souls. But for their resistance of the truth, it would sanctify them. And herein is seen the result:

Righteousness of God's Wrath—The wrath of God is revealed from heaven against all ungodliness and unrighteousness of men, and justly, too, "because that which may be known of God is manifest in them; for God hath shown it unto them." Note particularly the statement that that which may be known of God "is manifest in them." Although in the common version the margin gives "to them" as an alternative reading, the Greek gives no warrant for any such rendering. No matter how blindly men may sin, the fact remains that they are sinning against great light, "because that which may be known of God is manifest in them." With such knowledge not only before their eyes, but actually within them, it is easy to see the justice of God's wrath against all sin, no matter in whom it is found.

Even though it should not be perfectly clear to us how the knowledge of God is really placed in every man, we may accept the apostle's statement of the fact. In the wonderful description of the foolishness of idolatry, given in Isaiah, we are told that the man who makes an idol lies against the truth which he himself possesses. "He feedeth on ashes; a deceived heart hath turned him aside, that he can not deliver his soul, nor say, Is there not a lie in my right hand?" Isaiah 44:20.

Seeing the Invisible—It is said of Moses that "he endured, as seeing Him who is invisible." Hebrews 11:27. This was not a privilege peculiar to Moses. Every other man may do the same thing. How? Because the "invisible things of Him since the creation of the world are clearly seen, being perceived through the things that are made." There has not been a time since the world was created when all men did not have the knowledge of God within their grasp.

> "Lord, how Thy wonders are displayed
>   Where'er I turn my eye!
> If I survey the ground I tread,
>   Or gaze upon the sky.
>
> "There's not a plant or flower below
>   But makes Thy glories known."

Eternal Power and Divinity—The invisible things of God that are known by the things that are made are His everlasting power and divinity. "The heavens declare the glory of God; and the firmament showeth His handiwork." Psalm 19:1. Jesus Christ is "the power of God." 1 Corinthians 1:24. "For in Him were all things created, in the heavens and upon the earth, things visible and things invisible, whether thrones or dominions or principalities or powers; all things have been created through Him, and unto Him; and He is before all things, and in Him all things consist." Colossians 1:16, 17. "He spake, and it was." Psalm 33:9. He is "the firstborn of all creation." Colossians 1:15. He is the source, or beginning, of the creation of God. Revelation 3:14.

That is to say, all creation springs from Christ Jesus, who is the power of God. He spoke the worlds into existence from His own being. Therefore the external power and divinity of God are impressed upon everything that has been made. We can not open our eyes, we can not even feel the breeze upon our face, without having a clear revelation to us of the power of God.

"We Are His Offspring"—When Paul upon Mars' Hill rebuked the Athenians for their idolatry he said that God is not far from every one of us, "for in Him we live, and move, and have our being." The men to whom he was speaking were heathen, yet it was just as true of them as it is of us. Then he quoted one of their own poets, who had said, "For we are also His offspring," and placed upon it the stamp of truth, by saying, "Forasmuch then as we are the offspring of God, we ought not to think that the Godhead is like unto gold, or silver, or stone, graven by art and man's device." Acts 17:27-29.

Every movement of men, and every breath, is the working of the external power of God. Thus the eternal power and divinity of God are manifest to every man. *Not that man is in any sense divine*, or that he has any power in himself. Quite the contrary. Man is like the grass. "Every man at his best state is altogether vanity." Psalm 39:5. The fact that man is nothing in himself, and even "less than nothing, and vanity," is evidence of the power of God manifested in him.

God's Power in the Grass—Look at the tiny blade of grass just pushing its way through the hard ground to the sunlight. It is a very frail thing. Pull it up, and you will see that it has not power to stand alone. Even scrape the soil away from it as it stands in the earth, and it will at once lose its upright position. It depends upon the soil to hold it up, and yet it is pushing its way to the surface through that very hard soil. Dissect it as carefully as you please, and you will find nothing to indicate the possession of power. Rub it between your fingers, and you will see that there is scarcely any substance to it. It is about as frail a thing as there is in nature, and yet it will often remove quite large stones that are in the way of its growth.

Whence comes this power? It is not inherent in the grass, but is nothing less than the power of the life of God, working according to His word, which in the beginning said, "Let the earth bring forth grass."

The Gospel in Creation—We have seen that in every created thing the power of God is manifested. And we also learned from the scripture studied last week that the gospel is "the power of God unto salvation." God's power is ever the same, for the text before us speaks of "his eternal power." The power, therefore, which is manifested in the things which

God has made is the same power that works in the hearts of men to save them from sin and death. Therefore we may be assured that God has constituted every portion of His universe a preacher of the gospel. So then men may not only know the fact of God's existence from the things which He has made, but they may know His eternal power to save them. The twentieth verse of the first chapter of Romans is an expansion of the sixteenth. It tells us how we may know the power of the gospel.

The Stars as Preachers—"The heavens declare the glory of God; and the firmament showeth His handiwork. Day unto day uttereth speech, and night unto night showeth knowledge. There is no speech nor language, where their voice is not heard (margin, "without these their voice is heard"). Their line is gone out through all the earth, and their words to the end of the world." Psalm 19:1-4.

Now read Romans 10:13-18: "Whosoever shall call upon the name of the Lord shall be saved. How then shall they call on Him in whom they have not believed? and how shall they believe in Him of whom they have not heard? and how shall they hear without a preacher? and how shall they preach, except they be sent? as it is written, How beautiful are the feet of them that preach the gospel of peace, and bring glad tidings of good things! But they have not all obeyed the gospel. For Esaias saith, Lord, who hath believed our report? So then faith cometh by hearing, and hearing by the word of God. But I say, Have they not heard? Yes verily, their sound went into all the earth, and their words unto the ends of the world."

In this text all the objections which men raise against the punishment of the heathen are answered. As stated in the first chapter, they are without excuse. The gospel has been made known to every creature under heaven. It is admitted that men can not call on one in whom they have not believed, and that they can not believe in one of whom they have not heard, and that they can not hear without a preacher. And that which they ought to hear, and which they have not obeyed, is the gospel.

Having stated this, the apostle asks, "Have they not heard?" and at once answers his own question by repeating the words of the nineteenth psalm, "Yes verily, their sound went into all the earth, and their words unto the ends of the world." Thus we learn that the speech which the heavens utter from day unto day is the gospel; and the knowledge which they show from night unto night is the knowledge of God.

The Heavens Reveal Righteousness—With the knowledge that that which the heavens declare is the gospel of Christ, which is the power of God unto salvation, we can easily follow the nineteenth psalm through. It seems to the casual reader that there is a break in the continuity of this psalm. From talking about the heavens, the writer suddenly begins to speak of the perfection of the law of God, and its converting power. "The law of the Lord is perfect, converting the soul; the testimony of the Lord is sure, making wise the simple." Verse 7. But there is no break at all. The law of God is the righteousness of God, and the gospel reveals the righteousness of God, and the heavens declare the gospel; therefore it follows that the heavens reveal the righteousness of God. "The heavens declare His righteousness, and all the people see His glory." Psalm 97:6.

The glory of God is His goodness, because we are told that it is through sin that men come short of His glory. Romans 3:23. Therefore we may know that whoever looks upon the heavens with reverence, seeing in them the power of the Creator, and will yield himself to that power, will be led to the saving righteousness of God. Even the sun, moon, and stars, whose light is but a part of the glory of the Lord, will shine that glory into his soul.

Without Excuse—How evident it is, therefore, that men are without excuse for their idolatrous practices. When the true God reveals Himself in everything, and with His power makes known His love, what excuse can men have for not knowing and worshiping Him?

But is it true that God makes known His love to all men? Yes, it is just as true as that He makes Himself known, for "God is love." Whoever knows the Lord must know His love. This being the case with regard to the heathen, how utterly without excuse are people who live in lands where the gospel is preached with an audible voice from His written word.

The Cause of Idolatry—How is it that if God has so clearly revealed Himself and His truth, there are so many who are in utter ignorance of Him? The answer is given, "Because that, when they knew God, they glorified Him not as God, neither were thankful."

There is one thing which God has given as the seal and sign of His divinity, and that is the Sabbath. Speaking of men, He says, "Moreover also I gave them My Sabbaths, to be a sign between Me and them, that they might know that I am the Lord that sanctify them." Ezekiel 20:12. This is in keeping with what we have learned in Romans; for our text tells us that God's power and divinity are perceived by thoughtful people through the things that He has made; and the Sabbath is the great memorial of creation. "Remember the Sabbath day, to keep it holy. Six days shalt thou labour, and do all thy work; but the seventh day is the Sabbath of the Lord thy God; in it thou shalt not do any work; ... for in six days the Lord made heaven and earth, the sea, and all that in them is, and rested the seventh day; wherefore the Lord blessed the Sabbath day, and hallowed it." Exodus 20:8-11. If people had always kept the Sabbath as it was given, there would never have been any idolatry; for the Sabbath reveals the power of the word of the Lord to create and to work righteousness.

Vain Imaginations—Men became vain in their imaginations, and their foolish heart was darkened. Gibbon says of the speculations of the ancient philosophers that "their reason had often been guided by their imagination, and their imagination had been prompted by their vanity." The course of their fall was the same as that of the angel who became Satan. "How art thou fallen from heaven, O Lucifer, son of the morning! how art thou cut down to the ground, which didst weaken the nations! For thou hast said in thine heart, I will ascend into heaven, I will exalt my throne above the stars of God; I will sit also upon the mount of the congregation, in the sides of the north; I will ascend above the heights of the clouds; I will be like the Most High." Isaiah 14:12-14.

What was the cause of this self-exaltation and fall? "Thine heart was lifted up because of thy beauty, thou hast corrupted thy wisdom by reason of thy brightness." Ezekiel 27:17. Dependent entirely upon God for all the wisdom and glory that he had, he did not glorify God, but assumed that all his talents sprang from himself; and so, as he disconnected himself in his pride from the Source of light, he became the prince of darkness. Even thus it was with man.

Changing the Truth Into a Lie—"There is no power but of God." In nature we see the manifestation of mighty power, but it is the working of God. All the different forms of force which philosophers name, and which they declare to be inherent in matter, are but the working of the life of God in the things that He has made. Christ is "before all things, and by Him all things consist," or hold together. Colossians 1:17. Cohesion therefore is but the direct power of the life of Christ. Gravitation also is the same power, as we read of the heavenly bodies, "for that He is strong in power; not one faileth." Isaiah 40:26. But men looked upon all the operations of nature, and, instead of seeing the *power* of the one supreme God in them, they attributed divinity to the things themselves.

So, as they looked upon themselves; and saw what great things they could achieve, instead of honoring God as the giver and upholder of all things, the One in whom they lived and moved and had their being, they assumed that they themselves were by nature divine. Thus they changed the truth of God into a lie.

The truth is that the life and power of God are manifested in everything that He has made; the lie is that the force which is manifest in all things is *inherent* in the things themselves. So men put the creature in the place of the Creator.

Looking Within—Marcus Aurelius, who is accounted the best of the heathen philosophers, said: "Look within. Within is the fountain of good, and it will ever bubble up, if thou wilt ever dig." That expresses the spirit of all heathenism. Self was the supreme thing. But that spirit is not peculiar to what is known as heathenism, for it is very common in these days; nevertheless, it is nothing but the spirit of heathenism. It is a part of the worship of the creature instead of the Creator. It is but natural that they should put themselves in His place; and when they do that, it is a necessary consequence that they look to themselves, and not to God, for goodness.

When men look within, what is the only thing that they can see? "Evil thoughts, adulteries, fornications, murders, thefts, covetousness, wickedness, deceit, lasciviousness, an evil eye, blasphemy, pride, foolishness." Mark 6:21, 22. Even the apostle Paul said, "I know that in me (that is, in my flesh) dwelleth no good thing." Romans 7:18. Now, when a man looks at all this evil which is in him by nature, and thinks that it is good, and that he can get good out of himself, the result can be plainly seen: the vilest wickedness must be the result. He virtually says, "Evil, be thou my good."

The Wisdom of This World—"The world by wisdom knew not God." Keenness of intellect is not faith, nor is it a substitute for faith. A man may be a brilliant scholar, and still be the basest of men. Several years ago a man charged with half a score or more brutal murders was hanged, and yet he was a scholar and a scientist, and had held a high position in society. Learning is not Christianity, although a Christian may be a learned man. Modern inventions will never save men from perdition. Some modern philosopher has said that "idolatry can not live by the side of the highest art and culture that the world has ever known." But at the same time men were sunk in such wickedness as referred to by the apostle in the last part of the first chapter of Romans. Even the reputed wise men were such as are there described. It was the natural result of their looking at themselves for righteousness.

In the Last Days—Read the last verses of the first chapter of Romans if you wish to have a picture of the world in the last days. The one who believes in a millennium of peace and righteousness before the coming of the Lord will doubtless be shocked; but he needs to be. Read that list of sins carefully, and then see how exactly it tallies with the following:

"This know also, that in the last days perilous times shall come. For men shall be lover of their own selves, covetous, boasters, proud, blasphemers, disobedient to parents, unthankful, unholy, without natural affection, trucebreakers, false accusers, incontinent, fierce, despisers of those that are good, traitors, heady, high-minded, lovers of pleasures more than lovers of God; having a form of godliness, but denying the power thereof." 2 Timothy 3:1-5. This all springs from self, the very source of the evil with which Paul charged the heathen. Those things are the works of the flesh. See Galatians 5:19-21. They are the natural result of trusting in self.

In spite of the declaration of the apostle, there are very few who will believe that this state of things will ever be general, and especially among those who profess godliness. But the seed which produces such a crop is already sown broadcast. The Papacy, "that man of sin," "the son of perdition; who opposeth and exalteth himself above all that is called God, or that is worshiped," is the strongest force in professed Christendom, and its power is daily increasing. And how is it increasing? Not so much by the direct accessions as by the blind acceptance of its principles by professed Protestants. It has placed itself above God in thinking to change His law. Daniel 7:25. It boldly adopted the heathen sun festival day, Sunday, in the place of the Sabbath of the Lord, the memorial of creation, and defiantly points to it as its badge of authority. And the majority of Protestants follow in its train, accepting a custom which stands for the exaltation of man above God, the symbol of justification by works instead of by faith.

When professed Christians cling to a human ordinance in spite of the express command of the Lord, and support their custom by appeals to the Fathers, men who were learned in the philosophy of heathenism, the road to any evil which their hearts may choose is but a down grade. "He that hath ears to hear, let him hear."

NOTES

"And they that be wise shall shine as the brightness of the firmament; and they that turn many to righteousness as the stars for ever and ever." Daniel 12:3

Chapter 2

The Sin of Others Is Our Sin, Too

Introduction

"Blessed is the man that walketh not in the counsel of the ungodly, nor standeth in the way of sinners, nor sitteth in the seat of the scornful. But his delight is in the law of the Lord; and in His law doth he meditate day and night." Psalm 1:1, 2.

"My son, if thou wilt receive my words, and hide my commandments with thee; so that thou incline thine ear unto wisdom, and apply thine heart to understanding; yea, if thou criest after knowledge, and liftest up thy voice for understanding; if thou seekest her as silver, and searchest for her as for hid treasures; then shalt thou understand the fear of the Lord, and find the knowledge of God. For the Lord giveth wisdom; out of his mouth cometh knowledge and understanding." Proverbs 2:1-6.

Here we have the secret of the understanding of the Bible: study and meditation, coupled with an earnest desire to know the will of God in order to do it. "If any man will do His will, he shall know of the doctrine." John 7:17. Repetition—*review*—is one of the prime essentials to knowledge of the Bible. Not that any amount of study will compensate for lack of the Holy Spirit's guidance, but that the Holy Spirit witnesses through the word.

A Look Backward

In this study of Romans we wish to carry along with us as much as possible of what we learn. We will therefore take a view of the first chapter as a whole. We have found that it is naturally divided somewhat as follows:—

Verses 1-7, the salutation, containing an epitome of the whole gospel.

Verses 8-15, Paul's personal interest in the Romans, and his sense of obligation to them and to all mankind.

Verses 16, 17, what the gospel is, and what it contains.

Verses 21-23, the corruption of wisdom.

Verses 24-32, the result of unthankfulness and of forgetting God.

A careful reading of the chapter shows that the main thought is that God has made Himself known to every soul in His creation, and that even the most degraded heathen know that they are guilty and are worthy of death for their wickedness. "Who, knowing the judgment of God, that they which commit such things are worthy of death, not only do the same, but have pleasure in them that do them." Verse 32. So "they are without excuse." This leading thought of the first chapter should be well in mind before beginning the second chapter, for the second is a continuation of the first, and dependent upon it.

A Wider View—Romans 2:1-11

1 Therefore thou art inexcusable, O man, whosoever thou art that judgest; for wherein thou judgest another, thou condemnest thyself; for thou that judgest doest the same things. 2 But we are sure that the judgment of God is according to truth against them which commit such things. 3 And thinkest thou this, O man, that judgest them which do such things, and doest the same, that thou shalt escape the judgment of God? 4 Or despisest thou the riches of His goodness and forbearance and long-suffering; not knowing that the goodness of God leadeth thee to repentance? 5 But, after thy hardness and impenitent heart, treasurest up unto thyself wrath against the day of wrath and revelation of the righteous judgment of God; 6 Who will render to every man according to his deeds; 7 to them who by patient continuance in well-doing seek for glory and honor and immortality, eternal life; 8 but unto them that are contentious, and do not obey the truth, but obey unrighteousness, indignation and wrath, 9 tribulation and anguish, upon every soul of man that doeth evil; of the Jew first, and also of the Gentile; 10 but glory, honor, and peace to every man that worketh good; to the Jew first, and also to the Gentile; 11 for there is no respect of persons with God.

Acknowledging Their Guilt—The truth of the apostle's statement is easy of demonstration concerning the heathen and their deeds, that they know that they are worthy of death. When Adam and Eve had eaten the forbidden fruit, they were afraid to meet God, and hid themselves. Fear is a necessary accompaniment of guilt, and a proof of it. "Fear hath torment. He that feareth is not made perfect in love." 1 John 4:18. "The wicked flee when no man pursueth; but the righteous are bold as a lion." Proverbs 28:1. "But the fearful … shall have their part in the lake which burneth with fire." Revelation 21:8. If the heathen did not know that they were guilty, they would not expect punishment for murdering or stealing, and would not arm themselves for defense.

An Unanswerable Charge—There is wonderful shrewdness in the way that the apostle works up the charge made in the first verse. The first chapter is confined to the heathen. All will agree with the apostle's statement that they are guilty of most abominable wickedness. "They ought to know better," is the almost involuntary exclamation. "They do know better," is the apostle's reply or, at least, they have a chance to know better, and they do know that they are not doing right. "They are without excuse." Whatever men may think about the responsibility of the heathen, all agree that their practices are to be condemned.

Then comes the crushing rejoinder: "Therefore thou art inexcusable, O man, whosoever thou art that judgest; for wherein thou judgest another, thou condemnest thyself; for thou that judgest doest the same things." We are caught, and can not escape. If we know enough to condemn the unrighteous deeds of the heathen, we by that very judgment acknowledge ourselves to be without excuse for our own misdeeds.

All Alike Are Guilty—"Thou that judgest doest the same things." It is clear enough that anybody who knows enough to condemn evil in another is without excuse for his own sins; but all will not at once see that the one who judges another does the same things. Read, therefore the last verses of the first chapter again, and compare the list of sins with that found in Galatians 5:19-21, and it will be seen that the things which the heathen do, and for which we can readily see that they are guilty, are but the works of the flesh. They are the sins that come "from within, out of the heart of men." Mark 7:21-23. Whoever is included in the term "man" is subject to just such things. "The Lord looketh from heaven; He beholdeth all the sons of men. From the place of His habitation He looketh upon all the inhabitants of the earth. He fashioneth their hearts alike; He considereth all their works." Psalm 33:13-15.

All Are Self-condemned—Therefore, since all men are alike sharers in one common human nature, it is evident that whosoever in the world condemns another for any misdeed thereby condemns himself; for the truth is that all have the same evil in them, more or less fully developed; and the fact that they know enough to judge that a thing is wrong, is a declaration that they themselves are worthy of the punishment which they see that the other one deserves.

Sympathy, Not Condemnation—The robber often cries out, "Stop thief!" after some other man, in order to direct pursuit away from himself. So people condemn sin in others, in order that it may not be suspected that they are guilty of the same things. Often, too, people—

> "Compound for sins they are inclined to
> by damning those they have no mind to,"

but of which they are actually guilty by reason of their human nature.

Since all flesh of man is the same, we ought to be filled with humiliation, instead of contempt, when we hear of a gross sin that is committed; for it is really a picture of what is in our own hearts. Instead of saying, "God, I thank thee that I am not as other men," we should bear the burden of the erring, considering ourselves lest we also be tempted. Very often the man whose weakness we feel inclined to condemn, has not failed so badly as we should have done if we had been tempted in the same way, and to the same degree.

Outcry Against Sin—In *Pilgrim's Progress* when Talkative left Faithful to decide upon the subject of their conversation, Faithful proposed this question: "How doth the saving grace of God discover itself when it is in the heart of man?" And then Bunyan proceeds thus:

> "Talk—I perceive then that our talk must be about the power of things. Well, it is a very good question, and I shall be willing to answer you; and take my answer in brief thus: First, where the grace of God is in the heart, it causeth there a great outcry against sin. Secondly—

> "Faith—Nay, hold, let us consider of one at a time. I think you should rather say, It shows itself by inclining the soul to abhor its sin.

> "Talk—Why, what difference is there between crying out against and abhorring sin?

> "Faith—O, a great deal! A man may cry out against a sin, of policy; but he can not abhor it but by virtue of a godly antipathy

against it. I have heard many cry out against sin in the pulpit, who can yet abide it well enough in the heart, house, and conversation. Joseph's mistress cried out with a loud voice, as if she had been very chaste; but she would willingly, notwithstanding that, have committed uncleanness with him."

A keen perception of right and wrong, and a vigorous denunciation of sin, will never justify any man. On the contrary, they only deepen his condemnation. It is a sad fact that too many of the so-called reformers of the present day seem to think that gospel work consists largely in the denunciation of evil practices. A detective is not a minister of the gospel.

Judgment According to Truth—"But we are sure that the judgment of God is according to truth against them which commit such things." "Hold," says one, "I am not sure of that." Well, you may very easily assure yourself of it:

(1) God exists. We are agreed as to that.

(2) He is the source whence every created thing comes.

(3) Every creature is absolutely dependent upon Him. "In Him we live, and move, and have our being."

(4) Since all life depends on Him, it is evident that the continuation of man's life depends upon his agreement and union with God.

(5) Therefore God's own character must be the standard of judgment.

(6) But God Himself is truth. "There is no unrighteousness in Him."

(7) But He has made a revelation of Himself and His righteousness to all men. "His righteousness hath He openly showed in the sight of the heathen." Psalm 97:2.

(8) Therefore all men, from the least to the greatest, are without excuse for their sin.

(9) Then it is plain enough that when God judges all men, without exception, His judgment is according to truth. And earth will be constrained to join with heaven in saying, "Thou art righteous, O Lord, which art, and wast, and shalt be, because Thou hast judged thus." "Even so, Lord God Almighty, true and righteous are Thy judgments." Revelation 16: 5, 7.

No Escape—No one need think that he can escape the righteous judgment of God. It is usually the most enlightened who flatter themselves that they shall escape. It is so easy for us to think that our great knowledge of right and wrong will be counted for righteousness, to persuade ourselves that our condemnation of the sins of others will make the Lord believe that we could never be guilty of such things. But that only makes our condemnation the more clear.

The first chapter of Romans knocks all the props from under every man. If the lowest are justly held guilty, there is no escape for the "higher classes." "God shall bring every work into judgment, with every secret thing, whether it be good, or whether it be evil." Ecclesiastes 12:14.

God's Goodness Leads to Repentance—"Despisest thou the riches of His goodness and forbearance and long-suffering; not knowing that the goodness of God leadeth thee to repentance." God is the perfection of purity and holiness; man is altogether sinful. God knows every sin, yet He does not despise the sinner. "God sent not His Son into the world to condemn the world; but that the world through Him might be saved." John 3:17. Christ said, "If any man hear My words, and believe not, I judge him not." John 12:47.

In everything that He said and did, He was simply representing the Father. God "is long-suffering to usward;" and "the long-suffering of our God is salvation." 2 Peter 3:9, 15. Now it is impossible that one should consider the goodness and long-suffering of God without being humbled and moved to repentance. When we consider how tenderly God bears with us, it is not possible that we should deal harshly with our fellow-men. And if we do not judge, we shall not be judged. Luke 6:37.

Repentance Is a Gift—"By grace are ye saved through faith; and that not of yourselves; it is the gift of God." Ephesians 2:8. "The God of our fathers raised up Jesus, whom ye slew and hanged on a tree. Him hath God exalted with His right hand to be a Prince and a Saviour, for to give repentance to Israel, and forgiveness of sins." Acts 5:30, 31. But it was not to Israel alone that God gave repentance through Christ. "To Him give all the prophets witness, that through His name whosoever believeth in Him shall receive remission of sins." Acts 10:43. And so plainly did God make this appear that even the exclusive Jews were forced to exclaim, "Then hath God also to the Gentiles granted repentance unto life." Acts 11:18.

Incentives to Repentance—The goodness of God leads men to repentance. Therefore the whole earth is full of incentives to repentance, for "the earth is full of the goodness of the Lord." Psalm 33:5. "The earth, O

Lord, is full of Thy mercy." Psalm 119:64. God may be known through His works, and "God is love." All creation reveals the love and mercy of God.

And we need not try to improve on the Scriptures, and say that the goodness of God *tends* to lead men to repentance. The Bible says that it *does* lead them to repentance, and we may be sure that it is so. Every man is being led toward repentance as surely as God is good. But not all repent. Why? Because they despise the riches of the goodness and forbearance and long-suffering of God, and break away from the merciful leading of the Lord. But whoever does not resist the Lord, will surely be brought to repentance and salvation.

Treasuring Up Wrath—In the first chapter we learned that "the wrath of God is revealed from heaven against all ungodliness and unrighteousness of men." Therefore all who sin are treasuring up for themselves wrath. It should be noted that in the judgment God is clear. Men receive only what they have worked for. God is not arbitrary. He has not fixed arbitrary decrees, and declared that whoever violates them shall be visited with vengeance. The punishment that will come upon the wicked is the necessary result of their own choice. God is the only source of life.

His life is peace. Now when men reject Him, the only alternative for them is wrath and death. "For that they hated knowledge, and did not choose the fear of the Lord; they would none of my counsel; they despised all my reproof. Therefore shall they eat of the fruit of their own way, and be filled with their own devices. For the turning away of the simple shall slay them, and the prosperity of fools shall destroy them." Proverbs 1:29-32. Trouble and death are bound up in sin; they are what men choose when they refuse the Lord.

"According to His Deeds"—Unbelievers often say that it is not just for God to condemn a man simply because he does not believe a certain thing. But He does not do so. Not a word can be found in the Bible about judging a man according to his belief. Everywhere it is said that all will be judged according to their works. "For the Son of man shall come in the glory of His Father with His angels; and then He shall reward every man according to his works." Matthew 16:27. "Behold, I come quickly; and My reward is with Me, to give every man according as his work shall be." Revelation 22:12. He "judgeth according to every man's work." 1 Peter 1:17.

The man who says that his work is all right, sets himself up as judge in the place of God, who says that every man is all wrong. God is Judge alone, and He judges strictly according to a man's work, but a man's work is decided by his faith. "This is the work of God, that ye believe on Him whom He hath sent." John 6:29. It is not for any man to judge himself, and say that his work is all right. It is for him simply to trust the goodness and mercy of the Lord, that his work may be wrought in God.

Immortality and Eternal Life—God will render eternal life to them who seek for glory and honor and immortality. Christ "hath brought life and immortality to light through the gospel." 2 Timothy 1:10. Life and immortality are two different things. Whoever believes on the Son of God has eternal life. "This is life eternal, that they might know Thee the only true God, and Jesus Christ, whom Thou hast sent." John 17:3.

We have eternal life as soon as we know the Lord; but we can not have immortality until the Lord comes, at the last day. "We shall not all sleep, but we shall all be changed, in a moment, in the twinkling of an eye, at the last trump; for the trumpet shall sound, and the dead shall be raised incorruptible, and we shall be changed. For this corruptible must put on incorruption, and this mortal must put on immortality." 1 Corinthians 15:51-53.

We are to seek for immortality; that of itself is proof that no man has it now. Since Christ has brought it to light through the gospel, it is evident that immortality can be found in no other way than through the gospel. Therefore those who do not accept the gospel will never have immortality.

Tribulation and Anguish—Those who sin are the children of wrath. Ephesians 2:3. Indignation and wrath, tribulation and anguish, are sure to come upon evil doers. But tribulation and anguish will have an end. The fact that none receive immortality except the ones who are Christ's at His coming, shows that all others will eventually cease to exist. There will be torment in connection with the punishment of the wicked, but the torment, however long it may continue, will come to an end in the utter destruction of the wicked. God's indignation will come to an end. "For yet a very little while, and the indignation shall cease, and Mine anger in their destruction." Isaiah 10:25.

The call is: "Come, My people, enter thou into thy chambers, and shut thy doors about thee; hide thyself as it were for a little moment, until the indignation be overpast. For, behold, the Lord cometh out of His place to punish the inhabitants of the earth for their iniquity." Isaiah 16:20, 21. "He will not always chide; neither will He keep His anger forever." Psalm 103:9. His anger will cease, not because He will become reconciled to iniquity, but because iniquity will come to an end with its workers.

"To Every Soul"—Tribulation and anguish will come upon "every soul of man that doeth evil," and "glory, honor, and peace to every man that worketh good." None will be left out. There is not a soul so poor and ignorant that he will be passed by, nor one so wealthy and learned that he will be allowed to escape. Wealth and position will have no influence in that court. God has made the revelation of Himself so plain that every man has had an opportunity of knowing Him. "The wrath of God is revealed from heaven against all ungodliness and unrighteousness of men who hold down the truth in unrighteousness." Note well that His wrath is revealed against sin. Only those persons will suffer who cling to sin, and will not allow God to take it from them. In the final blotting out of sin, they are necessarily blotted out with it.[1]

To the Jew First—This statement is sufficient to show that God is no respecter of persons. Indeed, the apostle states as a necessary conclusion that "there is no respect of persons with God." "First" does not always refer to time. We speak of a man as being the first man in the country, not because there were no men before him, but because he is the chief man. In school a certain one is the first one in his class because he is the best scholar. The Jew is the one who has had the greatest revelation made to him, and therefore it is just that he should be chief in the judgment.

The text shows, however, that God has no special favor to the Jew over other men. If glory, honor, and peace come to the Jew first, so also do indignation and wrath, tribulation and anguish. The question is not, "What is the man's nationality?" but, "What has he done?" God will render to every man according to his deeds, "for there is no respect of persons with God."

A few words may suffice to bring to mind what we have already studied. The first chapter of Romans may be briefly summed up as setting forth the condition of those who know not God, and the way in which they lost their knowledge, together with the fact that they are wholly without excuse. Then, just as we are ready to hold up our hands in horror at their wickedness, and to launch forth severe condemnation upon them, the apostle turns to us, and shuts our mouths with the stinging words, "Therefore thou art inexcusable, O man, whosoever thou art that judgest; for wherein thou judgest another, thou condemnest thyself; for thou that judgest doest the same things."

And so the second chapter proceeds to show that all will be subjects of God's righteous judgment, "for there is no respect of persons with God." Thus we are brought to a confirmation of the fact that God is impartial, by a comparison of the two classes in the Judgment.

---

1. A.T. Jones, *Our God Is A Consuming Fire*, Appendix A, p. 213.

All Will Be Subjects to God's Righteous Judgment—Romans 2:12-16

12 For as many as have sinned without law shall also perish without law; and as many as have sinned in the law shall be judged by the law 13 (for not the hearers of the law are just before God, but the doers of the law shall be justified. 14 For when the Gentiles, which have not the law, do by nature the things contained in the law, these, having not the law, are a law unto themselves; 15 which show the work of the law written in their hearts, their conscience also bearing witness, and their thoughts the meanwhile accusing or else excusing one another); 16 in the day when God shall judge the secrets of men by Jesus Christ according to my gospel.

Without Law, and in the Law—Although it is quite certain that when the Lord comes the second time there will be no people on the earth who have not heard the preaching of the word, it is a fact that thousands and millions have died without ever having seen or heard of the Bible. They are the ones to whom the apostle refers as "without law." Yet it is plainly set forth that they are not absolutely without law, but only without the *written* law. The fact that they have some knowledge of the law is stated in the verses following, and is proved by the fact that they are counted sinners; but "sin is not imputed where there is no law." Romans 5:13.

All Sin Punished—Whether we have had the written law or not, all are alike counted sinners. "The wrath of God is revealed from heaven against all ungodliness and unrighteousness of men." Romans 1:18. The heathen are declared to be without excuse; and if they who have not the written law are without excuse, they who have the law in their hands are of course far more inexcusable. God is just. "We know that the judgment of God is according to truth against them which commit such things." Yet all who sin, whether in the law or without the law, are to be punished.

This is sufficient to show that "without law" does not mean without any knowledge of God. The first chapter settles that. The trouble with too many who read this statement that all shall be punished, and who think that it does not seem just, is that they forget, or are ignorant of, what is contained in the first chapter. It is a great mistake to take any single verse of the Bible and separate it from its connection.

They Shall Perish—That is declared to be the fate of the wicked. The apostle Peter tells us that the world is "reserved unto fire against the day of judgment and perdition of ungodly men." 2 Peter 3:7. What is meant by "perish?" It means just the opposite of living forever. On one occasion some people told Jesus of the Galileans whose blood Pilate had mingled with their sacrifices, and Jesus replied, "Except ye repent, ye shall all likewise perish." Luke 13:1-3. Again we read, "The wicked shall perish, and the enemies of the Lord shall be as the fat of lambs; they shall consume; into smoke shall they consume away." Psalm 37:20. Therefore the statement that those who sin shall perish means that they shall die, that they shall be utterly extinct, that "they shall be as though they had not been." Obadiah 16.

Strict Impartiality—That means strict justice. Sinners will be punished, whether they live in heathen lands or in so-called Christian lands. But no one will be judged by that of which he knew nothing. God does not punish men for violation of a law of which they knew nothing, nor does he hold them accountable for light that they have not had. It is very plain that those who have the law must know many things that are not known to those who do not have it in written form. All men have light enough to know that they are sinners; but the written word gives those who have it a knowledge of many particulars of which those are ignorant who do not have it.

Therefore God in His justice does not hold the latter accountable for many things for which the former will be judged. "As many as have sinned without law shall also perish without law; and as many as have sinned in the law shall be judged by the law." The man who has rejected light, whether it be little or much, is obviously guilty.

The Root of Sin—To some it seems unjust that those who have had but comparatively little light should suffer death for their sins, the same as those who have sinned against the greatest light. Their difficulty arises from the fact that they do not consider what sin really is. God alone is good. Luke 18:19. He is the source of goodness. Whatever goodness ever appears in man is only the working of God in him.

But He is also the source of life. With him is the fountain of life. Psalm 36:9. God's life is righteousness; therefore there can be no righteousness apart from the life of God. Now it is evident that if a man rejects God, he effectually cuts himself off from life. It matters not that he has had but comparatively little knowledge of God, if he rejects that light he rejects God, and thus rejects life. And by rejecting the little that he has seen of God, he shows that he would reject God in any case. Sin is simply separation from or rejection of God; and that means death.

"Thou Art the Man"—Romans 2:17-24

17 Behold, thou art called a Jew, and restest in the law, and makest thy boast of God, 18 and knowest His will, and approvest the things that are more excellent, being instructed out of the law; 19 and art confident that thou thyself art a guide of the blind, a light of them which are in darkness, 20 an instructor of the foolish, a teacher of babes, which hast the form of knowledge and of the truth in the law. 21 Thou therefore which teachest another, teachest thou not thyself? thou that preachest a man should not steal, dost thou steal? 22 Thou that sayest a man should not commit adultery, dost thou commit adultery? Thou that abhorrest idols, dost thou commit sacrilege? 23 Thou that makest thy boast of the law, through breaking the law dishonorest thou God? 24 For the name of God is blasphemed among the Gentiles through you, as it is written.

A Professed Jew—Are professed Christians to throw away this portion of the book of Romans as not applicable to them, since it is addressed to a professed Jew? By no means. Professed Christians are the very ones who are meant by the apostle. Read the description: Thou "restest in the law, and makest thy boast of God, and knowest His will, and approvest the things that are more excellent, being instructed out of the law; and art confident that thou thyself art a guide of the blind, a light of them which are in darkness, an instructor of the foolish, a teacher of babes, which hast the form of knowledge and of the truth in the law."

Whom does he address? Every one who professes to know the Lord, no matter by what name he is called; every one who thinks himself fully qualified to instruct others in the way of the Lord.

"Called a Jew"—It should not be overlooked as a trifling matter that the apostle does not say, "Behold, thou art a Jew," but, "Behold, thou art *called* a Jew." People are not always what they are called, nor what they call themselves. Beginning with the seventeenth verse the apostle settles the question of who are Jews. Before we have finished the chapter it will seem that by using the word "called" he meant to intimate that the one addressed and described in the following verses is not really a Jew, and is not considered so by the Lord.

Claiming to Be Jews—In Revelation 2:9 we read, "I know the blasphemy of them which say they are Jews, and are not, but are the synagogue of Satan." And again, "Behold, I will make them of the synagogue of Satan, which say they are Jews, and are not, but do lie; behold, I will make them to come and worship before thy feet, and to know that I have loved thee."

Revelation 3:9. From this we see that to be a Jew indeed is so high an honor that many will falsely claim it. Yet the people called Jews have been held in contempt by the greater part of the world, for many hundred years.

At no time and in no part of the world, since the New Testament was written, has it ever been an object for anybody to claim that he was a Jew, in the common acceptation of the term. The Jews as a class have never been in such honor that it would benefit one's prospects to be called one. But it has been and is very often an advantage for a man to be known as a Christian, and very many have falsely made the claim, in order to better their business prospects.

Jew and Christian—It is not straining the text at all to say that when "Jew" is used in these verses, it means what is now known as "Christian." This will be apparent if we consider what a real Jew is. We may quote enough to show that from the beginning a true Jew was one who believed in Christ. Of the head of the race the Lord Jesus said, "Your father Abraham rejoiced to see My day; and he saw it, and was glad." John 8:56. He believed in the Lord, and it was counted to him for righteousness; but righteousness comes only through the Lord Jesus. Moses, the leader of the Jews, esteemed "the reproach of Christ greater riches than the treasures in Egypt." Hebrews 11:26. The rebellious Jews in the wilderness tempted and rejected Christ. 1 Corinthians 10:9. When Christ came in the flesh, it was "His own" that received Him not. John 1:11. And to crown all, Christ said that no one could believe the writings of Moses unless he believed on Him. John 5:46, 47. Therefore it is evident that no one is or ever has been a real Jew unless he believes in Christ. He who is not a Jew indeed is of "the synagogue of Satan."

"Salvation Is of the Jews"—Jesus said to the woman of Samaria at the well of Jacob, "Ye worship ye know not what; we know what we worship; for salvation is of the Jews." John 4:22. Christ Himself was "made of the seed of David according to the flesh," and was therefore a Jew; and there is no other name than His "under heaven … whereby we must be saved."

No other people on earth, besides the Jews, have ever had so high a name. No other people have been so highly favored of God. "For what nation is there so great, who hath God so nigh unto them, as the Lord our God is in all things that we call upon Him for? And what nation is there so great, that hath statutes and judgments so righteous as all this law, which I set before you this day?" Deuteronomy 4:7, 8.

Resting in the Law—As stated in the verse last quoted, the Jews had committed to them the most perfect law in the universe, God's own. It was called "the testimony," because it was for a witness against them. They were not taught that they could get righteousness *out* of it, although it was perfect, but the contrary. Because it was so perfect, and they were sinners, it could have nothing but condemnation for them. It was designed only to drive them *to* Christ, in whom alone they could find the perfect righteousness that the law requires. "The law worketh wrath" (Romans 4:15), and Christ alone saves from wrath. But they "rested in the law," and therefore rested in sin. They "trusted in themselves that they were righteous." Luke 18:9. They found no righteousness, "because they sought it not by faith, but as it were by the works of the law." Romans 9:31, 32.

Boasting of God—This is something different from making one's boast in the Lord. Psalm 34:2. Instead of rejoicing in the Lord's salvation, the Jews boasted over their superior knowledge of God. They did indeed have more than others, but they had nothing that they had not received, yet they boasted as though they had not received it. They glorified themselves, rather than God, for the knowledge that they had; and therefore they put themselves in the condition of the heathen who "when they knew God, glorified Him not as God, neither were thankful, but became vain in their imaginations." Whatever reader is inclined to censure the ancient Jews for their vain boasting, let him remember how he himself has often felt on comparing himself with the inhabitants of heathen countries, and with the "lowest class" in his own land.

God's Will His Law—The apostle says that the Jew knows the will of God, because he is instructed out of the law. This is sufficient to show that the law of God is his will. Indeed, no argument should be needed on this point. The will of any government is expressed in its law. Where there is an absolute ruler, his will is always law. God is an absolute ruler, although not an arbitrary one, and as His will is the sole rule of right, it follows that His will is law. But His law is summed up in the Ten Commandments; therefore the Ten Commandments contain a summary statement of the will of God.

The Form of Knowledge and Truth—Although the Ten Commandments contain a statement of the will of God, which is the perfection of wisdom and truth, they are only a statement, and not the thing itself, just the same as a picture of a house is not a house, although it may be a perfect picture. Mere words written in a book or graven in stone have no life; but we know that the law of God is life everlasting. Only in Christ can the living law be found, since He is the only manifestation of the Godhead.

Whoever has the life of Christ dwelling in him, has the perfect law of God manifest in his life. But he who has only the letter of the law, and not Christ, has only the form of knowledge and of truth. Thus, the law is often rightly said to be a photograph of the character of God. But a photograph or other picture is only the shadow of the reality; it is not the very substance. He who has Christ has both the form and the substance, since one can not have a thing without also possessing its form. But he who has only the statement of the truth, without Christ who alone is the Truth has the form of godliness without the power thereof.

Hard Questions—In verses 21-23 the apostle asks some hard questions. Let each soul that has been wont to pride himself upon the correctness of his life answer these questions for himself. It is easy and natural for a man to pride himself upon his "morality." Men who are not Christians comfort themselves with the thought that they live "moral" lives, and that therefore they are as well off as though they were Christians. Let all such know that there is no morality except conformity to the law of God. Everything that is in any respect below the standard of that law is immorality. Knowing this, let them see if they have perfectly kept that law.

"Dost Thou Steal?"—Most people will say, "No; I am honest in all my dealing." Very well, but let us not decide the case offhand. Let us examine the Scripture. It says, "The law is spiritual." Romans 7:14. "The word of God is quick, and powerful, and sharper than any two-edged sword, piercing even to the dividing asunder of soul and spirit, and of the joints and marrow, and is a discerner of the thoughts and intents of the heart." Hebrews 4:12. No matter how correct we are in our outward acts, if in spirit or thought we have transgressed, we are guilty. The Lord looks at the heart, instead of the outward appearance. 1 Samuel 16:7.

Again, it is just as wrong to steal from God as to steal from man; have you given God His due? Have you dealt in a perfectly honest way with Him? Hear what He says: "Will a man rob God? Yet ye have robbed Me. But ye say, Wherein have we robbed Thee? In tithes and offerings. Ye are cursed with a curse; for ye have robbed Me, even this whole nation." Malachi 3:8, 9. Does this mean you? Have you rendered to God that which is His due in tithes and offerings? If not, what will you answer when the word of inspiration asks, "Thou that preachest a man should not steal, dost thou steal?"

"The Law Is Spiritual"—In the fifth chapter of Matthew the Saviour has set forth the spirituality of the law. He says that unless our righteousness shall exceed the righteousness of the scribes and Pharisees, we can not enter the kingdom of heaven. What was their righteousness? He said to them, "Ye also outwardly appear righteous unto men, but within ye are full of hypocrisy and iniquity." Matthew 23:28.

Therefore, unless we are righteous inwardly, we are nothing. God desires "truth in the inward parts." Psalm 51:6. Following on in the fifth chapter of Matthew, the Saviour shows that one may break the sixth commandment, which says, "Thou shalt not kill," by the utterance of a single word. He also shows that we may break the seventh commandment which says, "Thou shalt not commit adultery," by a look and a thought. The same principle of course obtains with all the commandments. This being the case, it becomes one to be very careful about saying that he has perfectly kept the law.

Some have said that the Ten Commandments are a very low standard, and that a man might keep them all and still not be worthy of admission into respectable society. Such know nothing about the law. As a matter of fact, a man may break all the commandments, and still figure as a shining light in the "best society."

The Name of God Blasphemed—"The name of God is blasphemed among the Gentiles through you, as it is written." Who has done this? The one who teaches the law, and who says that one who teaches the law, and who says that one should not take the name of the Lord in vain. When David sinned in the case of Uriah's wife, God said to him, "By this deed thou hast given great occasion to the enemies of the Lord to blaspheme." 2 Samuel 12:14. That is, he was a professed follower of the Lord, and by his violation of the law of the Lord he had given unbelievers a chance to say, "There, that is a specimen of Christianity."

Who is there that can say that as a professed follower of the Lord he has always correctly represented the truth? Who is there that must not admit to himself and God that either by his words or actions he has very often misrepresented the truth which he professed? Who is there that has not by his failures, either in teaching or acting, given people a miserably inadequate idea of what true godliness is?

In short, who is there that must not say yes to the apostle's question, "Through breaking the law, dishonorest thou God?" And since thus the name of God is blasphemed through professed Christians, who is there that can declare himself guiltless before God's law?

In these verses we have had some sharp questions to those who are "called Jews," that is, who profess to be followers of the Lord. Mere form and profession do not constitute one a proper teacher of the truth of God. He who does not exhibit in his life the power of that which he professes, is only a detriment to the cause. In the verses now before us we have a brief but explicit statement concerning—

Circumcision and Uncircumcision—Romans 2:25-29

> 25 For circumcision verily profiteth, if thou keep the law; but if thou be a breaker of the law, thy circumcision is made uncircumcision.

26 Therefore, if the uncircumcision keep the righteousness of the law, shall not his uncircumcision be counted for circumcision? 27 And shall not uncircumcision which is by nature, if it fulfill the law, judge thee, who by the letter and circumcision dost transgress the law? 28 For he is not a Jew, which is one outwardly; neither is that circumcision, which is outward in the flesh: 29 but he is a Jew, which is one inwardly; and circumcision is that of the heart, in the spirit, and not in the letter; whose praise is not of men, but of God.

Definition of Terms—The two terms "circumcision" and "uncircumcision" are here used not only to indicate the rite and the absence of it, but also to designate two classes of people. "The uncircumcision" evidently refers to those who were called Gentiles, those who worshiped other gods. This use of the terms is very plain in the following passage: "When they saw that the gospel of the uncircumcision was committed unto me, as the gospel of the circumcision was unto Peter (for he that wrought effectually in Peter to the apostleship of the circumcision, the same was mighty in me toward the Gentiles); and when James, Cephas, and John, who seemed to be pillars, perceived the grace that was given unto me, they gave to me and Barnabas the right hands of fellowship; that we should go unto the heathen, and they unto the circumcision." Galatians 2:7-9. Here we find that the terms "uncircumcision," "Gentiles," and "heathen," all refer to the same people.

Just what was the profit of circumcision, we are not told in this chapter. The statement of the fact was enough for this place, for the only point in the mind of the writer was to show what circumcision is, and who are the really circumcised. A great deal depends upon these few verses. They should be studied carefully, because upon them depends the proper understanding of a large portion of the prophecies of the Old Testament.

If these verses had received the consideration that they ought to have by professed Bible students, there would never have been any "Anglo-Israel" theory, and the unprofitable and misleading suppositions about the return of the Jews to Jerusalem before the coming of the Lord would never have been made.

What Is Circumcision?—This question is answered in plain language in Romans 4:11, where the apostle, speaking of Abraham, the first one who was circumcised, says: "And he received the sign of circumcision, a seal of the righteousness of the faith which he had yet being uncircumcised." To the question, "What is circumcision?" the answer must therefore be, The *sign* of circumcision is a *seal* of righteousness by faith.

When Circumcision Is Made Uncircumcision—This being the case, it is evident that where there was no righteousness, the sign of circumcision was worthless. So the apostle says, "If thou be a breaker of the law, thy circumcision is made uncircumcision." As in the previous verses we learned that the form without the fact amounts to nothing, so here we are told that the sign without the substance is of no account. It is very easy for a poor man to put out a sign advertising boots and shoes; but to fill the shop with goods requires capital. If he has the sign, but has no boots and shoes, he is worse off than if he had no sign.

The Mistake of the Jews—The Jews made a mistake of supposing that the sign was sufficient. They finally came to hold the idea that the sign would bring the reality, just as many professed Christians in these days suppose that the performance of certain rites will make them members of the body of Christ. But circumcision of the flesh alone could represent no righteousness, but sin. See Galatians 5:19-21. As a matter of fact, many of those whom they despised as "uncircumcised" were thus in reality "circumcised," while they themselves were not.

Circumcision of the Heart—Real circumcision is a matter of the heart, that is, of the inner life, and not at all of the flesh.[2] The apostle plainly declares that what is outward in the flesh is not circumcision, that is, which consists only in outward form; but "circumcision is that of the heart, in the spirit, and not in the letter." This is stated as a general truth.

This was not a new departure in the days of Paul, but was the case from the beginning. In Deuteronomy 30:6 we read the words of Moses to the children of Israel: "And the Lord thy God will circumcise thine heart, and the heart of thy seed, to love the Lord thy God with all thine heart, and with all thy soul, that thou mayest live." All true Jews recognized that true circumcision was only of the heart, for Stephen addressed those who rejected the truth as "stiffnecked and uncircumcised in heart and ears." Acts 7:51.

Righteousness in the Heart—The psalmist says, "Behold, thou desirest truth in the inward parts." Psalm 2:6. Mere outward righteousness is nothing. See Matthew 5:20; 23:27, 28. It is with the heart that man believeth unto righteousness. Romans 10:10. When Moses, at the command of the Lord, rehearsed the law to Israel, he said: "Thou shalt love the Lord thy God with all thine heart, and with all thy soul, and with all thy might. And these words, which I command thee this day, shall be in thine heart." Deuteronomy 6:5, 6. There can be no righteousness that is not real in the

---

2. E.J. Waggoner, *The Glad Tidings*, Appendix A, p. 214.

life. Therefore, since circumcision is but a sign of righteousness, it is evident that there can be no real circumcision except circumcision of the heart.

Circumcised by the Spirit—"For we know that the law is spiritual." Romans 7:14. That is, it is the nature of the Holy Spirit, for the word of God is the sword of the Spirit of God that can put the law of God into the heart of man. Therefore true circumcision is the work of the Holy Spirit. Stephen called the wicked Jews uncircumcised, because, said he, "Ye do always resist the Holy Ghost." Acts 7:51. It seems evident, therefore, that, although the word "spirit" in Romans 2:29 is not spelled with a capital "S," it refers to the Holy Spirit and not merely to the spirit of man. (Of course in the Greek there is nothing to indicate any difference, just as in English the word is spelled the same whether it refers to the Spirit of God or the spirit of man.)

If we remember that circumcision was given as the seal of righteousness by faith, and that the inheritance promised to Abraham and his seed was through the righteousness of the law (Romans 4:11, 13), we shall see that circumcision was the pledge of the inheritance. The apostle also says that we obtain the inheritance in Christ "in whom also, after that ye believed, ye were sealed with that Holy Spirit of promise, which is the earnest of our inheritance until the redemption of the purchased possession." Ephesians 1:10-13. The possession promised to Abraham and to his seed was assured only through the Spirit of righteousness; therefore, from the very beginning there was no real circumcision that was not of the Spirit.

Circumcision Through Christ—"Ye are complete in Him, which is the head of all principality and power; in whom also ye are circumcised with the circumcision made without hands, in putting off the body of the sins of the flesh by the circumcision of Christ." Colossians 2:8-11. Circumcision must have meant as much when first given as it ever did. Therefore from the very beginning it meant righteousness through Christ alone. This is sufficiently shown in the fact that circumcision was given to Abraham as the seal of the righteousness which he had by faith, and that "he believed in the Lord; and He counted it to him for righteousness." Genesis 15:6.

Who Are the "Circumcision"?—This question is answered in Philippians 3:3: "For we are the circumcision, which worship God in the spirit, and rejoice in Christ Jesus, and have no confidence in the flesh." And this is but saying in other words what we have in our text, "Circumcision is that of the heart, in the spirit, and not in the letter; whose praise is not of men, but of God." Nobody therefore was ever really circumcised who did not believe and rejoice in Christ Jesus. That is the reason why Stephen called the unbelieving Jews "uncircumcised."

The Meaning of Circumcision—We have not space to go into this question in detail, but the above texts put us on the track. A careful study of the chapters in Genesis which speak of God's covenant with Abraham will also help to clear up the matter.

We learn in Genesis 15 that God made a covenant with Abraham on the basis of his faith. The sixteenth chapter tells how Abraham listened to the voice of his wife instead of the voice of the Lord, and sought to work out the promise of God through the flesh and made a failure. His son was to be born of the Spirit, and not after the flesh. See Galatians 4:22, 23, 28, 29.

Then the seventeenth chapter shows the revival of Abraham's faith, and the renewal of the covenant, with circumcision as the seal. A portion of flesh was cut off to indicate that he was to have no confidence in the flesh, but was to expect righteousness and the inheritance only through the Spirit of God. The descendants of Abraham would thus have a continual reminder of his mistake and would be admonished to trust the Lord and not themselves.

But they perverted this sign. They regarded it as indicating that they were better than other people, instead of looking upon it as an evidence that "the flesh profiteth nothing." But the fact that the Jews perverted and misunderstood the sign does not destroy its original meaning.

Who Are Jews?—We have seen in a quotation from the second chapter of Galatians that the term "uncircumcised" refers to those who do not know the Lord, or who are "without God in the world." See Ephesians 2:11, 12. The Jews are "the circumcision." But only those who rejoice in Christ Jesus are the circumcision, who have no confidence in the flesh. Therefore the real Jews are none other than Christians. "He is a Jew, which is one inwardly." There never was a real Jew in the sight of God who was not a believer in Christ. And every true believer in Christ is a Jew in the Bible sense of the term. Abraham, the father of the Jewish nation, rejoiced in Christ. See John 8:56.

A Mark of Separation—Many have entertained the notion that circumcision was given as a distinguishing mark between the Jews and the Gentiles. The fallacy of this idea is sufficiently shown by a study of the giving of circumcision, and by the statement of the apostle Paul of what it really signified. Others suppose that it was given to keep the Jews separate, so that the genealogy of Christ could be ascertained. This also is simply an unfounded guess. Christ was to come from the tribe of Judah, but as all the tribes were circumcised, it is evident that circumcision could not by any means preserve His genealogy. Moreover, circumcision in the flesh never did make any separation between the Jews and the Gentiles.

It did not keep Israel from idolatry, and it did not keep them from joining the heathen in their idolatrous practices. Whenever the Jews forgot God, they mingled with the heathen, and there was no difference between them and the Gentiles. Circumcision did not separate them.

Still further, God did not wish the Jews to be separated from the Gentiles in the sense that they were to have no dealings with them. The object of His calling out the Jews from Egypt was that they should carry the gospel to the heathen. He did wish them to be separate in character, but outward circumcision could never effect this.

Moses said to the Lord, "Wherein shall it be known here that I and Thy people have found grace in Thy sight? is it not in that Thou goest with us? So shall we be separated, I and Thy people, from all the people that are upon the face of the earth." Exodus 33:16. The presence of the Lord in the heart of men will separate them from all others, although they live in the same house and eat at the same table. But if Christ is not in the heart of a man, he is not separated from the world, though he may have been circumcised and may live a hermit.

Literal and Spiritual Seed—Much of the confusion that has existed in regard to Israel has arisen through a misunderstanding of these terms. People suppose that to say that only those who are spiritual are really Jews is to deny the literalness of the seed and of the promise. But "spiritual" is not opposed to "literal." That which is spiritual is literal, and real. Christ is spiritual, but He is the real, literal Seed. God is spiritual, and is only Spirit, yet He is not a figurative Being, but a real, literal God. So the inheritance of which we are heirs in Christ, is a spiritual inheritance, yet it is real.

To say that only those who are spiritual constitute the true Israel is not to modify or turn aside the Scriptures, or to weaken in any way the directness and force of the promise, because the promise of God is only to those who have faith in Christ. "For the promise that he should be the heir of the world, was not to Abraham, or to his seed, through the law, but through the righteousness of faith." Romans 4:13. "And if ye be Christ's, then are ye Abraham's seed, and heirs according to the promise." Galatians 3:29.

NOTES

"And this I say, that the covenant, that was confirmed before of God in Christ, the law, which was four hundred and thirty years after, cannot disannul, that it should make the promise of none effect." Galatians. 3:17.

Chapter 3

The Free Grace of God

Introduction

It is not really correct to say that we have finished the study of these two chapters, because we can never finish the study of any portion of the Bible. After we have put the most profound study upon any portion of the Scripture, the most that we have done is only a beginning. If Newton, after a long life of study of natural science, could say that he seemed to be as a child playing on the seashore with the vast ocean before him unexplored, with much more aptness can the same be said by the greatest student of the Bible.

Let no one therefore think that we have by any means exhausted this portion of the book. When the reader has the text well in mind, so that he can quite distinctly recall any passage at will, and can locate it with reference to the connection, he has just got where he can begin to study with real profit. Therefore let the reader who is anxious to acquire an understanding of the Scriptures for himself, dwell upon the words as though he were digging in a sure place for treasure. An inexhaustible one awaits his search.

The second chapter is really summed up in the first verse, "Therefore thou art inexcusable, O man, whosoever thou art that judgest; for wherein thou judgest another, thou condemnest thyself; for thou that judgest doest the same things." The remaining verses are but an amplification of this statement. Thus, we find that there is no exception to the fact that the wrath of God is revealed from heaven against all ungodliness and unrighteousness of men. Hearing and knowing the truth is not a substitute for practicing it. God is no respecter of persons, but will punish sin wherever it is found.

Accepted With God—In the house of Cornelius the apostle Peter made a statement: "Of a truth I perceive that God is no respecter of persons;

but in every nation he that feareth Him, and worketh righteousness, is accepted with Him." Acts 10:34, 35. There are men in heathen lands who may never have heard the name of God, or seen a line of His written word, who will be saved.[3] God is revealed in the works of creation, and they who accept what they see of Him there are accepted with Him as surely as they who have learned much more of Him.

Objections Answered—The first part of the third chapter of Romans consists of questions and answers. The thoughtful reader of the epistles of Paul must have noticed the frequent occurrence of questions in the midst of an argument. Every possible objection is anticipated. The apostle asks the question that an objector might ask, and then answers it, making his argument more emphatic than before. So in the verses which follow it is very evident that the truths set forth in the second chapter would not be very acceptable to a Pharisee, and he would combat them with all his might. The questions raised by the apostle are not difficulties that lie in his own mind; this is clear from the parenthetical clause in verse 5, "I speak as a man." With this in mind, we may read Romans 3:1-18:

Questions and Answers—Romans 3:1-18

1 What advantage then hath the Jew? or what profit is there of circumcision? 2 Much every way; chiefly, because that unto them were committed the oracles of God. 3 For what if some did not believe? shall their unbelief make the faith of God without effect? 4 God forbid; yea, let God be true, but every man a liar; as it is written, That Thou mightest be justified in Thy sayings, and mightest overcome when Thou art judged. 5 But if our unrighteousness commend the righteousness of God, what shall we say? Is God unrighteous who taketh vengeance? (I speak as a man.) 6 God forbid; for then how shall God judge the world? 7 For if the truth of God hath more abounded through my lie unto His glory; why yet am I also judged as a sinner? 8 And not rather (as we be slanderously reported, and as some affirm that we say), Let us do evil, that good may come? whose damnation is just. 9 What then? are we better than they? No, in nowise; for we have before proved both Jews and Gentiles, that they are all under sin; 10 as it is written, There is none righteous, no, not one; 11 there is none that understandeth, there is none that seeketh after God. 12 They

---

3. E.G. White, *Christ's Object Lessons*, Appendix, p. 215.

are all gone out of the way, they are together become unprofitable; there is none that doeth good, no, not one. 13 Their throat is an open sepulcher; with their tongues they have used deceit; the poison of asps is under their lips; 14 whose mouth is full of cursing and bitterness; 15 their feet are swift to shed blood; 16 destruction and misery are in their ways; 17 and the way of peace have they not known; 18 there is no fear of God before their eyes.

"The Oracles of God"—An oracle is something spoken. That which was emphatically spoken by the mouth of the Lord is the Ten Commandments. See Deuteronomy 5:22. Stephen, speaking of Moses receiving the law, said, "This is he, that was in the church in the wilderness with the Angel which spake to him in the Mount Sina, and with our fathers; who received the lively oracles to give unto us." Acts 7:38. The Ten Commandments are primarily the oracles of God, because they were uttered by His own voice in the hearing of the people.

But the Holy Scriptures as a whole are the oracles of God, since they are the word of God, spoken "in divers manners" (Hebrews 1:1), and because they are but an expansion of the Ten Commandments. Christians are to shape their lives solely by the Bible. This is seen from the words of the apostle Peter: "If any man speak, let him speak as the oracles of God." 1 Peter 4:11.

The Law an Advantage—There are many who think that the law of God is a burden, and they imagine that the advantage of Christians is that they have nothing to do with it. But on the contrary, John says, "This is the love of God, that we keep His commandments; and His commandments are not grievous." 1 John 5:3. And Paul says that the possession of the law was a great advantage to the Jew. So Moses said: "What nation is there so great, that hath statutes and judgments so righteous as all this law, which I set before you this day?" Deuteronomy 4:8. All who truly love the Lord, count it a great blessing to have God's holy law made plain to them.

"Committed"—The advantage of the Jew was not simply in the fact that to them were made *known* the oracles of God, but that "unto them were *committed* the oracles of God," or "they were intrusted with the oracles of God." That is, the law was given to them to hold in trust for others, and not simply for their own benefit. They were to be the missionaries to the whole world. The advantage and the honor conferred upon the Jewish nation in intrusting them with the law of God to make it known to the world, can not be estimated.

Tell It to Others—When Peter and John were arrested and threatened for preaching Christ (who is simply the living law in perfection), they said,

"We can not but speak the things which we have seen and heard." Acts 4:20. They who appreciate the gift which God commits to them must tell it to others. Some think that it is useless to carry the gospel to the heathen when they hear that God justifies the heathen who walk according to the little light that shines to them just the same as he does the person who walks according to the light that shines from the written word. They think that the wicked heathen are in no worse case than the unfaithful professed Christians. None who appreciate the blessings of the Lord could think so. Light is a blessing. The more people know of the Lord, the more they can rejoice in Him, and all who truly know the Lord must be desirous of helping to spread the "good tidings of great joy" to all the people for whom it is designed.

God's Faithfulness—"What if some were without faith? Shall their want of faith make of none effect the faithfulness of God?" A very pertinent question. It is an appeal to the faithfulness of God. Will He break His promise, because of man's unbelief? Will He be unfaithful because man is unfaithful? Will our wavering cause God to waver? "That can not possibly be;" for this is the force of the expression which is incorrectly rendered, "God forbid." God will be true even though every man be a liar. "If we believe not, yet He abideth faithful; He can not deny Himself." 2 Timothy 2:13. "Thy mercy, O Lord, is in the heavens; and Thy faithfulness reacheth unto the clouds." Psalm 36:5.

Power and Faithfulness—Some one might hastily affirm that this overthrows the previous statements, that only those who have faith are heirs of the promise; for "how can it be that only the faithful are Abraham's seed, and thus heirs, if God will fulfill His promise even though every man disbelieves?" Very easily, when we consider the Scriptures and the power of God. Listen to the words of John the Baptist to the wicked Jews who could be fitly characterized only as "vipers": "Think not to say within yourselves, We have Abraham to our father; for I say unto you, that God is able of these stones to raise up children unto Abraham." Matthew 3:9. God will bestow the inheritance only on the faithful; but if every man should prove unfaithful, He who made man of the dust of the ground can of the stones raise other people, who will believe.

God Will Be Justified—"That Thou mightest be justified in Thy sayings, and mightest overcome when Thou art judged." God is now accused by Satan of injustice and indifference, and even of cruelty. Thousands have echoed the charge. But the judgment will declare the righteousness of God. His character, as well as that of man, is on trial. In the judgment every act, both of God and man, that has been done since creation will be seen by all in all its bearings. And when everything is seen in that perfect light, God will be acquitted of all wrongdoing, even by His enemies.[4]

Commending God's Righteousness—Verses 5 and 7 are but different forms of the same thought. God's righteousness stands out in bold relief in contrast with man's unrighteousness. So the caviler thinks that God ought not to condemn the unrighteousness which by contrast commends his righteousness. But that would be to destroy the righteousness of God, so that He could not judge the world. If God were what unbelieving men say He ought to be, He would forfeit even their respect, and they would condemn Him more loudly than they do now.

"I Speak as a Man"—Was not Paul a man? Most certainly. Was he ever anything other than a man? Never. Then why the expression, "I speak as a man"? Because the writings of Paul, like those of the ancient prophets, were given by inspiration of God. The Holy Spirit spoke by him. We are not reading Paul's view of the gospel, but the Spirit's own statement of it. But in these questions the Spirit speaks as a man; that is, the Spirit quotes the unbelieving words of man in order to show the folly of that unbelief.

Unbelieving Questions—There is a great difference in questions. Some are asked for the purpose of gaining instruction, and others are asked for the purpose of opposing the truth. So there must be a difference in answering them. Some questions deserve no more notice than would be given the same unbelief if uttered as a positive statement. When Mary asked, "How shall this be?" (Luke 1:34) with a desire for further information, she was told how. But when Zacharias asked, "Whereby shall I know this?" (Luke 1:18), thus plainly showing his disbelief of the angel's words, he was punished.

Wickedness Exposed—When the objector says, "If the truth of God hath more abounded through my lie unto His glory, why yet am I also judged as a sinner?" the swift retort comes, in effect: "You might rather say, what you really mean is, Let us do evil that good may come." The real intent of these unbelieving questions is that which is called evil is really good; people are really righteous, no matter what they may do, so that good will at last come out of evil. This is the substance of modern Spiritualism and of Universalism, which teach that all men will be saved.

Evil Is Not Good—There are many besides Spiritualists who virtually say, "Let us do evil that good may come." Who are they? All who claim that man is able of himself to do any good thing. The Lord declares that only God is good, and that good can come only from good. See Luke

---

4. Ellen G. White, *The Great Controversy*, Appendix A, p. 215.

18:19 and 6:43-45. From man only wickedness can come. Mark 7:21-23. Therefore he who thinks that of himself he alone can do good deeds, really says that good can come from evil.

The same thing is said by the one who refuses to confess that he is a sinner. Such an one is placing himself above God, for even He can not make evil into good. God can make an evil man good, but only by putting His own goodness in place of the evil.[5]

"All Under Sin"—The objector is silenced by the exposure of his infidel sentiments; the damnation of those who hold such positions is just; and now the conclusion is emphatically stated, namely, that all men, both Jews and Gentiles, are alike under sin.

Thus the way is fully prepared for the further conclusion that there is but one way of salvation for all men. The one who has been brought up within the sound of church bells and who hears the Scriptures read every day, has the same sinful nature and the same need of a Saviour, that the savage has. No one can justly despise another.

All Out of the Way—When the apostle wrote concerning both Jews and Gentiles, "They are all gone out of the way," he was but repeating what Isaiah had written hundreds of years before: "All we like sheep have gone astray; we have turned every one to his own way; and the Lord hath laid on Him the iniquity of us all." Isaiah 53:6.

"The Way of Peace"—"The way of peace have they not known" because they refused to know the God of peace. It has already been shown that God's law is His way; therefore, since He is the God of peace, His law is the way of peace. So He says, "O that thou hadst hearkened to My commandments! then had thy peace been as a river, and thy righteousness as the waves of the sea." Isaiah 48:18. "Great peace have they which love Thy law; and nothing shall offend them," or, "they shall have no stumbling-block." Psalm 119:162. So he who prepares the way of the Lord, by giving knowledge of remission of sins, guides our feet into the way of peace (Luke 1:76-79), because he brings us into the righteousness of God's law.

The portion of Romans thus far studied has shown us both Jews and Gentiles in the same sinful condition. No one has anything whereof to boast over another. Whoever, whether in the church or out, begins to judge and condemn another, no matter how bad that other one may be, thereby shows that he himself is guilty of the same things that he condemns in the other. Judgment belongs alone to God, and it shows a most daring spirit of usurpation for a man to presume to take the place of God. Those who have

---

5. E.J. Waggoner, *Christ and His Righteousness*, Appendix A, p. 215.

the law committed to them have a wonderful advantage over the heathen; nevertheless they must say: "Are we better than they? No, in no wise; for we have before proved both Jews and Gentiles, that they are all under sin." Romans 3:9.

The Grand Conclusion—Romans 3:19-22

19 Now we know that what things soever the law saith, it saith to them who are under the law; that every mouth may be stopped, and all the world may become guilty before God. 20 Therefore by the deeds of the law there shall no flesh be justified in His sight; for by the law is the knowledge of sin. 21 But now the righteousness of God without the law is manifested, being witnessed by the law and the prophets; 22 even the righteousness of God which is by faith of Jesus Christ unto all and upon all them that believe.

Within the Law—This is not the place to consider the force of the term "under the law," since it does not really occur here. It should be "in the law," as in Romans 2:12, for the Greek words are the same in both places. The words for "under the law" are entirely different. Why the translators have given us "under the law" in this place, and also in 1 Corinthians 9:21, where the term is also "in the law," as noted in *Young's Concordance*, it is impossible to determine. There certainly is no reason for it. The rendering is purely arbitrary. What the verse before us really says is, "Now we know that what things soever the law saith, it saith to them who are in the law," or, "within the sphere or jurisdiction of the law." This is an obvious fact, and in view of what immediately follows, it is a very important fact to keep in mind.

"What the Law Saith"—The voice of the law is the voice of God. The law is the truth, because it was spoken with God's own voice. In the covenant which God made with the Jews concerning the Ten Commandments, He said of the law, "Now therefore, if ye will obey My voice," etc. Exodus 19:5. The commandments were spoken "in the mount out of the midst of the fire, of the cloud, and of the thick darkness, with a great voice." Deuteronomy 5:22. Therefore when the law of God speaks to a man, it is God Himself speaking to that man. Satan has invented a proverb, which he has induced many people to believe, to the effect that "the voice of the people is the voice of God." This is a part of his great lie by which he causes many to think themselves above the law of God. Let every one who loves the truth, substitute for that invention of Satan the truth that the voice of the law of God is the voice of God.

Every Mouth Stopped—The law speaks that "every mouth may be stopped." And so every mouth would be, if men would only consider that it is God that is speaking. If men realized that God Himself speaks in the law, they would not be so ready to answer back when it speaks to them, and they would not frame so many excuses for not obeying it.

When some servant of the Lord reads the law to people, they often seem to think that it is only man's word to which they are listening, and so they feel themselves privileged to parley, and debate, and object, and to say that, although the words are all right, they do not feel under obligation to obey, or that it is not convenient. They would not think of doing this if they heard the voice of God speaking to them.

But when the law is read, it is the voice of God now just as much as it was to the Israelites who stood at the base of Sinai. People often open their mouths against it now, but the time will come when every mouth will be stopped, because "our God shall come, and shall not keep silence." Psalm 50:3.

The Law's Jurisdiction—What things soever the law says, it says to them who are within its sphere, or jurisdiction. Why? "That every mouth may be stopped, and all the world may become guilty before God." How extensive, then, is the jurisdiction of the law? It includes every soul in the world. There is no one who is exempt from obedience to it. There is not a soul whom it does not declare to be guilty. The law is the standard of righteousness, and "there is none righteous, no, not one."

No Justification by the Law—"Therefore by the deeds of the law there shall no flesh be justified in His sight; for by the law is the knowledge of sin." One of two things must be the case whenever a man is justified by the law, namely, either the man is not guilty, or else the law is a bad law. But neither of these things is true in this case. God's law is perfectly righteous, and all men are sinners. "By the law is the knowledge of sin." It is obvious that a man can not be declared righteous by the same law that declares him to be a sinner. Therefore it is a self-evident truth that by the deeds of the law there shall no flesh be justified.

A Double Reason—There is a double reason why no one can be justified by the law. The first is that all have sinned. Therefore the law must continue to declare them guilty, no matter what their future life might be. No man can ever do more than his duty to God, and no possible amount of good deeds can undo one wrong act.[6]

But more than this, men have not only sinned, but they are sinful. "The carnal mind is enmity against God; for it is not subject to the law of God, neither indeed can be." Romans 8:7. "For the flesh lusteth against the Spirit, and the Spirit against the flesh; and these are contrary the one to

---

6. Waggoner, *Christ and His Righteousness*, Appendix A, p. 215.

the other; so that ye can not do the things that ye would." Galatians 5:17. Therefore, no matter how much a man may try to do the righteousness of the law, he will fail to find justification by it.

Self-justification—If one were justified by the deeds of the law, it would be because he always did all that the law requires. Note well that it would be he that did it, and not the law. It would not be that the law itself does something to justify the man, but that the man himself does the good deeds required. Therefore if a man were justified by the law, it would be because he has in him by nature all the righteousness that the law requires. He who imagines that he can do the righteousness of the law, imagines that he himself is as good as God is, because the law requires and is a statement of the righteousness of God.

Therefore for a man to think that he can be justified by the law, is to think that he is so good that he needs no Saviour. Every self-righteous person, no matter what his profession, exalts himself above the law of God, and therefore identifies himself [in principle] with the Papacy.[7]

Righteousness Without the Law—Since because of man's weak and fallen condition no one can get righteousness out of the law, it is evident that if any man ever has righteousness he must get it from some other source than the law. If left to themselves and the law, men would truly be in a deplorable condition. But here is hope. The righteousness of God without the law or apart from the law, is manifested. This reveals to man a way of salvation.

Righteousness "Manifested"—Where? Why, of course where it most needs to be manifested, in people, that is, in a certain class described in the next verse. But it does not originate in them. The Scriptures have already shown us that no righteousness can come from man. The righteousness of God is manifested in Jesus Christ. He himself said through the prophet David: "I delight to do Thy will, O My God; yea, Thy law is within My heart. I have preached righteousness in the great congregation; lo, I have not refrained My lips, O Lord, Thou knowest." Psalm 40:8, 9.

"Witnessed by the Law"—Let no one imagine that in the gospel he can ignore the law of God. The righteousness of God which is manifested apart from the law, is witnessed by the law. It is such righteousness as the law witnesses to, and commends. It must be so, because it is the righteousness which Christ revealed; and that came from the law, which was in His heart. So, although the law of God has no righteousness to impart to any man, it does not cease to be the standard of righteousness. There can be no

---

7. A.T. Jones, *1893 General Conference Bulletin*, Appendix A, p. 217.

righteousness that does not stand the test of the law. The law of God must put its seal of approval upon every one who enters heaven.

Witnessed by the Prophets—When Peter preached Christ to Cornelius and his family, he said, "To Him give all the prophets witness, that through His name whosoever believeth in Him shall receive remission of sins." Acts 10:43. The prophets preached the same gospel that the apostles did. See 1 Peter 1:12. There is but one foundation, and that is "the foundation of the apostles and prophets, Jesus Christ Himself being the chief corner stone." Ephesians 2:20.

This also suggests another thought about "witnessed by the law." It is not simply that the righteousness which is manifested in Christ is *approved* by the law, but it is *proclaimed* in the law. In the portion of Scripture specifically known as "the law," the portion written by Moses, Christ is preached. Moses was a prophet, and therefore he testified of Christ the same, "for he wrote of Me." John 5:46. More than this, the very giving of the law itself was a promise and an assurance of Christ. This will appear when we come to the fifth chapter of Romans.

The Righteousness of God—While there is no chance for the despiser of God's law to evade its claims under cover of the expression, "the righteousness of God apart from the law," there is also no need for the lover of that law to fear that the preaching of righteousness by faith will tend to bring in a spurious righteousness. Such is guarded against by the statement that the righteousness must be *witnessed* by the law, and further by the statement that this righteousness which is manifested apart from the law is the righteousness of God. No one need fear that he will be wrong if he has *that* righteousness! To seek the kingdom of God and His righteousness is the one thing required of us in this life. Matthew 6:33.

"By Faith of Jesus Christ"—In another place Paul expresses his desire when the Lord comes to be found "not having mine own righteousness which is of the law, but that which is through the faith *of* Christ, the righteousness which is of God by faith." Philippians 3:9. Here again we have "the faith of Christ." Still further, it is said of the saints, "Here are they that keep the commandments of God, and the faith of Jesus." Revelation 14:12. God is faithful (1 Corinthians 1:9) and Christ is faithful, for "He abideth faithful." 2 Timothy 2:13. God deals to every one a measure of faith. Romans 12:3; Ephesians 2:8.

He imparts to us His own faithfulness. This He does by giving us Himself. So that we do not have to get righteousness which we ourselves manufacture; but to make the matter doubly sure, the Lord imparts to us in Himself the faith by which we appropriate His righteousness. Thus the faith of Christ must bring the righteousness of God, because the possession of that faith is the possession of the Lord Himself. This faith is dealt to every man, even as Christ gave Himself to every man. Do you ask what then can prevent every man from being saved? The answer is, Nothing, except the fact that all men will not keep the faith. If all would keep all that God gives them, all would be saved.[8]

Within and Without—This righteousness of God, which is by the faith *of* Jesus Christ, is *unto*, literally *into*, and *upon* all them that believe. Man's own righteousness, which is of the law, is only on the outside. Matthew 23:27, 28. But God desires truth in the inward parts. Psalm 51:6. "These words, which I command thee this day, shall be in thine heart." Deuteronomy 6:6. And so the promise of the new covenant is, "I will put My law in their inward parts, and write it in their hearts." Jeremiah 31:33. He does it, because it is impossible for man to do it. The most that men can do is to make a fair show in the flesh, to gain the applause of their fellow men. God puts His glorious righteousness *in the heart*.

But He does more than that—He covers men with it. "I will greatly rejoice in the Lord, my soul shall be joyful in my God; for He hath covered me with the robe of righteousness." Isaiah 51:10. "He will beautify the meek with salvation." Psalm 149:4. Clothed with this glorious dress, which is not merely an outward covering, but the manifestation of that which is within, God's people may go forth, "fair as the moon, clear as the sun; and terrible as an army with banners." Song of Solomon 6:10.

The Justice of Mercy—Romans 3:22-26

> 22 There is no difference; 23 for all have sinned, and come short of the glory of God; 24 being justified freely by His grace through the redemption that is in Christ Jesus; 25 whom God hath set forth to be a propitiation through faith in His blood, to declare His righteousness for the remission of sins that are past, through the forbearance of God; 26 to declare, I say, at this time His righteousness; that He might be just, and the justifier of him which believeth in Jesus.

"No Difference"—In what is there no difference? There is no difference in the way in which men receive righteousness. And why is no difference made in the manner of justifying men? Because "all have sinned." Peter, in relating to the Jews his experience in first preaching the gospel to the

---

8. Waggoner, *The Glad Tidings*, Appendix A, p. 217.

Gentiles, said, "God, which knoweth the hearts, bare them witness, giving them the Holy Ghost, even as He did unto us; and put no difference between us and them, purifying their hearts by faith." Acts 15:8, 9. "Out of the heart of men," not of one class of men, but of all men, "proceed evil thoughts," etc. Mark 7:21. God knows the hearts of all men, that all are alike sinful, and therefore He makes no difference in the gospel to different men.

"One Blood"—This lesson is one of the most important to be learned by the missionary, whether laboring at home or abroad. Since the gospel is based on a principle that there is no difference in men, it is absolutely essential that the gospel worker should recognize the fact, and always keep it in mind. God "hath made of one blood all nations of men for to dwell on all the face of the earth." Acts 17:26. Not only are all men of one blood, but they are also of "one kind of flesh." 1 Corinthians 15:39.

The great burden of the Epistle to the Romans, as has appeared up to this point, is to show that so far as sin and salvation therefrom are concerned, there is absolutely no difference between men of all races and conditions in life. The same gospel is to be preached to the Jew and to the Gentile, to the slave and to the freeman, to the prince and to the peasant.

Coming Short—People are fond of imagining that what are called "shortcomings" are not so bad as real sins. So it is much easier for them to confess that they have "come short" than that they have sinned and done wickedly. But since God requires perfection, it is evident that "shortcomings" are sins. It may sound pleasanter to say that a bookkeeper is "short" in his accounts, but people know that the reason for it is that he has been taking that which is not his, or stealing. When perfection is the standard, it makes no difference in the result, how much or how little one comes short, so long as he comes short. The primary meaning of sin is "to miss the mark." And in an archery contest, the man who has not strength to send his arrow to the target, even though his aim is good, is a loser just as surely as he who shoots wide of the mark.

"The Glory of God"—From the text we learn that the glory of God is His righteousness. Notice, the reason why all have come short of the glory of God is that all have sinned. The fact is plain that if they had not sinned they would not have come short of it. The coming short of the glory itself consists in sin. Man in the beginning was "crowned with glory and honor" (Hebrews 2:7) because he was upright. In the fall he lost the glory, and therefore now he must "seek for glory and honor and immortality." Christ could say to the Father, "The glory which Thou gavest Me, I have given them," because in Him is the righteousness of God which He has given as a free gift to every man. It is the part of wisdom to receive righteousness; and "they that be wise shall shine."

"**Being Justified**"—In other words, being made righteous. To justify means to make righteous. God supplies just what the sinner lacks. Let no reader forget the simple meaning of justification. Some people have the idea that there is a much higher condition for the Christian to occupy than to be justified. That is to say, that there is a higher condition for one to occupy than to be clothed within and without with the righteousness of God. That can not be.

"**Freely**"—"Whosoever will, let him take the water of life freely." That is, let him take it as a gift. So in Isaiah 55:1: "Ho, every one that thirsteth, come ye to the waters, and he that hath no money; come ye, buy, and eat; yea, come, buy wine and milk without money and without price."

It was the Epistle to the Romans that accomplished the Reformation in Germany. Men had been taught to believe that the way to get righteousness was to purchase it either by hard work or by the payment of money. The idea that men may purchase it with money is not so common now as then; but there are very many who are not Catholics who think that some work must be done in order to obtain it.

Making Prayer to Be a Work—The writer was once talking with a man in regard to righteousness as the free gift of God, the man maintaining that we could not get anything from the Lord without doing something for it. When asked what we must do to win forgiveness of sins, he replied that we must pray for it.

It is with this idea of prayer that the Roman or Hindu devotee "says" so many prayers a day, putting in an extra number some days to make up for omissions. But the man who "says" a prayer, does not pray. Heathen prayer, as for instance when the prophets of Baal leaped and cut themselves (1 Kings 18:26-28), is work; but true prayer is not. A man comes to me and says that he is starving. Afterwards he is asked if anything was given him, and he says that he received some dinner, but that I made him work for it. When asked what he had to do for it, he replies that he asked for it. He could hardly make any one believe that he worked for his dinner! True prayer is simply the thankful acceptance of God's free gifts.

Redemption in Christ Jesus—We are made righteous "through the redemption that is in Christ Jesus." That is, through the purchasing power that is in Christ Jesus, or "through the unsearchable riches of Christ." Ephesians 3:8. This is the reason why it comes to us as a gift.

Some one may say that everlasting life in the kingdom of God is too great a thing to be given to us for nothing. So it is, and therefore it had to be *purchased*, but since we had nothing that could buy it, Christ has purchased it for us and He gives it to us freely, in Himself. But if we had to purchase it from Him, we might as well have bought it in the first place, and saved Him the task.[9] "If righteousness come by the law, then Christ is dead in vain." Galatians 2:21. "Ye were redeemed, not with corruptible things, with silver or gold, from your vain manner of life handed down from your fathers; but with precious blood, as of a Lamb without blemish and without spot, even the blood of Christ." 1 Peter 1:18, 19. The blood is the life. Leviticus 17:11-17. Therefore the redemption that is in Christ Jesus is His own life.

Christ Set Forth—Christ is the one whom God has set forth to declare His righteousness. Now since the only righteousness that is real righteousness is the righteousness of God, and Christ is the only One who has been ordained of God to declare it upon men, it is evident that it can not be obtained except through Him. "There is none other name under heaven given among men, whereby we must be saved." Acts 4:12.

A Propitiation—A propitiation is a sacrifice. The statement then is simply that Christ is set forth to be a sacrifice for the remission of our sins. "Once in the end of the world hath He appeared to put away sin by the sacrifice of Himself." Hebrews 9:26. Of course the idea of a propitiation or sacrifice is that there is wrath to be appeased. But take particular notice that it is *we* who require the sacrifice, and not God. He *gives* the sacrifice. The idea that God's wrath has to be propitiated in order that we may have forgiveness finds no warrant in the Bible.

It is the height of absurdity to say that God is so angry with men that He will not forgive them unless something is provided to appease His wrath, and that therefore He Himself gives the gift to Himself, by which He is appeased. "And you, that were sometime alienated and enemies in your mind by wicked works, yet now hath He reconciled in the body of His flesh through death." Colossians 1:21, 22; 2 Corinthians 5:21.

Heathen and Christian Propitiation—The Christian idea of propitiation is that set forth above. The heathen idea, which is too often held by professed Christians, is that men must provide a sacrifice to appease the wrath of their god. All heathen worship is simply a bribe to their gods to be favorable to them. If they thought that their gods were very angry with them, they would provide a greater sacrifice, and so human sacrifices were offered in extreme cases. They thought, as the worshipers of Siva in India do today, that their god was gratified by the sight of blood.

The persecution that was carried on in so-called Christian countries in times past and is to some extent even now, is but the outcropping of this

---

9. Waggoner, *The Glad Tidings*, Appendix A, p. 218.

heathen idea of propitiation. Ecclesiastical leaders imagine that salvation is by works and that men by works can atone for sin, and so they offer the one whom they think rebellious as a sacrifice to their god—not to the true God, because He is not pleased with such sacrifices.

Righteousness Declared—To declare righteousness is to speak righteousness. God speaks righteousness to man, and then he is righteous. The method is the same as in the creation in the beginning. "He spake, and it was." "We are His workmanship, created in Christ Jesus unto good works, which God hath before ordained that we should walk in them." Ephesians 2:10.

God's Justice in Redemption—Christ is set forth to declare God's righteousness for the remission of sins, in order that He might be just and at the same time the justifier of him who believes in Jesus. God justifies sinners, for they are the only ones who need justification. The justice of declaring a sinner to be righteous lies in the fact that he is actually made righteous.[10] Whatever God declares to be so, is so. And then he is made righteous by the life of God given him in Christ.

The sin is against God, and if He is willing to forgive it, He has the right to do so. No unbeliever would deny the right of a man to overlook a trespass against him. But God does not simply overlook the trespass; He gives His life as a forfeit. Thus He upholds the majesty of the law, and is just in declaring that man righteous who was before a sinner. Sin is remitted—sent away—from the sinner, because sin and righteousness can not exist together, and God puts His own righteous life into the believer. So God is merciful in His justice, and just in His mercy.

> "There's a wideness in God's mercy,
>   Like the wideness of the sea;
> There's a kindness in His justice,
>   That is more than liberty."

We now come to the close of the third chapter of Romans. We found that righteousness is the free gift of God unto every one who believes. It is not that God gives a man righteousness as a reward for believing certain dogmas; the gospel is something entirely different from that. It is this, that true faith has Christ alone as its object, and it brings Christ's life actually into the heart; and therefore it must bring righteousness.

This act of mercy on the part of God is eminently just, because in the first place the sin is against God, and He has a right to pass by offenses

---

10. Waggoner, *Christ and His Righteousness*, Appendix A, p. 219.

against Him; and, further, it is just, because He gives His own life as an atonement for the sin, so that the majesty of the law is not only maintained, but is magnified. "Mercy and truth are met together; righteousness and peace have kissed each other." Psalm 85:10. God is just and the justifier of him who believes in Jesus. All righteousness is from Him alone.

Establishing the Law—Romans 3:27-31

27 Where is boasting then? It is excluded. By what law? of works? Nay; but by the law of faith. 28 Therefore we conclude that a man is justified by faith without the deeds of the law. 29 Is He the God of the Jews only? is He not also of the Gentiles? Yes, of the Gentiles also; 30 seeing it is one God, which shall justify the circumcision by faith, and uncircumcision through faith. 31 Do we then make void the law through faith? God forbid; yea, we establish the law.

No Boasting—Since righteousness is a free gift of God through Jesus Christ, it is evident that no one can justly boast of any righteousness that he has. "For by grace are ye saved through faith; and that not of yourselves; it is the gift of God; not of works, lest any man should boast." Ephesians 2:8, 9. "Who maketh thee to differ from another? and what hast thou that thou didst not receive? now if thou didst receive it, why dost thou glory, as if thou hadst not received it?" 1 Corinthians 4:7.

What Boasting Proves—"Behold, his soul which is lifted up is not upright in him; but the just shall live by his faith." Habakkuk 2:4. Boasting therefore is an evidence of a sinful heart. But suppose a man boasts of his righteousness, as, for instance, when a man says that he has lived without sin for so many years? "If we say that we have no sin, we deceive ourselves, and the truth is not in us." 1 John 1:8.

But are not the grace and power of God manifested in Christ to cleanse and *keep* us from sin? Most certainly; but only when in humility we acknowledge that we are sinners. "If we confess our sins, He is faithful and just to forgive us our sins, and to cleanse us from all unrighteousness." 1 John 1:9. When we say that we have no sin, that very thing is evidence that we have; but when with faith in the word of the Lord we say that we are sinners, then the blood of Christ cleanses us from all sin. In the plan of salvation there is no place for human pride and boasting.

No Boasting in Heaven—The result of boasting in heaven is seen in the case of Satan. Once he was one of the covering cherubs above the throne of God. But he began to contemplate his own glory and goodness, and his fall was the consequence. "Thou hast sinned; therefore I will cast thee as profane out of the mountain of God; and I will destroy thee, O covering cherub, from the midst of the stones of fire. Thine heart was lifted up because of thy beauty, thou hast corrupted thy wisdom by reason of thy brightness." Ezekiel 28:16, 17.

If the saints after their translation should begin to boast of their sinlessness, they would be as bad as they ever were. But that will never be. All who are admitted to heaven will have fully learned the lesson that God is all and in all. There will not be a voice or a heart silent in the song of praise, "Unto Him that loved us, and washed us from our sins in His own blood, and hath made us kings and priests unto God and His Father; to Him be glory and dominion forever and ever."

The "Law" of Works—The law of works does not exclude boasting. If a man were justified by works, he would have whereof to boast over another who had the same privilege, but did not use it. In that case the righteous could boast over the wicked; and people would continually be comparing themselves with one another to see who had done the most. The law of works is simply the Ten Commandments in form only. Compliance with the law of works enables one to appear outwardly righteous, while within he is full of corruption. Yet the one who follows the law of works is not always necessarily a hypocrite. He may have an earnest desire to keep the Commandments, but may be deceived into thinking that he can work them out of himself.

The "Law" of Faith—This has for its object the same thing as the law of works, namely, [obedience to] the Commandments of God, but the result is different. The law of works deceives a man with a form; the law of faith gives him the substance. The law of faith is the law "as it is in Jesus." The one may be a sincere attempt to keep the law; the other is the actual accomplishment of that desire, through the redemption that is in Christ Jesus.

The Ten Commandments as given by the Lord are only a law of faith, since God never designed that they should be taken in any other way; and He never expected that anybody could get righteousness from them in any other way than by faith. The law of works is man's perversion of the law of God.

Faith Without Works—"Therefore we conclude that a man is justified by faith without the deeds of the law." Because there is no other means by which he could be justified! We have before seen that all men are sinners, and that no man has power in himself to perform the deeds of the law, no matter how strong his desires. "Not the hearers of the law are just before God, but the doers of the law shall be justified." Romans 2:13.

But "by the deeds of the law shall no flesh be justified in His sight; for by the law is the knowledge of sin." Romans 3:20. Therefore whoever is justified, or made righteous at all, must be made righteous by faith alone, wholly apart from the deeds of the law. This is of universal application. It means that justification, first, last, and all the time, is by faith alone. The Christian can not be justified by works any more than the sinner can be. No man can ever get so good and strong that his own deeds can justify him.

Faith and Works—But that is not to say that works have nothing to do with faith. Justification means making just, or making righteous. Righteousness is right doing. Faith which justifies, therefore, is faith which makes a man a doer of the law, or, rather, which puts the doing of the law into him. "For we are His workmanship, created in Christ Jesus unto good works, which God hath before ordained that we should walk in them." Ephesians 2:10. "It is God which worketh in you both to will and to do of His good pleasure." Philippians 2:13. "This is a faithful saying, and these things I will that thou affirm constantly, that they which have believed in God might be careful to maintain good works." Titus 3:8. A man is not justified by faith *and* works, but by faith alone, *which works*. Galatians 5:6.

One God for All—There is but "one God and Father of all." Ephesians 4:6. He "hath made of one blood all nations of men," "for we are also His offspring." Acts 16:26, 28. "There is no respect of persons with God." Romans 2:11. "In every nation He that feareth Him, and worketh righteousness, is accepted with Him." Acts 10:35. The Scripture saith: "Whosoever believeth on Him shall not be ashamed. For there is no difference between the Jew and the Greek; for the same Lord over all is rich unto all that call upon Him." Romans 10:11, 12.

One Means of Justification for All—The fact that justification is only by faith, and that God "commandeth all men everywhere to repent" (Acts 17:30), shows that God regards Jew and Gentile alike. Nor is there any evidence that He ever did put any difference between them. A believing Gentile was always accounted righteous, and an unbelieving Jew was never considered by the Lord any better than any other unbeliever. Remember that Abraham, the father of the whole Jewish nation, was a Chaldean. The Jews were related to the Chaldeans who remained in their native land, just as surely as they were to one another in the land of Canaan. Unfortunately, they forgot this; but they are not the only ones in the world who have forgotten that all men are their brethren.

In the statement, "It is one God, which shall justify the circumcision by faith, and uncircumcision through faith," there is no need of stumbling over the prepositions. Bear in mind how often we use the words "by" and "through" interchangeably, to indicate means, and there will be no difficulty.

The emphatic word is "faith." Both circumcision and uncircumcision are justified through, or by means of, faith.

Making Void the Law—Making void the law does not mean abolishing it. There is no question as to the perpetuity of the law. It is so plainly eternal that the apostle Paul never wastes space in arguing about it. The only question is how its claim may be satisfied. The Saviour said that the Jews made the commandment of God of none effect through their tradition. So far as they were concerned, they made it void. No man could by any action or lack of action abolish or in any way affect the law of God. But anybody may by his unbelief obliterate it from his own heart. The question then is, Do we by faith make the law of God of none effect? Or, more plainly still, Does faith lead to the transgression of the law? The answer is, "Not by any means."

Establishing the Law—That which has been said in regard to making void the law of God will apply here also. That is, no action of man can make the law anything different from what it actually is. It is the foundation of the throne of God, and as such it will ever abide, in spite of demons and men.

But it is left for us to say whether or not we will have it obliterated from our hearts, or have it established there. If we choose to have it established in our hearts, we have only to accept Christ by faith. Faith brings Christ to dwell in the heart. Ephesians 3:17. The law of God is in the heart of Christ (Psalm 40:8), so that the faith which brings Christ into the heart establishes the law there. And since the law of God is the establishment of His throne, the faith which brings the law into the heart, enthrones God there. And thus it is that God works in men "both to will and to do of His good pleasure."

NOTES

"In whom we have redemption through His blood, the forgiveness of sins, according to the riches of His grace; wherein He hath abounded toward us in all wisdom and prudence." Ephesians 1:7, 8.

Chapter 4

Believing God's Tremendous Promise

The ultimate object of studying any Bible book in detail is to be able to take in the entire book at one glance. The second chapter and the first portion of the third chapter of Romans have given us the information that all men are in the same deplorable condition. Then comes the brighter side in the last part of the third chapter, in which the free grace of God is set forth in Christ as the Saviour of sinners. And now in the fourth chapter we have the final argument concerning justification by faith.

The Blessing of Abraham—Romans 4:1-12

1 What shall we say then that Abraham our father, as pertaining to the flesh, hath found? 2 For if Abraham were justified by works, he hath whereof to glory; but not before God. 3 For what saith the Scripture? Abraham believed God, and it was counted unto him for righteousness. 4 Now to him that worketh is the reward not reckoned of grace, but of debt. 5 But to him that worketh not, but believeth on Him that justifieth the ungodly, his faith is counted for righteousness. 6 Even as David also describeth the blessedness of the man, unto whom God imputeth righteousness without works, 7 saying, Blessed are they whose iniquities are forgiven, and whose sins are covered. 8 Blessed is the man to whom the Lord will not impute sin. 9 Cometh this blessedness then upon the circumcision only, or upon the uncircumcision also? for we say that faith was reckoned to Abraham for righteousness. 10 How was it then reckoned? when he was in circumcision, or in uncircumcision? Not in circumcision, but in uncircumcision. 11 And he received the sign of circumcision, a seal of the righteousness of the faith

which he had yet being uncircumcised; that he might be the father of all them that believe, though they be not circumcised; that righteousness might be imputed unto them also: 12 and the father of circumcision to them who are not of the circumcision only, but who also walk in the steps of that faith of our father Abraham, which he had being yet uncircumcised.

"As Pertaining to the Flesh"—Abraham was not the father, or ancestor, according to the flesh, of all those to whom Paul addressed the epistle. The question under consideration is justification by faith. If now it can be shown that even Abraham received no righteousness through the flesh, but that it was only by faith, the case will be practically settled.

No Place for Glorying—If in the plan of salvation there were any such thing as righteousness by works, then there would be provision made for boasting. For if one may be saved by works, then all men may be; and then those who were saved might boast of their superiority to others in like circumstances. But we have already learned that boasting is excluded. "God hath chosen the foolish things of the world to confound the wise; and God hath chosen the weak things of the world to confound the things which are mighty; and base things of the world, and things which are despised, hath God chosen, yea, and things which are not, to bring to naught things that are; that no flesh should glory in His presence."

Glorying In, and Glorying Before—If Abraham were justified by works, he might glory; but the fact is that he can not glory before God; and the proof of this is found in the words of Scripture: "Abraham believed God, and it was counted unto him for righteousness." A man can be justified by works when it can be shown that he has done no wrong. In that case he needs no faith; his works speak for themselves. But Abraham was justified by faith, and therefore it is evident that he was not justified by any works. He who is justified only by the works of God, will glory only in those works. That is glorying in God, and is far different from glorying before God.

Paul and James—Here is where nearly everybody quotes the words of James, "Was not Abraham our father justified by works, when he had offered Isaac his son upon the altar?" James 2:21. Unfortunately this text is usually quoted as a disparagement of the words of Paul. It seems to be taken for granted that there is a contradiction between Paul and James; and sympathy naturally leans to James, because people like to believe that there is some merit in their own works, and they imagine that this is what James teaches. Indeed, there are some who hold that James wrote for the purpose of correcting Paul's "extreme views" of justification by faith.

We may well throw all such foolish and wicked ideas to the winds. No one need hope to come to an understanding of the Scriptures until he approaches them with the settled conviction that "all Scripture is given by inspiration of God." The Holy Spirit does not at one time inspire words which must later on be corrected.

Faith Working—The trouble with those who thus read the words of James is that they suppose that the apostle says that Abraham was justified by his own works of faith. "Seest thou how faith wrought?" That is ever the mark of living faith, as the apostle is showing. And that is just the statement of the apostle Paul. The last verse of the third chapter of Romans tells us that by faith we establish the law.

Moreover, the very term "justification" shows that faith performs the requirement of the law. Faith makes a man a doer of the law,[11] for that is the meaning of the term "justification by faith." So in James we read that the works of Abraham simply showed the perfection of his faith. "And the Scripture was fulfilled which saith, Abraham believed God, and it was imputed unto him for righteousness." The apostle James, therefore, teaches the same kind of justification that Paul does. If he did not, one or the other or both of them would be discredited as apostles. Justification by faith which works is the only kind of justification known in the Bible.

Debt and Grace—"Now to him that worketh is the reward not reckoned of grace, but of debt." It is necessary to keep in mind what the apostle is writing about. The subject is the means by which a man is justified. To him that works for justification, the reward of righteousness is not a gift of grace, but the payment of a debt. That is, it would be so if there were any righteousness by works. In that case, the man would come to the Lord and demand of Him his due.

But no man can put the Lord under obligation to him. "Who hath first given to Him, and it shall be recompensed unto him again?" Romans 11:35. If any one could do something for the Lord for which the Lord would be under obligation to him, then all things would not be from Him. That is to say, the idea of justification by works is opposed to the fact that God is the Creator of all things. And, conversely, the recognition of God as Creator is the acknowledgment that righteousness comes from Him alone.

Justifying the Ungodly—God justifies the ungodly. No others need justification. But mark that He does not justify *ungodliness*. That would be to call evil good, and to deny Himself. But He justifies or makes righteous the ungodly, and that is just what they need. He justifies the believing

---

11. Waggoner, *The Glad Tidings*, Appendix A, p. 219.

sinner by making him a new man in Christ Jesus, and this He can do and still be just. To make a new man in righteousness is perfectly in harmony with His own character as Creator.

Working Not—"But to him that worketh not, but believeth on Him that justifieth the ungodly, his faith is counted for righteousness." Bear in mind that justification is the subject under consideration. When the apostle speaks of not working, it is evident that he means not working in order to be justified. A man is not made just by works, but the just man works—yet always by faith. "The just shall live by faith." It is faith that makes him continue to live justly. The reality of the works of faith is made more prominent in the latter part of this chapter.

The Blessedness Described—The blessedness of the man unto whom God imputeth righteousness without works is the blessedness of sins forgiven, and of freedom from the power of sin. God will not impute sin to the man who lives by faith in Christ, so that Christ's works are his works. "As ye have therefore received Christ Jesus the Lord, so walk ye in Him; … for in Him dwelleth all the fullness of the Godhead bodily. And ye are complete in Him." Colossians 2:6-10.

Blessings to Jew and Gentile—This blessedness comes alike to the circumcision and to the uncircumcision. We have here a repetition of the truth set forth in the third chapter, namely, that there is no difference in the matter of justification. Abraham is the father of the Jewish nation after the flesh, but the blessing which he received was while he was uncircumcised, the same as any other Gentile. Therefore he can be the father of both the Jews and the Gentiles. His blessing was received by faith, and therefore "they which be of faith are blessed with faithful Abraham." Galatians 3:9.

How the Blessing Comes—We have some time ago seen that the blessing came to Abraham through Christ. In another place the apostle Paul tells us that "Christ hath redeemed us from the curse of the law, being made a curse for us; for it is written, Cursed is every one that hangeth on a tree; that the blessing of Abraham might come on the Gentiles through Jesus Christ; that we might receive the promise of the Spirit through faith." Galatians 3:13, 14.

Whatever was promised to Abraham was all contained in the blessing which David described. God sent His Son to bless us in turning every one of us away from our iniquities. Acts 3:26. It is the cross of Christ that transmits the blessings of Abraham to us. Therefore the blessings are spiritual. None of the blessings promised to Abraham were merely temporal. And this further shows that the inheritance promised to Abraham and his seed is only to those who are the children of God through faith in Christ Jesus.

Circumcision Is Nothing—The advantage of those who are circumcised was that to them were intrusted the oracles of God; but that did not come to them through circumcision. Circumcision was only a sign; it was not the thing itself. It was given to Abraham as a token of the righteousness by faith which he already possessed. Therefore it could not signify anything more to anybody else. If any who were circumcised did not have righteousness, then their circumcision did not signify anything. "Circumcision is nothing, and uncircumcision is nothing, but the keeping of the commandments of God." 1 Corinthians 7:19. So Abraham was the father of the circumcised, provided they were not of the circumcision only, but had righteousness by faith, which is the one necessary thing.

Everything in Christ—Speaking of Christ, the apostle says, "All the promises of God in Him are yea, and in Him Amen, unto the glory of God by us." 2 Corinthians 1:20. There is no promise of God to any man—

The Inheritance and the Heirs—Romans 4:13-15

13 For the promise, that he should be the heir of the world, was not to Abraham, or to his seed, through the law, but through the righteousness of faith. 14 For if they which are of the law be heirs, faith is made void, and the promise made of none effect; 15 because the law worketh wrath; for where no law is, there is no transgression.

Where Is the Promise?—A very natural inquiry upon reading the thirteenth verse would be, Where is there any promise that Abraham and his seed should be heirs *of the world*? Many think that no such promise is contained in the Old Testament. But there can be no doubt about the matter, for the apostle says that there was such a promise. If we have not found it, it is because we have read the Old Testament too superficially, or with minds biased by preconceived opinions. If we consider the connection, we shall have no difficulty in locating the promise

Of what is the apostle speaking in this connection? Of an inheritance through the righteousness of faith, and also of the fact that circumcision was given to Abraham as a seal of this righteousness which he had by faith, and therefore as the seal of the inheritance which was to come thereby.

Where in the Old Testament do we find the account of the giving of circumcision, and of a promise in connection therewith? In the seventeenth chapter of Genesis. Then that must be the place for us to look for the promise that Abraham should be the heir of the world. Let us turn and read:—

> "And I will establish My covenant between Me and thee and thy seed after thee in their generations, for an everlasting covenant,

to be a God unto thee and to thy seed after thee. And I will give unto thee, and to thy seed after thee, the land wherein thou art a stranger, all the land of Canaan, for an everlasting possession; and I will be their God. ... And ye shall circumcise the flesh of your foreskin; and it shall be a token of the covenant betwixt Me and you." Genesis 17:7-11.

The reader will at once say: "Yes; it is plain enough that there is a promise here; but what we are looking for is the promise that Abraham and his seed should inherit *the earth*; and I do not see that here. All that I can see is a promise that they should inherit the land of Canaan."

But it is certain from the connection in Romans that we are on the right track, and we shall soon see that this is indeed the promise that Abraham and his seed should be heirs of the world. We must study the details of this promise. And first let us note the fact that the inheritance promised is an everlasting inheritance.

Abraham himself is to have it for an everlasting possession. But the only way in which both Abraham and his seed may have everlasting possession of an inheritance is by having everlasting life. Therefore we see that in this promise to Abraham we have the assurance of everlasting life in which to enjoy the possession.[12]

This will appear still more clearly when we consider that the inheritance is an inheritance of righteousness: "For the promise, that he should be the heir of the world, was not to Abraham, or to his seed, through the law, but through the righteousness of faith." Romans 4:13. That is just what we have in the promise recorded in the seventeenth of Genesis. For that covenant was sealed by circumcision (see verse 11), and circumcision was the seal of righteousness by faith. See Romans 4:11.

Someone may say that this does not appear from the Old Testament itself, and that therefore the Jews could not be expected to have understood it; we have the New Testament to enlighten us. It is true that in studying the Old Testament we owe much to the New Testament, but it is also a fact that there is no new revelation in it. One may see from the Old Testament alone that the inheritance promised to Abraham and to his seed was only on the condition of righteousness by faith.

This is the natural conclusion from the fact that the inheritance is to be an everlasting possession. Now the Jews well knew that everlasting life belongs to the righteous alone. "The righteous shall never be removed; but

---

12. Waggoner, *The Glad Tidings*, Appendix A p. 220–222.

the wicked shall not inhabit the earth." Proverbs 10:30. "For evildoers shall be cut off; but those that wait upon the Lord, they shall inherit the earth." Psalm 37:9. "For such as be blessed of Him shall inherit the earth; and they that be cursed of Him shall be cut off." Verse 22.

The fifth commandment reads, "Honor thy father and thy mother; that thy days may be long upon the land which the Lord thy God giveth thee." The keeping of the commandments has never made any difference in the length of men's lives in this present world. But the inheritance which God promised to Abraham is one that will be everlasting because of the righteousness of its possessors.

The Promise and the Resurrection—Another point from the promise is recorded in Genesis, if we read carefully. The promise was to Abraham and to his seed. Now Stephen stated as a well-known fact that Abraham did not have so much of the promised land as he could set his foot on. Acts 7:5. We may learn this from the Old Testament record, because we are told that he had to buy from the Canaanites, whom God had promised to drive out, a spot of land in which to bury his wife. As for his immediate descendants, we know that they dwelt in tents, wandering from place to place, and that Jacob died in the land of Egypt.

Further than this, we read the words of David, whose reign was at the time of the highest prosperity of the children of Israel in the land of Canaan: "Hear my prayer, O Lord, and give ear unto my cry; hold not Thy peace at my tears; for I am a stranger with Thee, and a sojourner, as all my fathers were." Psalm 39:12. See also his prayer at the consecration of the gifts to the temple, when Solomon was made king. 1 Chronicles 29:15.

Still further, and this is most positive of all, we have the words of God to Abraham when He made the promise. After telling him that He would give the land of Canaan to him and to his seed, the Lord said that his seed should first be slaves in a strange land. "And thou shalt go to thy fathers in peace; thou shalt be buried in a good old age. But in the fourth generation they shall come hither again." Genesis 15:7, 13-16. Thus we see that Abraham was plainly told that he should die before he had any inheritance in the land, and that it would be at least four hundred years before any of his seed could inherit it.

But Abraham died in faith, and so did his seed. See Hebrews 11:13. "These all died in faith, not having received the promises, but having seen them afar off, and were persuaded of them, and embraced them, and confessed that they were strangers and pilgrims on the earth." They died in faith, because they knew that God could not lie. But since God's promise must be fulfilled, and they did not receive the promised inheritance in this present life, we are shut up to the conclusion that it can be obtained only through the resurrection from the dead.

This was the hope that sustained the faithful Israelites. Abraham had faith to offer Isaac upon the altar because his faith was in God's power to raise the dead. When Paul was a prisoner on account of "the hope and resurrection of the dead" (Acts 23:6), he said, "And now I stand and am judged for the hope of the promise made of God unto our fathers; unto which promise our twelve tribes, instantly serving God day and night, hope to come." And then, to show the reasonableness of this hope, he asked, "Why should it be thought a thing incredible with you, that God should raise the dead?" Acts 26:6-8.

The resurrection of Jesus Christ is the pledge and surety of the resurrection of those who believe on Him. See 1 Corinthians 15:13-20. The apostles "preached through Jesus the resurrection from the dead." Acts 4:2. And one of them says for our benefit, "Blessed be the God and Father of our Lord Jesus Christ, which according to His abundant mercy hath begotten us again unto a lively hope by the resurrection of Jesus Christ from the dead, to an inheritance incorruptible, and undefiled, and that fadeth not away, reserved in heaven for you, who are kept by the power of God through faith unto salvation ready to be revealed in the last time." 1 Peter 1:3-5.

And then he adds that this faith is tried that it may "be found unto praise and honor and glory at the appearing of Jesus Christ." And this brings us to the conclusion of the matter, namely, that the promise to Abraham and to his seed that they should be heirs of the world, is the promise of Christ's coming.

The apostle Peter says that it is necessary to remind us of the words that were spoken by the holy prophets because "there shall come in the last days scoffers, walking after their own lusts, and saying, Where is the promise of His coming? for since the fathers fell asleep, all things continue as they were from the beginning of the creation." Therefore they do not believe in the promise at all.

But they do not reason well, "for this they willingly are ignorant of, that by the word of God the heavens were of old, and the earth standing out of the water and in the water, whereby the world that then was being overflowed with water, perished; but the heavens and the earth, which are now, by the same word are kept in store, reserved unto fire against the day of judgment and perdition of ungodly men." 2 Peter 3:5-7.

Take notice that not only has the promise something to do with the fathers, but it concerns the whole earth. The complaint of the scoffers is that since the fathers fell asleep all things continue as they were from the beginning of the creation. But the apostle shows that when they say so they shut their eyes to the fact that the same word that in the beginning made the heavens and the earth, also destroyed the earth by the flood. Also the earth is by the same word now preserved until the day of judgment and perdition of ungodly men, when it will be destroyed by fire. "Nevertheless we, according to His promise, look for new heavens and a new earth, wherein dwelleth righteousness." 2 Peter 3:13.

According to What Promise?—Why, according to the promise to the fathers, which was that Abraham and his seed should inherit the earth. It has been a long time, as men count, since that promise was made, but "the Lord is not slack concerning His promise." It has not been so long since it was made that He has forgotten it; for "one day is with the Lord as a thousand years, and a thousand years as one day." The reason why He has waited this long is that He is not willing that any should perish in the fires that will renew the earth, but He desires that all should come to repentance.

And so we find that we have as great an interest in the promise to Abraham as he himself had. That promise is still open for all to accept. It embraces nothing less than an eternal life of righteousness in the earth made new as it was in the beginning. The hope of the promise of God unto the fathers was the hope of the coming of the Lord to raise the dead, and thus to bestow the inheritance.

Christ was once here on the earth, but then He did not have any more of the inheritance than Abraham had. He had not where to lay His head. God is now sending His Holy Spirit to seal the believers for the inheritance, even as He did to Abraham; and when all the faithful shall have been sealed by the Spirit, "He shall send Jesus Christ, which before was preached unto you; whom the heaven must receive until the times of restitution of all things, which God hath spoken by the mouth of all His holy prophets since the world began." Acts 3:20, 21.

We have learned what Abraham found, and how he found it. At the same time we have learned what God has promised us as well as Abraham, if we believe His word. God has promised to every man who believes Him nothing less than the freedom of the world. This is not an arbitrary thing. God has not said that if we will believe certain statements and dogmas, He will in return give us an everlasting inheritance. The inheritance is one of righteousness; and since faith means the reception of the life of Christ into the heart, together with God's righteousness, it is evident that there is no other way in which the inheritance can be received. This is further made clear by a statement in the last section, which was not noted, that "the law worketh wrath."

Therefore whoever thinks to get righteousness by the law is putting his trust in that which will destroy him.[13] God has promised a grant of land to every one who will accept it on His conditions, namely, that he shall also accept the righteousness which goes with it, because righteousness is the characteristic of the land. Righteousness is to "dwell" in it.[14] But this righteousness can be found only in the life of God, which is manifested in Christ.

Now the man who thinks that he himself can get righteousness out of the law is in reality trying to substitute his own righteousness for God's righteousness. In other words, he is trying to get the land by fraud. Therefore when he comes in the court to prove his claim to the land, it appears that there is a criminal charge against him; and he finds "wrath" instead of blessing. "Where no law is, there is no transgression;" but there is law everywhere, and therefore transgression. All have sinned, so that the inheritance can not be by the law.

The Great Joy of Believing the Promise—Romans 4:16-25

> 16 Therefore it is of faith, that it might be by grace; to the end the promise might be sure to all the seed; not to that only which is of the law, but to that also which is of the faith of Abraham, who is the father of us all 17 (as it is written, I have made thee a father of many nations), before Him whom he believed, even God, who quickeneth the dead, and calleth those things which be not as though they were. 18 Who against hope believed in hope, that he might become the father of many nations, according to that which was spoken, So shall thy seed be. 19 And being not weak in faith, he considered not his own body now dead, when he was about an hundred years old, neither yet the deadness of Sarah's womb; 20 he staggered not at the promise of God through unbelief; but was strong in faith, giving glory to God; 21 and being fully persuaded, that what He had promised, He was able also to perform. 22 And therefore it was imputed to him for righteousness. 23 Now it was not written for his sake alone, that it was imputed to him; 24 but for us also, to whom it shall be imputed, if we believe on Him that raised up Jesus our Lord from the dead; 25 who was delivered for our offenses, and was raised again for our justification.

---

13. Waggoner, *The Glad Tidings*, Appendix A, p. 222.
14. Ibid., Appendix A, p. 222.

Sure to All—Since the inheritance is through the righteousness of faith, it is equally sure to all the seed, and equally within the reach of all. Faith gives all an equal chance, because faith is just as easy for one person as for another. God has dealt to every man a measure of faith, and to all the same measure, for the measure of grace is the measure of faith, and "unto every one of us is given grace according to the measure of the gift of Christ." Ephesians 4:7. Christ is given without reserve to every man. Hebrews 2:9. Therefore, as the same measure of faith and grace is given to all men, all have an equal opportunity to gain the inheritance.

Jesus Is the Surety—Faith makes the promise sure to all the seed, because it has Christ alone for its object, and He is the surety of the promises of God. 2 Corinthians 1:20. We read also of the oath of God, by which Jesus was made High Priest, that "by so much was Jesus made a surety of a better testament," or covenant. Hebrews 7:22. Now Jesus was not given for a certain class, but for all without distinction. "God so loved *the world*, that He gave His only-begotten Son, that whosoever believeth in Him should not perish, but have everlasting life." John 3:16. Jesus by the grace of God tasted death for every man. Hebrews 2:9. He says, "Him that cometh to me I will in no wise cast out." John 6:37. Christ dwells in the heart by faith. Ephesians 3:17. Therefore, since Christ is the surety of the promise, it must be sure to every one who believes.

The Oath of God—It may seem to some a little far-fetched to say that the oath by which Jesus was made priest is the surety of the promise to Abraham. But a little consideration will enable any one to see that it can be no other way. In the sixth chapter of Hebrews we read:

> "When God made a promise to Abraham, because He could swear by no greater, He sware by Himself, saying, Surely blessing I will bless thee. … God, willing more abundantly to show unto the heirs of promise the immutability of his counsel, confirmed it by an oath; that by two immutable things, in which it was impossible for God to lie, we might have a strong consolation, who have fled for refuge to lay hold upon the hope set before us; which hope we have as an anchor of the soul, both sure and steadfast, and which entereth into that within the vail, whither the forerunner is for us entered, even Jesus, made a High Priest forever after the order of Melchizedek."

It's All for Our Sakes—Why did God confirm His promise to Abraham by an oath? That we might have a strong consolation. It was not for Abraham's sake, because Abraham believed fully without the oath. His faith was shown to be perfect before the oath was given. It was altogether for our sakes.

When does that oath give us strong consolation? When we flee for refuge to Christ as priest in the most holy place. Within the vail He ministers as High Priest; and it is the oath of God that gives us courage to believe that His priesthood will save us. Then our consolation comes from Christ's priesthood, and so from the oath which made Him priest.

Therefore the oath of God to Abraham was identical with the oath that made Christ High Priest. This shows most plainly that the promise of God to Abraham is as wide as the gospel of Christ. And so our text, speaking of the righteousness that was imputed to Abraham, says, "Now it was not written for his sake alone, that it was imputed to him; but for us also, to whom it shall be imputed, if we believe on Him that raised up Jesus our Lord from the dead."

The Power of God's Word—God "calleth those things which be not as though they were." Sometimes men do the same thing, but we soon lose confidence in them. When men speak of things that are not as though they were, there is only one proper name for it. It is a lie. But God calls those things that be not as though they were, and it is the truth. What makes the difference? Simply this: Man's word has no power to make a thing exist when it does not exist. He may say that it does, but that does not make it so. But when God names a thing, the very thing itself is in the word that names it. He speaks, and it is. It was by this power of God that Abraham was made the father of many nations, even of us, if we believe that Jesus died and rose again.

Quickening [Making Alive] the Dead—It is by the power of God's word which can speak of those things that be not as though they were and have it true, that the dead are raised. His word makes them live. It was Abraham's faith in the resurrection of the dead that made him the father of many nations. God's oath to Abraham was on the occasion of his offering Isaac. Genesis 22:15-18. And "by faith Abraham, when he was tried, offered up Isaac; and he that had received the promises offered up his only-begotten son, of whom it was said, that in Isaac shall thy seed be called; accounting that God was able to raise him up, even from the dead." Hebrews 11:17-19.

Righteousness and the Resurrection of Jesus—The right-eousness which was imputed to Abraham will be imputed to us also if we believe on Him who raised up Jesus our Lord from the dead. Therefore it follows that righteousness was imputed to Abraham because of his faith in the resurrection of the dead, which comes only through Jesus. Acts 4:2. That was what the apostles preached the promises to the fathers. The power by which a man is made righteous is the power of the resurrection. See Philippians 3:9-11. This power of the resurrection, which works righteousness in a man, is the surety of the final resurrection to immortality at the last day by which he enters upon his inheritance.

Not Weakened in Faith—Some versions of Romans 4:19 give the idea, "Without being weakened in faith, he considered his own body now as good as dead." That is to say, after God had made the promise to him, a full consciousness of his weakness and of all the difficulties and seeming impossibilities in the way did not have any effect in weakening his faith. Nothing is impossible with God, and there are no difficulties for Him. Whenever a person is inclined to doubt the possibility of His salvation, let him stop and consider that God made the world by His word, and that He raises the dead, and that it is by that same power that God will save him—if he is willing. To doubt God's promise to deliver us from all evil is to doubt the fact that He created all things by His word, and that He is able to raise the dead.

NOTES

"The LORD recompense thy work, and a full reward be given thee of the LORD God of Israel, under whose wings thou art come to trust." Ruth 2:12.

Chapter 5

Grace Which Much More Abounds

The fourth chapter has taken up the case of Abraham as an illustration of righteousness by faith. The faith which was imputed to him, faith in the death and resurrection of Christ, will bring us the same righteousness, and make us heirs with him of the same promise. But the fourth chapter is really a parenthetical illustration, so that the fifth begins where the third closes.

Peace With God—Romans 5:1-11

1 Therefore being justified by faith, we have peace with God through our Lord Jesus Christ; 2 by Whom also we have access by faith into this grace wherein we stand, and rejoice in hope of the glory of God. 3 And not only so, but we glory in tribulations also; knowing that tribulation worketh patience; 4 and patience, experience; and experience, hope; 5 and hope maketh not ashamed; because the love of God is shed abroad in our hearts by the Holy Ghost which is given unto us. 6 For when we were yet without strength, in due time Christ died for the ungodly. 7 For scarcely for a righteous man will one die; yet peradventure for a good man some would even dare to die.

8 But God commendeth His love toward us, in that, while we were yet sinners, Christ died for us. 9 Much more then, being now justified by His blood, we shall be saved from wrath through Him. 10 For if, when we were enemies, we were reconciled to God by the death of His Son, much more, being reconciled, we shall be saved by His life. And not only so, but we also joy in God through our Lord Jesus Christ, by whom we have now received the atonement. 11 And not only so, but we also joy in God through our Lord Jesus Christ, by whom we have now received the atonement.

Faith Works Real Righteousness—The first verse of the fifth chapter begins with "therefore." The word indicates that what follows is a natural conclusion of what goes before. What has gone before? The story of what Abraham gained by faith. He gained righteousness by faith, but it was by faith in the promise that he should have a son. That son was the child of faith. But the same faith that resulted in the birth of Isaac, also brought righteousness to Abraham. And the same will also be imputed to us, if we have the same faith. Therefore, we are taught that the righteousness of faith is as real as was the son that was born to Abraham through faith. Righteousness by faith is not a myth.

What Is Peace?—Most people have the idea that it is a sort of ecstatic feeling. They think that peace with God means an indescribable heavenly feeling; and so they always look for that imaginary feeling as evidence that they are accepted with God.

But peace with God means the same thing that it means with men: it means simply the absence of war. As sinners we are enemies of God. He is not our enemy, but we are His enemies. He is not fighting against us, but we are fighting against Him. How then may we have peace with Him? Simply by ceasing to fight, and laying down our arms. We may have peace whenever we are ready to stop fighting.

"Peace With God"—Note that when we have peace with God we are not simply at peace with Him, but we have His peace. This peace has been left on the earth for men; for the Lord has said, "Peace I leave with you, My peace I give unto you." John 14:27. He has given it to us. It is ours, therefore, already. It has always been ours. The only trouble has been that we have not believed it. As soon as we believe the words of Christ, then we have in very deed the peace which He has given. And it is peace with God, because we find the peace in Christ, and Christ dwells in the bosom of the Father. John 1:18.

Peace and Righteousness—"Great peace have they which love Thy law." Psalm 119:165. "O that thou hadst hearkened to My commandments! then had thy peace been as a river, and thy righteousness as the waves of the sea." Isaiah 48:18. Righteousness is peace, because our warfare against God was our sins that we cherished. God's life is righteousness, and He is the God of peace. Since the enmity is the carnal mind and its wicked works, peace must be the opposite, namely, righteousness. So it is simply the statement of an obvious fact, that being justified by faith we have peace with God. The righteousness that we have by faith carries peace with it. The two things can not be separated.

Peace and Feeling—The question is asked, "Can one have peace with God and not have a feeling of peace?" What says the Scripture? "Being justified by faith, we have peace with God." What brings the peace? The faith. But faith is not feeling. If it were necessarily the case that there must be a certain feeling with peace, then if we did not have that feeling we should know that we were not justified; and then justification would be a matter of feeling, and not of faith. The verses which follow show us that we may have peace in tribulation as well as when everything goes smoothly.

Glory in Tribulations—This does not mean that we are to seek for martyrdom, as some in the early centuries did. But it means, as it says, that in the midst of tribulations our peace and joy continue the same. This must necessarily be the case with peace that comes by faith. Peace that depends on feeling will depart as soon as we begin to feel tribulation. But nothing can make any difference with the peace that comes by faith. "These things I have spoken unto you, that in Me ye might have peace. In the world ye shall have tribulation; but be of good cheer; I have overcome the world." John 16:33.

Tribulation Worketh Patience—What is patience? It is endurance of suffering. The root of the word "patience" means suffering. We see this in the fact that one who is ill is called "a patient." That is, he is a sufferer. People often excuse their petulance by saying that they have so much to endure. They think that they would be patient if they did not have to suffer so much. No, they would not be. There can be no patience where there is no suffering. Trouble does not destroy patience, but develops it. When trouble seems to destroy one's patience, it is simply showing the fact that the person had no patience.

When Does It Work?—The statement is that tribulation worketh patience. Yet there are many who become more and more irritable the more trouble they have. It does not work patience with them. Why not? Simply because they are not in the condition that the apostle is describing. It is only those who are justified by faith that tribulation works patience. Nothing but faith in God can keep one perfectly patient under all circumstances.

Will It Always Work?—Yes, invariably. "Well," says one, "I am sure that anybody would be impatient if he had as much to trouble him as I have." Question: Would Christ become impatient if He had the things to endure that you have? Did He not have as much to endure, and more? You must admit that He did. Was He impatient? "He was oppressed, and He was afflicted, yet He opened not His mouth." Isaiah 53:7. Then if He were in your place, He would be patient. Why, then, do you not let Him be in your place?

Faith brings Christ into the heart, so that He is identified with us, and therefore He bears the burdens. "Cast thy burden upon the Lord, and He shall sustain thee; He shall never suffer the righteous to be moved." Psalm 55:22.

"All Patience"—There is no limit to the patience that comes by faith in Christ. This is the inspired prayer: "That ye might walk worthy of the Lord unto all pleasing, being fruitful in every good work, and increasing in the knowledge of God; strengthened with all might, according to His glorious power, unto all patience and long-suffering with joyfulness." Colossians 1:10, 11. That is, we may be so strengthened by the glorious power by which Christ endured suffering, that we may have all patience even though suffering long, and may rejoice in the midst of it.

Patience Works Experience—In what does it work experience? It works experience in the peace of God through our Lord Jesus Christ. Many people confuse Christian experience with Christian profession. They speak of having had so many years of "Christian experience," when it may be that they have never really experienced the blessedness of the life of Christ. They have made a profession of religion; but real experience means the actual proving of the power of the life of Christ. When one has that experience, it is not a difficult matter for him to tell something of his experience when occasion calls for it.

"Not Ashamed"—Hope makes not ashamed. Why? Because the love of God is shed abroad in our hearts. "And now, little children, abide in Him; that, when He shall appear, we may have confidence, and not be ashamed before Him at His coming." 1 John 2:28. "Herein is our love made perfect, that we may have boldness in the day of judgment; because as He is, so are we in this world." 1 John 4:17. There can not possibly be a more trying day than the day of judgment. Therefore it is certain that those who will then not be ashamed or afraid, will have boldness now. And he who has boldness with God ought certainly not to be afraid of man.

"The Love of God"—The reason why hope makes not ashamed is that the love of God is shed abroad in our hearts by the Holy Spirit. Note that it does not say love *for* God, but the love *of* God. What is the love of God? "This is the love of God, that we keep His commandments." 1 John 5:3. The Holy Spirit, then, puts into our hearts obedience to the law of God; and it is that which gives us boldness in the day of judgment, and at all other times. It is sin that makes men afraid. When sin is taken away, then fear is gone. "The wicked flee when no man pursueth; but the righteous are bold as a lion." Proverbs 28:1.

"Christ Died for the Ungodly"—"This is a faithful saying, and worthy of all acceptation, that Christ Jesus came into the world to save sinners." 1 Timothy 1:15. "This man receiveth sinners." Luke 15:2. Strange that people will allow a sense of their sinfulness to keep them away from the Lord, when Christ came for the one purpose of receiving and saving *them*. He is able to save them to the uttermost that come unto God by Him (Hebrews 7:25); and He says that those who come to Him He will in no wise cast out (John 6:37).

"Without Strength"—It was when we were yet without strength, that Christ died for the ungodly. Of course; because He died for the purpose that we might be strengthened with might by the Spirit. If He waited for us to gain some strength before giving Himself for us, then we should be lost. When were we without strength? Just now; and even now Jesus Christ is set forth evidently crucified among us. Galatians 3:1. "Surely, shall one say, in the Lord have I righteousness and strength." Isaiah 45:24.

Righteous Versus Good—"For scarcely for a righteous man will one die; yet peradventure for a good man some would even dare to die." Our English translation does not indicate the difference between the two words used here. The righteous man is the just man, the man who is careful to give every one his due. The good man is the benevolent man, the one who has done us many favors, and who does for us more than we could justly claim. Now, no matter how just a man may be, his integrity of character would scarcely lead one to die for him. Yet it is possible that for a man of great kindness some would even dare to die.

The Greatest Love—That is the highest measure of love among men. One may lay down his life for his friends, "but God commendeth His love toward us, in that, while we were yet sinners," and therefore enemies, "Christ died for us."

> "For the love of God is broader
> Than the measure of man's mind;
> And the heart of the Eternal
> Is most wonderfully kind."

"Reconciled by His Death"—God is not our enemy, but we are or have been enemies to Him. Therefore He does not need to be reconciled to us, but we need reconciliation to Him. And He Himself, in the kindness of His heart, makes the reconciliation. We "are made nigh by the blood of Christ." Ephesians 2:13. How so? Because it was sin that separated us from Him, and made us enemies; and "the blood of Jesus Christ His Son cleanseth us from all sin." 1 John 1:7. Being cleansed from sin, we must necessarily be reconciled to God.

The Gift of Life—"The life of the flesh is in the blood." "For it is the life of all flesh." Leviticus 17:11, 14. In that Christ shed His blood *for* us, He gave His life for us. But inasmuch as the blood is applied *to* us, to cleanse us from all sin, He gives His life to us. In the death of Christ therefore, if we are crucified with Him, we receive His life as a substitute for our sinful life, which He takes upon Himself. Our sins are remitted through faith in His blood, not as an arbitrary act, but because by faith we exchange lives with Him, and the life which we get in exchange has no sin. Our sinful life is swallowed up in His boundless life, because He has life so abundantly that He can die because of our transgressions, and still live again to give life to us.

"Saved by His Life"—Christ did not go through the pangs of death for nothing, nor did He give His life to us for the purpose of taking it away again. When He gives us His life, He designs that we shall keep it forever. How do we get it? By faith. How do we keep it? By the same faith. "As ye have therefore received Christ Jesus the Lord, so walk ye in Him." Colossians 2:6. His life can never end, but we may lose it by unbelief.

Let it be remembered that we have not this life in ourselves, but "this life is in His Son." "He that hath the Son hath life; and he that hath not the Son of God hath not life." 1 John 5:11, 12. We keep the everlasting life by keeping Christ. Now it is a very simple proposition that if we have been reconciled to God by the death of Christ, if His life has been given to us for the remission of our sins, then we shall much more be saved by that life since He has risen from the dead.

People sometimes say that they can believe that God forgives their sins, but they find it difficult to believe that He can *keep them from* sin. Well, if there is any difference, the latter is the easier of the two; for the forgiveness of sins requires the death of Christ, while the saving *from* sins requires only His continued life.

By What Life Are We Saved?—By the life of Christ, and He has but one. He is "the same yesterday, and today, and forever." Hebrews 13:8. It is by His present life that we are saved, that is, by His life in us from day to day. But the life which He now lives is the very same life that He lived in Judea eighteen hundred years ago. He took again the same life that He laid down. Think what was in the life of Christ, as we have the record in the New Testament, and we shall know what ought to be in our lives now. If we allow Him to dwell in us, He will live just as He did then. If there is something in our lives that was not then in His, we may be sure that He is not living it in us now.

A Series of Contrasts—Romans 5:12-19

12 Wherefore, as by one man sin entered into the world, and death by sin; and so death passed upon all men, for that all have sinned: 13 (for until the law sin was in the world; but sin is not imputed when there is

no law. 14 Nevertheless death reigned from Adam to Moses, even over them that had not sinned after the similitude of Adam's transgression, who is the figure of Him that was to come. 15 But not as the offence, so also is the free gift. For if through the offence of one many be dead, much more the grace of God, and the gift by grace, which is by one Man, Jesus Christ, hath abounded unto many. 16 And not as it was by one that sinned, so is the gift: for the judgment was by one to condemnation, but the free gift is of many offences unto justification.

17 For if by one man's offence death reigned by one; much more they which receive abundance of grace and of the gift of righteousness shall reign in life by One, Jesus Christ.) 18 Therefore as by the offence of one judgment came upon all men to condemnation; even so by the righteousness of One the free gift came upon all men unto justification of life. 19 For as by one man's disobedience many were made sinners, so by the obedience of One shall many be made righteous.

Joy in God—The eleventh verse should have been included in last week's lesson, as the thought is the same as in the preceding verses. By the same life by which we receive the reconciliation and salvation, "we also joy in God." Christ's life is a joyous life. When David had fallen, he prayed, "Restore unto me the joy of Thy salvation; and uphold me with Thy free Spirit." Psalm 61:12. The brightness of the heavens, the beauty of the infinite variety of flowers with which God clothes the earth, and the glad songs of the birds, all indicate that God delights in joy and beauty. Brightness and song are but the natural expressions of His life. "Let them also that love Thy name be joyful in Thee." Psalm 5:11.

There is probably no passage in Romans more difficult to understand than verses 12-19. The reason is that there is so long a parenthesis in the midst of the main statement, and there is so much repetition of the same form of expression. There is really no greatly involved argument. In this study we shall not attempt to deal with every particular, but will note the main thought running through the whole, so that the reader can read and study it more satisfactorily for himself.

First Principles—It will be seen from verse 12 that the apostle goes back to the very beginning. "By one man sin entered into the world, and death by sin; and so death passed upon all men, for that all have sinned." There can never be any presentation of the gospel, if these facts are ignored.

Death by Sin—Death came by sin, because sin is death. Sin, when it is full grown, bringeth forth death. See James 1:15. "To be carnally minded is death." Romans 8:6. "The sting of death is sin." 1 Corinthians 15:56. There could be no death if there were no sin. Sin carries death in its bosom. So it was not an arbitrary act on the part of God that death came upon men because of sin. It could not possibly be otherwise.

Righteousness and Life—"To be spiritually minded is life and peace." Romans 8:6. "There is none good but one, that is, God." Matthew 19:17. He is goodness itself. Goodness is His life. Righteousness is simply God's way. Therefore righteousness is life. It is not merely a conception of what is right, but it is the right thing itself. Righteousness is active. As sin and death are inseparable, so are righteousness and life. "See, I have set before thee this day life and good, and death and evil." Deuteronomy 30:15.

Death Passed Upon All Men—Note the justice here. Death passed upon all men, "for that all have sinned." "The soul that sinneth, it shall die. The son shall not bear the iniquity of the father, neither shall the father bear the iniquity of the son; the righteousness of the righteous shall be upon him, and the wickedness of the wicked shall be upon him." Ezekiel 18:20. And this is also a necessary consequence of the fact that sin contains death in it, and that death can not come in any other way than by sin.

The Conclusion—It will be noticed that the twelfth verse begins a proposition that is not completed. Verses 13-17 are parenthetical; we must pass on to the eighteenth verse to find the conclusion. But as the mind would naturally lose the first part of the statement on account of the long parenthesis, the apostle repeats the substance of it, so that we may perceive the force of the conclusion. So the first part of verse 18 is parallel to verse 12. "As by one man sin entered into the world, and death by sin; and so death passed upon all men to condemnation." The conclusion is, "Even so by the righteousness of One the free gift came upon all men unto justification of life."

The Reign of Death—"Death reigned from Adam to Moses." That does not imply that death did not reign just as much afterwards. But the point is that Moses stands for the giving of the law; "for the law was given by Moses." John 1:17. Now since death reigns through sin, and sin is not imputed when there is no law, it is evident from the statement that "death reigned from Adam to Moses," that the law was in the world just as much before Sinai as it was afterwards. "The sting of death is sin; and the strength of sin is the law." 1 Corinthians 15:56. There can be no sin imputed when there is no law; but wherever there is sin, there death reigns.

Adam a Figure—"Death reigned from Adam to Moses, even over them that had not sinned after the similitude of Adam's transgression, who is the figure of Him that was to come." How is Adam a figure of Him that was to come, namely, Christ? Just as the following verses indicate, that is, Adam was a figure of Christ in that his action involved many besides himself. It is evident that Adam could not give his descendants any higher nature than he had himself, so Adam's sin made it inevitable that all his descendants should be born with sinful natures. Sentence of death, however, does not pass on them for that, but because they have sinned.

A Figure by Contrast—Adam is a figure of Christ, but only by contrast. "Not as the offense, so also is the free gift." Through the offense of one many are dead; but through the righteousness of One, many receive life. "The judgment was by one to condemnation, but the free gift is of many offenses unto justification. For if by one man's offense death reigned by one; much more they which receive abundance of grace and of the gift of righteousness shall reign in life by One, Jesus Christ." There is contrast all the way through. Everything that came through Adam's fall is undone in Christ; or, better still, all that was lost in Adam is restored in Christ.

"Much More"—This might be taken as the keynote of this chapter. Not only is everything that is lost in Adam restored in Christ, but "much more." "If, when we were enemies, we were reconciled to God by the death of His Son; much more, being reconciled, we shall be saved by His life."

And there is no chance of finding fault with the inevitable fact that we are inheritors of a sinful nature through Adam. We can not complain that we are unjustly dealt with. It is true that we are not to blame for having a sinful nature, and the Lord recognizes the fact. So He provides that just as in Adam we were made partakers of a sinful nature, even so in Christ we shall be made partakers of the divine nature.

But "much more." "For if by one man's offense death reigned by one; *much more* they which receive abundance of grace and of the gift of righteousness shall reign in life by One, Jesus Christ." That is, the life of which we are made partakers in Christ is much stronger for righteousness than the life which we received from Adam is for unrighteousness. God does not do things by halves. He gives "abundance of grace."

The Condemnation—"Death passed upon all men;" or, as stated later, "judgment came upon all men to condemnation." "The wages of sin is death." Romans 6:23. All have sinned, and, therefore, all are in condemnation. There has not a man lived on earth over whom death has not reigned, nor will there be until the end of the world. Enoch and Elijah, as well as those who shall be translated when the Lord comes, are no exceptions.

There are no exceptions, for the Scripture says that "death passed upon all men." For the reign of death is simply the reign of sin. "Elias was a man of like passions with us." Enoch was righteous only by faith; his nature was as sinful as that of any other man. So that death reigned over them as well as over any others. For be it remembered that this present going into the grave, which we so often see, is not the punishment of sin. It is simply the evidence of our mortality. Good and bad alike die. This is not the condemnation, because men die rejoicing in the Lord, and even singing songs of triumph.

"Justification of Life"—"By the righteousness of One the free gift came upon all men unto justification of life."[15] There is no exception here. As the condemnation came upon all, so the justification comes upon all. Christ has tasted death for every man. Hebrews 2:9. He has given Himself for all. Nay, He has given Himself to every man. The free gift has come upon all. The fact that it is a free gift is evidence that there is no exception. If it came upon only those who have some special qualification, then it would not be a free gift.[16]

It is a fact, therefore, plainly stated in the Bible, that the gift of righteousness and life in Christ has come to every man on earth. There is not the slightest reason why every man that has ever lived should not be saved unto eternal life, except that they would not have it. So many spurn the gift given so freely.[17]

"The Obedience of One"—By the obedience of One shall many be made righteous. Men are not saved through their own obedience, but through the obedience of Christ. Here is where the skeptic cavils, and says that it is not just that one man's obedience should be counted as another's. But the man who rejects the counsel of the Lord does not know anything about justice, and is not qualified to speak in the case.

The Bible does not teach us that God calls us righteous simply because Jesus of Nazareth was righteous eighteen hundred years ago. It says that by His obedience we are made righteous. Notice that it is present, actual righteousness. The trouble with those who object to the righteousness of Christ being imputed to believers is that they do not take into consideration the fact that Jesus lives. He is alive today, as much as when He was in Judea. "He ever liveth," and He is "the same yesterday and today, and forever." His life is as perfectly in harmony with the law now as it was then. And He lives in the hearts of those who believe on Him.

Therefore it is Christ's present obedience in believers that makes them righteous. They can of themselves do nothing, and so God in His love does

---

15. See Appendix A, p. 223.
16. *The Glad Tidings*, Appendix A, p. 223.
17. Ibid., Appendix A, p. 223.

it in them. Here is the whole story: "I am crucified with Christ; nevertheless I live; yet not I but Christ liveth in me; and the life which I now live in the flesh I live by the faith of the Son of God, who loved me, and gave Himself for me." Galatians 2:20.

Why Not All?—The text says that "by the obedience of One shall many be made righteous." Some one may ask, "Why are not all made righteous by the obedience of One?" The reason is that they do not wish to be. If men were counted righteous simply because One was righteous eighteen hundred years ago, then all would have to be righteous by the same obedience. There would be no justice in counting righteousness to one and not to all, if it were in that way. But we have seen that it is not so.

People are not simply counted righteous, but actually made righteous by the obedience of Christ,[18] who is as righteous as He ever was, and who lives today in those who yield to Him. His ability to live in any human being is shown in the fact that He took human flesh eighteen hundred years ago. What God did in the person of the Carpenter of Nazareth, He is willing and anxious to do for every man that believes. The free gift comes upon all, but all will not accept it, and therefore all are not made righteous by it. Nevertheless, "many" will be made righteous by His obedience.

In studying the two remaining verses of this chapter, it will be sufficient for our present purpose if we remember that the main thought running through the chapter is life and righteousness. Sin is death, and righteousness is life. Death has passed upon all men, because all have sinned, and the gift of righteousness has come to all men in the life of Christ. Sin is not imputed when there is no law, yet sin was imputed to Adam and to all who lived after him, even till the time of the giving of the law, in the days of Moses.

Grace and Truth—Romans 5:20, 21

20 Moreover the law entered, that the offense might abound. But where sin abounded, grace did much more abound; 21 that as sin hath reigned unto death, even so might grace reign through righteousness unto eternal life by Jesus Christ our Lord.

"The Law Entered"—This statement indicates that there was offense before the particular time spoken of as the "entering" of the law. Taking into consideration verses 13, 14, we have no difficulty in seeing that the

---

18. Waggoner, *Christ and His Righteousness*, Appendix A, p. 224.

giving of the law upon Sinai is the time referred to. "Until the law," the time of Moses, and the entering of the law, evidently refer to the one event.

Sin Abounds—The law entered that the offense already existing might abound. "But sin is not imputed when there is no law." Therefore we must know that the law was in the world before the time spoken of as the "entering" of the law, that is, before it was spoken from Sinai. This is what we learned from verses 13 and 14. It was not possible that the law should actually make any more sin than already existed. It could only emphasize it, that is, more plainly show its true nature.

As stated in chapter 7:13, it was "that sin by the commandment might become exceeding sinful." There was not one whit more of the law of God in the world after it was spoken from Sinai than there was before; neither was anything that was right before made sinful by the giving of the law; nor was any act that was sinful before made more sinful by the giving of the law. But the circumstances under which the law was spoken tended to show the awfulness of sin, and to impress the hearers with a greater sense of their sinfulness than ever before.

Grace Superabounds—It would be well if every person knew this fact. We should hear less talk about being discouraged because we are so sinful. Is the heart full of sin? Know that where sin abounds, there does grace much more abound. This is shown in the fact that Christ, who is full of grace, stands at the door of the heart that is sinfulness itself, and knocks for admission. See Revelation 3:15-20. "This is a faithful saying, and worthy of all acceptation, that Christ Jesus came into the world to save sinners; of whom I am chief." 1 Timothy 1:15. When Wesley sang,

> "Plenteous grace with Thee is found,
> Grace to cover all my sin,"

he had the authority of Romans 5:20 for it!

Grace at Sinai—Since the law entered that the offense might abound, it is evident that at the very time of the entering of the law the offense must have greatly abounded. There never was a time when the awfulness of sin was made to stand out more prominently. "But where sin abounded, grace did much more abound." Therefore it is as plain as the Scripture can make it, that grace was superabounding at the giving of the law from Sinai.

It is a mistake, therefore, to suppose that God designed that any should think that righteousness was to be obtained by their own works of obedience.[19]

---

19. E.G. White, *Faith and Works*, Appendix A, p. 224.

On the contrary, the law was spoken to emphasize the boundless grace of God, in pardoning sin, and in working righteousness in men.

The Law and God's Throne—We read that "righteousness and judgment are the habitation of His throne." Psalm 97:2. Righteousness dwells in His throne. It is the foundation of it. The law of God is righteousness, even His own righteousness. This is shown by Isaiah 51:6 and 7, where God speaks of His righteousness, and says, "Hearken unto Me, ye that know righteousness, the people in whose heart is My law." That is, only they in whose heart is God's law, know His righteousness. Therefore His law is His righteousness. And the statement that righteousness is the habitation or establishment of His throne, indicates that the law of God is in His throne. He sits upon the throne of righteousness.

Evidence From the Tabernacle—The tabernacle built by Moses was for a dwelling place for God. "Let them make Me a sanctuary; that I may dwell among them." Exodus 25:8. In that sanctuary, in the most holy place, was the ark of the testament. This ark is described in Exodus 25:10-22. The cover of the ark was called the mercy-seat. Upon this mercy-seat were the two cherubim of gold. Within the ark, under the mercy-seat, were the tables of the law. See Exodus 25:16-21; Deuteronomy 10:1-5. Between the cherubim, upon the mercy-seat, and above the tables of the law, was where the glory of God was seen, and where God spoke to the people. Exodus 25:22. In 2 Kings 19:15 and Psalm 80:1 God is addressed as sitting between the cherubim.

Therefore we learn that the ark of the testament, with the mercy-seat, or the cover, was a representation of the throne of God. As the Ten Commandments were in the ark in the earthly tabernacle, so the Ten Commandments are the very foundation of the throne of God in heaven. We may note, in passing, that since the earthly tabernacle was a figure of the true tabernacle in heaven, therefore we are taught that the law as it stands in heaven, in the throne of God, is identical with the law as spoken from Sinai, and written on the tables of stone that were placed in the ark.

God's Throne and Sinai—We have learned that the law of God is the very basis of His throne. This is no more than might reasonably be expected, since the basis of any government is its law, and the throne simply stands for the law.

Mount Sinai, when the law was spoken from it, was the seat of God's law. It represented the awfulness of the law, since no one could touch it without dying. The Lord was there with all His angels. See Deuteronomy 33:2; Acts 7:53. Therefore Mount Sinai, at the time of the giving of the law, was designed to represent the throne of God. Indeed, it was for the time the throne of God, the place whence the law goes forth, out of which proceed "lightnings and thunderings and voices" (Revelation 4:5), and around which stand "ten thousand times ten thousand, and thousands of thousands" of angels. Here again we learn that the righteousness which is the habitation of the throne of God is the righteousness described by the Ten Commandments, just as they were spoken from the top of Sinai, as recorded in Exodus 20:3-17.

The Throne of Grace—But although the throne of God is the habitation of His law, that law which is death to sinners, yet it is a throne of grace. We are exhorted to "come boldly unto the throne of grace, that we may obtain mercy, and find grace to help in time of need." Hebrews 4:16. Note that we are to come to obtain mercy. Note also that the top of the ark of the testimony, in which were the tables of the law, was called the mercy-seat. It was the place where God appeared to speak to His people, so that the ark of the earthly tabernacle not only represented the throne where God's law is enshrined, but it represented that throne as the throne of grace.

The Law and the Mediator—We are told that the law was ordained "in the hand of a Mediator." Galatians 3:19. Who was the Mediator in whose hand the law was ordained? "There is one God, and one Mediator between God and men, the Man Christ Jesus; who gave Himself a ransom for all." 1 Timothy 2:5 and 6. The law, therefore, was given from Sinai by Christ, who is and always was the manifestation of God to men. He is the Mediator, that is, the One through whom the things of God are brought to men. The righteousness of God is conveyed to men through Jesus Christ. The statement that the law was given in the hand of a Mediator, reminds us that where sin abounded grace did much more abound.

The fact that the law was in the hand of a Mediator at Sinai shows us this: (1) That God did not mean that any one should suppose that he must get the righteousness of the law by his own power, but only through Christ. (2) That the gospel of Christ was displayed at Sinai as well as at Calvary. (3) That the righteousness of God which is revealed in the gospel of Christ, is the identical righteousness that is described in the law as given from Sinai, without the alteration of a letter. The righteousness which we are to obtain in Christ is none other than that.

The Fountain of Life—In Psalm 36:7-9 we read: "How excellent is Thy loving-kindness, O God! Therefore the children of men put their trust under the shadow of Thy wings. They shall be abundantly satisfied with the fatness of Thy house; and Thou shalt make them drink of the river of Thy pleasures. For with Thee is the fountain of life." It is because with God is the fountain of life that He makes those who trust in Him to drink of the river of His pleasure.

What is that river? "And He showed me a pure river of water of life, clear as crystal, proceeding out of the throne of God and of the Lamb." Revelation 22:1. Think of it! A river flowing out of the throne of God. He is the fountain of life. The invitation is to every one that is athirst to drink of the water of life freely. Revelation 22:17; John 4:10-14, and 7:37-39, will help to an understanding of the matter. We take the living water by receiving the Holy Spirit.

Drinking in Righteousness—The Saviour says, "Blessed are they which do hunger and thirst after righteousness; for they shall be filled." Matthew 5:6. If one is thirsty, how only can he be filled? By drinking. Therefore the Saviour means that we can drink righteousness, if we thirst for it. Remember that God's throne is the seat of righteousness, and that from it flows the river of life, and we shall see the fitness of the assurance that we may drink in righteousness.

Since the throne is the seat of righteousness, the river that proceeds from the throne must, so to speak, be charged with the righteousness of the law. Whosoever therefore believes on Christ, and drinks in of His Spirit, must drink in of the righteousness of the law as it is in the throne, or as it was spoken from Sinai.

Drinking at Sinai—Whoever will read Exodus 17:1-6 together with Deuteronomy 4:10-12 (which show that Horeb and Sinai are the same), will learn that at the very time when the law was spoken from Sinai, there was a river of water flowing from its base. That river flowed from Christ. See 1 Corinthians 10:4. Christ, the living Rock, stood upon that rock in the desert, from which the water flowed for the thirst of the people, and He it was from Whom it came. With Him is the fountain of life. And so we have the complete likeness of the throne of God in Sinai. It was the embodiment of the law of God, so that no one could approach it without death, and yet they could drink the living water that flowed from it. And in this figure we again see that the righteousness which those who accept Christ's invitation are to drink in, is the righteousness that is described in the Ten Commandments.

The Heart of Christ—Through David, Christ spoke thus of His coming to this earth: "Then said I, Lo, I come; in the volume of the book it is written of Me, I delight to do Thy will, O My God; yea, Thy law is within My heart." Psalm 40:7, 8. He said that He had kept His Father's commandments. John 15:10. So closely did He keep the commandments that He observed the seventh-day Sabbath, which is sometimes stigmatized as "the Jewish Sabbath."

Canon Knox-Little says, "It is certain that our Lord when on earth did observe Saturday, and did not observe Sunday."—*Sacerdotalism*, p. 75.

This is not true because Canon Knox-Little said it, but it is true because the Bible teaches it. It is so clear a fact that there is no chance for discussion about it. We have never yet heard of any one who had the hardihood to assert that Jesus ever kept any other day than the seventh, the day enjoined in the fourth commandment. The keeping of "the Sabbath day according to the commandment" was part of the righteousness which was in the heart of Christ. And since Christ is the same today that He ever was, it is in His heart still.

Eternal Life through Christ—"Even so might grace reign through righteousness unto eternal life by Jesus Christ our Lord." Christ's life was given for us and to us on the cross. It is by being crucified with Him that we live with Him. Galatians 2:20; Romans 6:8. "God was in Christ, reconciling the world unto Himself." 2 Corinthians 5:19. In His heart was the law, so that the heart of Christ was really the throne of God. Thus we sing of "Christ enthroned within."

When Christ hung upon the cross, "one of the soldiers with a spear pierced His side, and forthwith came there out blood and water." John 19:34. This was the fountain of life, that freely flows for all. It flowed from the heart of Christ, in which the law of God was enshrined. So we find that Sinai, Calvary, and Mount Sion all present the same thing. Sinai and Calvary are not in opposition, but are united. Both present the same gospel and the same law. The life which flows for us from Calvary, bears to us the righteousness of the law that was proclaimed from Sinai.

Grace Through Righteousness—Thus we see how grace reigns through righteousness unto eternal life. Eternal life is in Christ, because His life is the life of the self-existent God, who is "from everlasting to everlasting." But the life of God is the law. The grace of God flows to us through the life of Christ, and bears to us the righteousness of it. Thus in Christ we receive the law as it was ordained, namely, to life.

To accept the unspeakable gift of God's grace, therefore, is simply to yield ourselves to Him, that Christ may dwell in us, and live in us the righteousness of the law as spoken from Sinai, and treasured in the throne of God. From Christ that living stream still flows, so that, receiving Him, we shall have in us that well of water spring up unto everlasting life.

Chapter 6

Christ's Yoke Is Easy, His Burden Light

In beginning the study of the sixth chapter of Romans, it must be remembered that we have but a continuation of the fifth. The subject of that chapter is superabounding grace, and the gift of life and righteousness by grace. As sinners we are enemies of God, but are reconciled, that is, freed from sin, by receiving the righteousness of Christ's life, which has no limit. No matter how greatly the sin may abound, grace does much more abound.

Crucified, Buried, and Risen "With Christ"— Romans 6:1-11

1 What shall we say then? Shall we continue in sin, that grace may abound? 2 God forbid. How shall we, that are dead to sin, live any longer therein? 3 Know ye not, that so many of us as were baptized into Jesus Christ were baptized into His death?

4 Therefore we are buried with Him by baptism into death; that like as Christ was raised up from the dead by the glory of the Father, even so we also should walk in newness of life. 5 For if we have been planted together in the likeness of His death, we shall be also in the likeness of His resurrection: 6 knowing this, that our old man is crucified with Him, that the body of sin might be destroyed, that henceforth we should not serve sin. 7 For he that is dead is freed from sin.

8 Now if we be dead with Christ, we believe that we shall also live with Him; 9 knowing that Christ being raised from the dead dieth no more; death hath no more dominion over Him. 10 For in that He died, He died unto sin once; but in that He liveth, He liveth

unto God. 11 Likewise reckon ye also yourselves to be dead indeed unto sin, but alive unto God through Jesus Christ our Lord.

An Important Question—"Shall we continue in sin, that grace may abound?" The student will doubtless recall a similar question in the third chapter, verses 5 and 7, and the answer in verses 6 and 8. It is another form of the question, "Shall we do evil, that good may come?" The answer must be apparent to all, "Not by any means," for this is really the force of the words improperly rendered, "God forbid."

Although grace superabounds where sin abounds, that is no reason why we should willfully pile up the sin. That would be most emphatically to receive the grace of God in vain. 2 Corinthians 6:1.

The Reason Why—"How shall we, that are dead to sin, live any longer therein?" It is simply an impossibility, and there is really no question as to whether or not we may do it; for it is certain that if we are dead to sin, we can not live in it at the same time. A man can not at the same time be both dead and alive.

Now the previous chapter has emphasized the fact that we are reconciled to God by the death of Christ, and are saved by His life. Reconciliation to God means being freed from sin; so that being "saved by His life" means that we have "passed from death unto life." The life of sin that was enmity has been ended in the life of Christ.

"Baptized Into Jesus Christ"—Baptism is the symbol of putting on Christ. "For as many of you as have been baptized into Christ have put on Christ." Galatians 8:27. "For as the body is one, and hath many members, and all the members of that one body, being many, are one body; so also is Christ. For by one Spirit are we all baptized into one body, whether we be Jews or Gentiles." 1 Corinthians 12:12, 13.

Where Christ Touches Us—It is in death that we come into contact with Christ. He touches us at the lowest possible point. That is what makes our salvation so sure, and so sure for every one without any exception. Sin and sickness are tributary to death. Death is the sum of all the evils possible to man. It is the lowest depth, and it is there that Christ comes in contact with us. We become united to Him in death. As the greater includes the lesser, the fact that Christ humbled Himself even to death proves that there is no ill possible to us that He does not take upon Himself.

Baptized Into His Death—"So many of us as were baptized into Jesus Christ were baptized into His death." And what is it to be baptized into His death? Verse 10 tells us: "For in that He died, He died unto sin once." He died unto sin, *not His own*, because He had none; but He "bare *our* sins in His own body on the tree." 1 Peter 2:24. "He was wounded for our transgressions, He was bruised for our iniquities." Isaiah 53:5. Since in that He died, He died unto sin, it follows that if we are baptized into His death, we also die to sin.

A New Life—"Christ being raised from the dead dieth no more." "If we be dead with Christ, we believe that we shall also live with Him." It was impossible for the grave to hold Christ. Acts 2:24. Therefore, just as surely as we are baptized into the death of Christ, so surely shall we be raised from a life of sin to a life of righteousness in Him. "For if we have been planted together in the likeness of His death, we shall be also in the likeness of His resurrection."

Crucifixion With Him—As Christ was crucified, therefore, being baptized into His death means that we are crucified with Him. So we read, "I am crucified with Christ; nevertheless I live; yet not I, but Christ liveth in me." Galatians 2:20. Crucified, yet living, because crucified with Christ, and yet he lives. Christ said, "Because I live, ye shall live also." John 14:19. How can we live a new life? We have no power at all of ourselves; but Christ was raised from the dead by the glory of the Father; and in His prayer to the Father He said, "The glory which Thou gavest Me I have given them." John 17:22. Therefore, the power that raised Jesus from the dead is exercised to raise us from the death of sin. If we are willing to allow the old life to be crucified, we may be sure of the new.

"Our Old Man" Crucified—We shall be in the likeness of His resurrection. If we are crucified with Christ, our sins must also be crucified with Christ, for they are a part of us. Our sins were on Him as He was crucified, so of course our sins are crucified if we are crucified with Him.

But here is a difference between us and our sins when crucified. We are crucified in order that we may live again; our sins are crucified in order that they may be destroyed. Christ is not "the minister of sin" (Galatians 2:17). It was the life of God that raised Him from the dead, and in that life there is no sin.

A Separation From Sin—The reader will notice that the separation from sin is in death. That is because death is in sin. "Sin, when it is finished, bringeth forth death." James 1:15. Therefore nothing less than death will effect a separation.[20] We could not separate ourselves from sin, because sin was our very life. If it had been possible for us to effect the destruction of

---

20. A.T. Jones, *1893 General Conference Bulletin*, Appendix A, p. 225.

sin, it could have been only by the giving up of our lives, and that would have been the end of us. That is why there will be no future for the wicked who die in their sins; their life having been given up (or rather, taken from them), they are out of existence. But Christ had the power to lay down His life, and to take it again; and therefore when we lay down our lives in Him, we are raised again by His endless life.

Remember that He does not give us our own life back again, but that He gives us His own life. In that life there never was a sin; and so it is that our crucifixion and resurrection with Him is the separation of sin from us. This thought must be borne in mind when we come to study the next chapter.

Living With Him—When shall we live with Him? Why, as soon as we are buried and risen with Him, of course. Our life with Christ in the world to come is assured to us only by our living with Him now in this world. We are separated from sin, by death with Him, in order that we may be joined to life in Him. The reader is asked to bear this in mind also until we come to the study of the next chapter.

"Buried with Him by Baptism"—Baptism, therefore, is burial. If people were content to follow the plain reading of the Scriptures, there never would be a question concerning "the mode of baptism." No one from reading the Bible could ever get any other idea than that baptism is immersion. "Buried with Him in baptism, wherein also ye are risen with Him through the faith of the operation of God, who hath raised Him from the dead." Colossians 2:12. Baptism represents the death and resurrection of Christ, and by it we show our acceptance of His sacrifice; and the very act is an actual burial, in order to make the lesson the more impressive.

Why the Change in Baptism?—How is it that there has been a change from Scripture baptism to sprinkling? The answer is very easy. Baptism is a memorial of the resurrection of Christ. But "the church," by which is meant the bishops who loved the praise of men more than the praise of God and who wished to curry favor with the "better class" of the heathen, adopted the pagan sun festival. And in order to appear to justify themselves in so doing, they claimed that the rising sun which was worshipped by the heathen was a symbol of the resurrection of "the Sun of Righteousness," namely, Christ, and that by observing Sunday they were celebrating His resurrection.

But they did not need two memorials of the resurrection, and so they dropped the one that the Lord had given. In order, however, not to appear to throw baptism away, they claimed that the heathen sprinkling with "holy water" which they very naturally adopted with the heathen sun festival, was the baptism enjoined in the Scriptures.

The people trusted in the "fathers" instead of reading the Bible for themselves, and so it was very easy to make them believe that the Bible was obeyed. It is true that there are some who follow the word in regard to immersion, who also observe Sunday; but the two practices are inconsistent. The word is neglected in one particular (observing Sunday) in order to provide a memorial for an event which they already celebrate in accordance with the word (baptism). Scriptural baptism is falling into disuse among many who observe the first day of the week. It must be the case that sooner or later they will wholly give up one or the other.

Instruments of Righteousness—Romans 6:12-23

12 Let not sin therefore reign in your mortal body, that ye should obey it in the lusts thereof. 13 Neither yield ye your members as instruments of unrighteousness unto sin; but yield yourselves unto God, as those that are alive from the dead, and your members as instruments of righteousness unto God. 14 For sin shall not have dominion over you; for ye are not under the law, but under grace. 15 What then? shall we sin, because we are not under the law, but under grace? God forbid. 16 Know ye not, that to whom ye yield yourselves servants to obey, his servants ye are to whom ye obey; whether of sin unto death, or of obedience unto righteousness?

17 But God be thanked, that ye were the servants of sin, but ye have obeyed from the heart that form of doctrine which was delivered you. 18 Being then made free from sin, ye became the servants of righteousness. 19 I speak after the manner of men because of the infirmity of your flesh; for as ye have yielded your members servants to uncleanness and to iniquity unto iniquity; even so now yield your members servants to righteousness unto holiness. 20 For when ye were the servants of sin, ye were free from righteousness. 21 What fruit had ye then in those things whereof ye are now ashamed? For the end of those things is death. 22 But now being made free from sin, and become servants to God, ye have your fruit unto holiness, and the end everlasting life. 23 For the wages of sin is death; but the gift of God is eternal life through Jesus Christ our Lord.

The Reign of Sin—In the fifth chapter we learned that the reign of sin is the reign of death, because death comes by sin. But we also learned that the gift of life is given to all, so that whoever has Christ has life. Instead of death reigning over such, they themselves "shall reign in life by One, Jesus

Christ." The exhortation, "Let not sin therefore reign in your mortal body," is therefore equal to an exhortation to abide in Christ, or to keep His life. We gained the life by faith, and so we are to keep it by faith.

Whose Servants Are We?—That is very easy to answer. "To whom ye yield yourselves servants to obey." If we yield ourselves to sin, then we are the servants of sin, for "whosoever committeth sin is the servant of sin." John 8:34. But if we yield ourselves to righteousness, then we are the servants of righteousness. "No man can serve two masters." Matthew 6:24. We can not serve both sin and righteousness at the same time. No man can at once be both a sinner and a righteous man. Either sin or righteousness must rule.

Instruments—We have in this chapter two terms to describe people—servants and instruments. It takes both to illustrate our relation to sin and righteousness. Sin and righteousness are rulers. We are but instruments in their hands. The kind of work a given instrument will do depends entirely upon the one who uses it.

For instance, here is a good pen; what kind of work will it do? It will do good work if it is in the hands of a skillful penman, but in the hands of a bungler its work will be poor. Or, in the hands of a good man it will write only what is good; but in the hands of a bad man it will exhibit that which is evil. But man is not a mere tool. No, not by any means. There is this difference between men and ordinary instruments: the latter have no choice as to who shall use them, while the former have full choice as to whom they will serve. They must yield themselves, not once only, but all the time. If they yield to sin, they will commit sin. If they yield to God, to be instruments in His hands, they can do nothing else but good so long as they are yielded to Him.

A Parallel—In the nineteenth verse we are exhorted to yield ourselves as servants of righteousness just as we have yielded ourselves servants to sin. This being done, we are assured in the following verses that just as surely as the fruit was sin and death when we were yielded to sin, so surely will the fruit be holiness when we yield ourselves servants to righteousness. Yea, even more sure; for "where sin abounded, grace did much more abound; that as sin hath reigned unto death, even so might grace reign through righteousness unto eternal life by Jesus Christ our Lord." Righteousness is stronger than sin, even as God is stronger than Satan. God can pluck out of the hands of Satan the soul that cries out for deliverance; but none can pluck God's children out of His hand.

Not Under the Law—Many people are fond of quoting this expression, thinking that it forever absolves them from any observance of the law of God.

Strange to say, this expression is used as a cover only for non-observance of the fourth commandment. Repeat the fourth commandment to a man who objects to keeping the Sabbath of the Lord, the seventh day, and he will say, "We are not under the law." Yet that same man will quote the third commandment to a man whom he hears swearing, or the first and second against the heathen, and will acknowledge the sixth, seventh, and eighth commandments. Thus it appears that men do not really believe that the statement that we are "not under the law" means that we are at liberty to break it. Let us study the whole verse, and its different parts.

What Is Sin?—"Whosoever committeth sin transgresseth also the law; for sin is the transgression of the law." 1 John 3:4. "All unrighteousness is sin." 1 John 5:17. This is definite; let us hold it well in our minds.[21]

What Is Righteousness?—Righteousness is the opposite of sin, because "all unrighteousness is sin." But "sin is the transgression of the law." Therefore righteousness is the keeping of the law. So when we are exhorted to yield our members as instruments of righteousness unto God, it is the same as telling us to yield ourselves to obedience to the law.

The Dominion of Sin—Sin has no dominion over those who yield themselves servants to righteousness, or to obedience to the law; because sin is the transgression of the law. Now read the whole of the fourteenth verse: "For sin shall not have dominion over you; for ye are not under the law, but under grace." That is to say, transgression of the law has no place in them who are not under the law. Then those who are not under the law are those who obey the law. Those who break it are under it. Nothing can be plainer.

Under Grace—"Ye are not under the law, but under grace." We have seen that those who are not under the law are the ones who are keeping the law. Those therefore who are under the law are the ones who are breaking it, and who are therefore under its condemnation.[22] But "where sin abounded, grace did much more abound." Grace delivers from sin.

Distressed by the threatenings of the law which we have broken, we flee for refuge to Christ, who is "full of grace and truth." There we find freedom from sin. In Him we not only find grace to cover all our sin, but we find the righteousness of the law because He is full of truth, and the law is the truth. Psalm 119:142. Grace "reigns" in our life through righteousness (or obedience to the law), unto eternal life *by* Jesus Christ our Lord.

---

21. *Christ and His Righteousness*, Appendix, p. 225.
22. *The Glad Tidings*, Appendix, p. 226.

The Wages of Sin—In the second chapter we learned that those who reject the goodness of God are treasuring up to themselves wrath. Now wrath comes only on the children of disobedience. Ephesians 5:6. Those who sin are laying up wages for themselves. "The wages of sin is death." Sin has death in it, therefore "sin, when it is finished, bringeth forth death." There can be no other end to sin than death, because sin is the absence of righteousness, and righteousness is the life and character of God. Persistent and final choice of sin is therefore choice of complete separation from the life of God, and so from *all* life, since he is the only source of life. Christ, who is the wisdom of God, says, "All they that hate Me love death." Proverbs 8:36. Those who suffer death at last will be only those who have worked for it.

The Gift of God—But we do not work for eternal life. No works that we could do would make the smallest part of payment towards it. It is the gift of God. True, it comes only through righteousness, but righteousness is a gift. "By grace are ye saved through faith; and that not of yourselves; it is the gift of God; not of works, lest any man should boast. For we are His workmanship, created in Christ Jesus unto good works, which God hath before ordained [prepared] that we should walk in them." Ephesians 2:8–10.

"O how great is Thy goodness, which Thou hast laid up for them that fear Thee; which Thou hast wrought for them that trust in Thee before the sons of men!" Psalm 31:19. When people sin God gives them only what they have bargained for. But if any yield themselves as servants of righteousness, He provides the righteousness for them, and gives them eternal life with it, all as a free gift. "The way of the transgressor is hard," but the yoke of Christ is easy, and His burden is light.

Chapter 7

Married to the Wrong Man

The seventh chapter of Romans is really all contained in the sixth. He who understands the sixth chapter will have no difficulty with the seventh. By Christ's obedience we are made righteous. This is because His life is now given to us, and He lives in us.

This union with Christ we get by being crucified with Him. In that death the body of sin is destroyed, that henceforth we should not serve sin or, in other words, that we should no more transgress the law. So closely are we identified with sin, it being our very life, that it can not be destroyed without our dying. But in Christ there is no sin, so that while we have a resurrection with Him, sin remains dead. So, being raised with Him, we live with Him, a thing that was formerly impossible on account of sin; sin can not dwell with Him.

A Striking Illustration—Romans 7:1-7

1 Know ye not, brethren (for I speak to them that know the law), how that the law hath dominion over a man as long as he liveth? 2 For the woman which hath an husband is bound by the law to her husband so long as he liveth; but if the husband be dead, she is loosed from the law of her husband. 3 So then if, while her husband liveth, she be married to another man, she shall be called an adulteress; but if her husband be dead, she is free from that law; so that she is no adulteress, though she be married to another man. 4 Wherefore, my brethren, ye also are become dead to the law by the body of Christ; that ye should be married to another, even to Him who is raised from the dead, that we should bring forth fruit unto God. 5 For when we were in the flesh, the motions of sins, which

were by the law, did work in our members to bring forth fruit unto death. 6 But now we are delivered from the law, that being dead wherein we were held; that we should serve in newness of spirit and not in the oldness of the letter. 7 What shall we say then? Is the law sin? God forbid. Nay, I had not known sin, but by the law; for I had not known lust, except the law had said, Thou shalt not covet.

The Illustration—It is a very simple one, and one which every one can understand. The law of God says of man and woman, "They two shall be one flesh." It is adultery for either one to be married to another while the other is living. The law will not sanction such a union.

For reasons that will appear later, the illustration cites only the case of a woman leaving her husband. The law unites them. That law holds the woman to the man as long as he lives. If while her husband lives she shall be united to another man, she will find herself under the condemnation of the law. But if her husband dies, she may be united to another, and be perfectly free from any condemnation.

The woman is then "free from the law," although the law has not changed in one particular. Least of all has it been abolished; for the same law that bound her to the first husband and which condemned her for uniting with another in his lifetime, now unites her to another and binds her to him as closely as it did to the first. If we hold to this simple illustration, we shall have no difficulty with what follows.

The Application—As in the illustration there are four subjects—the law, the woman, the first husband, and the second husband—so also in the application.

We are represented as the woman. This is clear from the statement that we are "married to another, even to Him who is raised from the dead," which is Christ. He therefore is the second husband. The first husband is indicated in verse 5: "When we were in the flesh, the motions of sins, which were by the law, did work in our members to bring forth fruit unto death." Death is the fruit of sin. The first husband, therefore, was the flesh, or "the body of sin."

"Dead to the Law"—This is the expression that troubles so many. There is nothing troublesome in it, if we but keep in mind the illustration and the nature of the parties to this transaction. Why are we dead to the law? In order that we might be married to another. But how is it that we become dead in order to be married to another? In the illustration it is the first husband that dies before the woman may be married to another. Even so it is here, as we shall see.

"One Flesh"—The law of marriage is that the two parties to it "shall be one flesh." How is it in this case? The first husband is the flesh, the body of sin. Well, we were truly one flesh with that. We were by nature perfectly united to sin. It was our life. It controlled us. Whatever sin devised, that we did. We might have done it unwillingly at times, but we did it nevertheless. Sin reigned in our mortal bodies, so that we obeyed it in the lusts thereof. Whatever sin wished, was law to us. We were one flesh. Romans 6:16.

Seeking a Divorce—There comes a time in our experience when we wish to be free from sin. It is when we see something of the beauty of holiness. With some people the desire is only occasional; with others it is more constant. Whether they recognize the fact or not, it is Christ appealing to them to forsake sin, and to be joined to Him, to live with Him. And so they endeavor to effect a separation. But sin will not consent. In spite of all that we can do, it still clings to us. We are "one flesh," and it is a union for life since it is a union of our life to sin. There is no divorce in that marriage.

Freedom in Death—There is no hope of effecting a separation from sin by any ordinary means. No matter how much we may desire to be united to Christ, it can not be done while we are joined to sin; for the law will not sanction such a union, and Christ will not enter into any union that is not lawful.

If we could only get sin to die, we should be free, but it will not die. There is only one way for us to be freed from the hateful union, and that is for us to die. If we wish freedom so much that we are willing for self to be crucified, then it may be done. In death the separation is effected; for it is by the body of Christ that "we" become dead. We are crucified with Him. The body of sin is also crucified. But while the body of sin is destroyed, we have a resurrection in Christ. The same thing that frees us from the first husband, unites us to the second.

A New Creature—Now we see how it is that we are dead to the law. We died in Christ, and were raised in Him. But "if any man be in Christ, he is a new creature; old things are passed away; behold, all things are become new. And all things are of God." 2 Corinthians 5:17, 18. Now we may be united to Christ, and the law will witness to the union, and sanction it. For not only is the first husband dead, but we also died, so that, although alive, we are not the same creature that we were before. "I am crucified with Christ; nevertheless I live; yet not I, but Christ liveth in me." Galatians 2:20. We are one. The same law that formerly declared us to be sinners now binds us to Christ.

A Different Service—Now that the union with Christ has been effected, we serve in newness of spirit and not in the oldness of the letter. In marriage, the woman is to be subject to the husband. So when we were united to sin, we were in all things subject to sin. For a time it was willing service; but when we saw the Lord, and were drawn to Him, the service became irksome. We tried to keep God's law, but were bound, and could not. But now we are set free. Sin no longer restrains us, and our service is freedom. We gladly render to Christ all the service that the law requires of us. We render this service because of the perfect union between us. His life is ours, since we were raised only by the power of His life. Therefore our obedience is simply His loyalty and faithfulness working in us.

Sin by the Law—The apostle says that when we were in the flesh, "the motions of sins, which were by the law, did work in our members to bring forth fruit unto death." What shall we say then? Is the law sin? Far from it. The law is righteousness. But it is only by the law that sin is known. "Sin is not imputed when there is no law." "The sting of death is sin; and the strength of sin is the law." 1 Corinthians 15:56. "Sin is the transgression of the law." So there can be no sin but by the law. But the law is not sin; for if it were, it would not reprove sin. To convince of sin is the work of the Spirit of God, and not of Satan. He would make us believe that sin is right.

"Thou Shalt Not Covet"—It once seemed very strange that the apostle should have quoted only this one commandment as the one that convicted him of sin. But the reason is plain. It was because this one includes every other. We learn (Colossians 3:5) that covetousness is idolatry. Thus the law ends just where it begins. It is a complete circle, including every duty of every person in the universe. "I had not known lust," or unlawful desire, "except the law had said, Thou shalt not covet." Now lust is the beginning of every sin, for "when lust hath conceived, it bringeth forth sin." James 1:15. And sin is the transgression of the law.

But the tenth commandment is that one which forbids lust or unlawful desire. Therefore, if it is perfectly kept, all the others must be. And if it is not kept, no part of the law is kept. So we see that in quoting the tenth commandment as that which convinced him of sin, the apostle really included the whole law.

Living With Him—Before leaving this portion we must call attention to the force of the eighth verse of chapter 6: "Now if we be dead with Christ, we believe that we shall also live with Him." We can see how apt this is when we know that it is our death with Christ that frees us from the union with the monster sin, and unites us in marriage to Christ. People get married in order to live together. So we become united to Christ in order that we may live with Him here and in the world to come. If we would live with Him in the world to come, we must live with Him in this world.

In the first seven verses of the seventh chapter of Romans we have had the relation which we by nature sustain to sin, and which by grace we afterwards sustain to Christ, represented under the figure of marriage to a first and second husband. The union with the second husband can not take place while the first husband is living; and in this case the marriage is so perfect, the two parties being literally one flesh and blood, that one can not die without the other; therefore we must needs die with sin, before we can be separated from it.

But we die *in Christ,* and as He lives, although He was dead, we also live *with Him.* Galatians 2:20. But in His life there is no sin, and so the body of sin is destroyed, while *we* are raised. Thus in death we are separated from the first husband, sin, and united to the second husband, Christ.

In the verses which follow the apostle has pictured the struggle with the sin that has become distasteful. It is really an enlargement of that which has been presented in the first verses.

The Struggle for Freedom—Romans 7:8-25

8 Sin, taking occasion by the commandment, wrought in me all manner of concupiscence. For without the law sin was dead. 9 For I was alive without the law once; but when the commandment came, sin revived, and I died. 10 And the commandment, which was ordained to life, I found to be unto death. 11 For sin, taking occasion by the commandment, deceived me, and by it slew me. 12 Wherefore the law is holy, and the commandment holy, and just, and good.

13 Was then that which is good made death unto me? God forbid. But sin, that it might appear sin, working death in me by that which is good; that sin by the commandment might become exceeding sinful. 14 For we know that the law is spiritual; but I am carnal, sold under sin. 15 For that which I do, I allow not; for what I would, that do I not; but what I hate, that do I. 16 If then I do that which I would not, I consent unto the law that it is good. 17 Now then it is no more I that do it, but sin that dwelleth in me.

18 For I know that in me (that is, in my flesh) dwelleth no good thing; for to will is present with me; but how to perform that which is good, I find not. 19 For the good that I would, I do not; but the evil which I would not, that I do. 20 Now if I do that I would not, it is no more I that do it, but sin that dwelleth in me.

21 I find then a law, that, when I would do good, evil is present with me. 22 For I delight in the law of God after the inward man; 23 but I see another law in my members, warring against the law of my mind, and bringing me into captivity to the law of sin which is in my members.

24 O wretched man that I am! who shall deliver me from the body of this death? 25 I thank God through Jesus Christ our Lord. So then with the mind I myself serve the law of God; but with the flesh the law of sin.

Sin Personified—It will be noticed that in this entire chapter sin is represented as a person. It is the first husband to which we are united. But the union has become distasteful because, having seen Christ and having been drawn to Him by His love, we have seen that we were joined to a monster. The marriage bond has become a galling yoke, and our whole thought is how to get away from the monster to which we are united and which is dragging us down to a certain death. The picture presented in this chapter is one of the most vivid in the whole Bible.

The Strength of Sin—"The sting of death is sin; and the strength of sin is the law." 1 Corinthians 15:56. "Without the law sin was dead." "Sin is not imputed when there is no law." "Where no law is, there is no transgression." So it is that "sin, taking occasion by the commandment, wrought in me all manner of concupiscence." Sin is simply the law transgressed, "for sin is the transgression of the law." 1 John 3:4. Sin has no strength, therefore, except that which it gets from the law. The law is not sin, and yet it binds us to sin, that is, the law witnesses to the sin and will not grant us any escape, simply because it can not bear false witness.

The "Law of Life," and the "Law of Death"—"The commandment, which was ordained to life, I found to be unto death." The law of God is the life of God. "Be ye therefore perfect, even as your Father which is in heaven is perfect." Matthew 5:48. His life is the rule for all His creatures. Those in whom the life of God is made perfectly manifest, keep His law. It is very evident therefore that the design of the law is life, since it is life itself. But the opposite of life is death. Therefore when the law is transgressed, it is death to the transgressor.

The Deadly Enemy—"For sin, taking occasion by the commandment, deceived me, and by it slew me." It is not the law that is the enemy; the enemy is sin. Sin does the killing, for "the sting of death is sin." Sin has the poison of death in it. Sin deceived us so that for a time we thought that it was our friend, and we embraced it and delighted in the union. But when the law enlightened us, we found that sin's embrace was the embrace of death.

The Law Cleared—The law pointed out the fact that sin was killing us. "Therefore the law is holy, and the commandment holy, and just, and good." We have no more reason to rail at the law than we have to hate the man who tells us that the substance which we are eating, thinking it to be food, is poison. He is our friend. He would not be our friend if he did not show us our danger. The fact that he is not able to heal the illness that the poison already eaten has caused does not make him any the less our friend. He has warned us of our danger, and we can now get help from the physician. And so, after all, the law itself was not death to us, but its office was "that sin by the commandment might become exceeding sinful."

"The Law Is Spiritual"—"For we know that the law is spiritual." If this fact were more generally recognized, there would be much less religious legislation among so-called Christian nations. People would not try to enforce the commandments of God. Since the law is spiritual, it can be obeyed only by the power of the Spirit of God. "God is Spirit" (John 4:24); therefore the law is the nature of God. Spiritual is opposed to carnal, or fleshly. Thus it is that the man who is in the flesh can not please God.

A Slave—"But I am carnal, sold under sin." One who is sold is a slave; and the evidence of the slavery in this instance is very plain. Free men do that which they wish to do. Only slaves do that which they do not wish to do, and are continually prevented from doing what they wish to do. "For that which I do, I allow not; for what I would, that do I not; but what I hate, that do I." A more disagreeable position can not be imagined. Life in such a state can be only a burden.

Convicted, but Not Converted—"If then I do that which I would not, I consent unto the law that it is good." The fact that we do not wish to do the sins that we are committing shows that we acknowledge the righteousness of the law which forbids them. But conviction is not conversion, although a very necessary step to that condition. It is not enough to *wish* to do right. The blessing is pronounced upon those who *do* His commandments, and not upon those who wish to do them, or who even try to do them.[23] Indeed, if there were no higher position for a professed follower of the Lord than that described in these verses, he would be in a far worse condition than the careless sinner. Both are slaves, only the latter is so hardened that he finds pleasure in his slavery.

Now if one must all his life be a slave, it is better for him to be unconscious of his bondage than to be continually fretting over it. But there is something better; therefore it is a blessing that we are convicted of sin, and that our slavery is thereby made as disagreeable as possible.

Two "Laws"—"I find then a law, that, when I would do good, evil is present with me. For I delight in the law of God after the inward man; but I see another law in my members, warring against the law of my mind,

---

23. A.T. Jones, *1893 General Conference Bulletin*, Appendix A, p. 227.

and bringing me into captivity to the law of sin which is in my members." Compare this with verse 5.

Remember also that all this is written to them that know the law. It is not addressed to the heathen who have not the law, but to those who profess to know God. While knowing the law, we are united in marriage to sin. This sin is in our flesh, since they who are married are one flesh. It is the law that witnesses to the fact that we are sinners, and that will not grant us any escape from it. But we are slaves. Whosoever commits sin is the slave of sin. John 8:34. Therefore it is the law that will not let us be anything but what we are, that is really holding us in bondage. While we are in that condition, it is not to us a law of liberty.

A Body of Death—We are joined in marriage to sin. But sin has in it death; for "the sting of death is sin." Sin is that with which death kills us. Therefore the body of sin, to which we are joined when in the flesh, is but a body of death. What a terrible condition! Joined in such close union that we are one flesh with that which is in itself death. A living death!

And "the strength of sin is the law." It witnesses to our union, and thus holds us in that bondage of death. If there were no hope of escape, we might curse the law for not allowing us to die in ignorance. But although the law seems to be pitiless, it is nevertheless our best friend. It holds us to a sense of the dreadfulness of our bondage until in anguish we cry out, "O wretched man that I am! who shall deliver me from the body of this death?" We must be delivered, or we perish.

There Is a Deliverer—The pagan proverb has it that God helps those who help themselves. The truth is that God helps those who can not help themselves: "I was brought low, and He helped me." No one ever cries in vain for help. When the cry goes up for help, the Deliverer is at hand; and so, although sin is working death in us by all the power of the law, we may exclaim, "Thanks be to God, which giveth us the victory through our Lord Jesus Christ." 1 Corinthians 15:57. "There shall come out of Zion the Deliverer, and shall turn away ungodliness from Jacob." Romans 11:26. "Unto you first God, having raised up His Son Jesus, sent Him to bless you, in turning away every one of you from his iniquities." Acts 3:26. "Thanks be unto God for His unspeakable gift."

A Divided Man—"So then with the mind I myself serve the law of God; but with the flesh the law of sin." That is, of course, while in the condition described in the preceding verses. In purpose he serves the law of God, but in actual practice he serves the law of sin. As described in another place, "The flesh lusteth against the Spirit, and the Spirit against the flesh; and these are contrary the one to the other; so that ye can not do the things that ye would." Galatians 5:17. It is not a state of actual service to God, because we read in our next chapter that "they that are in the flesh can not please God." It is a state from which one may well pray to be delivered, so that he can serve the Lord not merely with the mind, but with his whole being. "The very God of peace sanctify you wholly; and I pray God your whole spirit and soul and body be preserved blameless unto the coming of our Lord Jesus Christ. Faithful is He that calleth you, who also will do it." 1 Thessalonians 5:23, 24.

NOTES

"For the love of Christ constraineth us; because we thus judge, that if One died for all, then were all dead: and that He died for all, that they which live should not henceforth live unto themselves, but unto Him which died for them, and rose again." 2 Corinthians 5:14, 15.

Chapter 8

Glorious Freedom From a Bad "Marriage"

We now come to the conclusion of the whole matter. In the eighth chapter of Romans the epistle reaches its highest point. The seventh chapter has presented to us the deplorable condition of the man who has been awakened by the law to a sense of his condition, bound to sin by cords that can be loosened only by death. It closes with a glimpse of the Lord Jesus Christ as the One who alone can set us free from the body of death.

Freedom from Condemnation—Romans 8:1-9

1 There is therefore now no condemnation to them which are in Christ Jesus, who walk not after the flesh, but after the Spirit. 2 For the law of the Spirit of life in Christ Jesus hath made me free from the law of sin and death. 3 For what the law could not do, in that it was weak through the flesh, God sending His own Son in the likeness of sinful flesh, and for sin, condemned sin in the flesh; 4 that the righteousness of the law might be fulfilled in us, who walk not after the flesh, but after the Spirit. 5 For they that are after the flesh do mind the things of the flesh; but they that are after the Spirit, the things of the Spirit. 6 For to be carnally minded is death; but to be spiritually minded is life and peace. 7 Because the carnal mind is enmity against God; for it is not subject to the law of God, neither indeed can be. 8 So then they that are in the flesh cannot please God. 9 But ye are not in the flesh, but in the Spirit, if so be that the Spirit of God dwell in you. Now if any man have not the Spirit of Christ, he is none of His.

"No Condemnation"—There is no condemnation to them which are in Christ. Why? Because He received the curse of the law, that the blessing might come on us. Nothing can come to us while we are in Him, without first passing through Him; but in Him all curses are turned to blessings, and sin is displaced by righteousness. His endless life triumphs over everything that comes against it. We are made "complete in Him."

"Looking Unto Jesus"—Some say, "I do not find this Scripture fulfilled in my case, because I find something to condemn me every time I look at myself." To be sure; for the freedom from condemnation is not in ourselves, but in Christ Jesus. We are to look at Him, instead of at ourselves. If we obey His orders, and trust Him, He takes the responsibility of making us clear before the law. There will never be a time when one will not find condemnation in looking at himself.

The fall of Satan was due to his looking at himself. The restoration for those whom he has made to fall, is only through looking to Jesus. "As Moses lifted up the serpent in the wilderness, even so must the Son of man be lifted up." John 3:14. The serpent was lifted up to be looked at. Those who looked were healed. Even so with Christ. In the world to come the servants of the Lord "shall see His face," and they will not be drawn away to themselves. The light of His countenance will be their glory and it is in that same light that they will be brought to that glorious state.

Conviction, Not Condemnation—The text does not say that those who are in Christ Jesus will never be reproved.

> "Do you think He ne'er reproves me?
> What a false friend He would be
> If He never, never told me
> Of the faults that He must see!"

Getting into Christ is only the beginning, not the end, of Christian life. It is the entrance to the school where we are to learn of Him. He takes the ungodly man with all his evil habits and forgives all his sins, so that he is counted as though he never had sinned.[24] Then He continues to give him His own life, by which he may overcome his evil habits.

Association with Christ will more and more reveal to us our failings, just as association with a learned man will make us conscious of our ignorance. As a faithful witness, He tells us of our failings. But it is not to

---

24. Waggoner, *Christ and His Righteousness*, Appendix A, p. 227.

condemn us. We receive sympathy, not condemnation, from Him. It is this sympathy that gives us courage, and enables us to overcome.

When the Lord points out a defect in our characters, it is the same as saying to us, "There is something that you are in need of, and I have it for you." When we learn to look at reproof in this way, we shall rejoice in it, instead of being discouraged.

Law of Life in Christ—The law without Christ is death. The law in Christ is life. His life is the law of God; for out of the heart are the issues of life, and the law was in His heart. The law of sin and death works in our members. But the law of the Spirit of life in Christ gives us freedom from this. Mark that it is the life in Christ that does this. It does not give us freedom from obedience to the law, for we had that before, and that was bondage, and not freedom. What He gives us freedom from is the transgression of the law.

Christ's Work—This is made very plain in verses 3 and 4. God sent His Son in the likeness of sinful flesh, and for sin, "that the righteousness of the law might be fulfilled in us." "The law is holy, and the commandment holy, and just, and good." There is no fault to be found with it but with us, because we have transgressed it. Christ's work is not to change the law in any particular, but to change us in every particular. It is to put the law into our hearts in perfection, in place of the marred and broken copy.

The Weakness of the Law—The law is strong enough to condemn, but it is weak, even powerless, with respect to what man needs—namely, salvation. It was and is "weak through the flesh." The law is good, and holy, and just, but man has no strength to perform it. Just as an ax may be of good steel, and very sharp, yet unable to cut down a tree because the arm that has hold of it has no strength, so the law of God could not perform itself. It set forth man's duty; it remained for him to do it. But he could not, and therefore Christ came to do it in him. What the law could not do, God did by His Son.

Likeness of Sinful Flesh—There is a common idea that this means that Christ simulated sinful flesh; that He did not take upon Himself actual sinful flesh, but only what appeared to be such. But the Scriptures do not teach such a thing. "In all things it behooved Him to be made like unto His brethren, that He might be a merciful and faithful High Priest in things pertaining to God, to make reconciliation for the sins of the people." Hebrews 2:17. He was "born of a woman, born under the law," that He might redeem them that were under the law. Galatians 4:4, 5.

He took the same flesh that all have who are born of woman. A parallel text to Romans 8:3, 4 is found in 2 Corinthians 5:21. The former says that Christ was sent in the likeness of sinful flesh, "that the righteousness of the law might be fulfilled in us." The latter says that God "made Him to be sin for us," although He knew no sin, "that we might be made the righteousness of God in Him."

"Compassed With Infirmity"—All the comfort that we can get from Christ lies in the knowledge that He was made in all things as we are. Otherwise we should hesitate to tell Him of our weaknesses and failures. The priest who makes sacrifices for sins must be one "who can have compassion on the ignorant, and on them that are out of the way; for that He Himself also is compassed with infirmity." Hebrews 5:2.

This applies perfectly to Christ; "for we have not an High Priest which cannot be touched with the feeling of our infirmities; but was in all points tempted like as we are, yet without sin." Hebrews 4:15. This is why we may come boldly to the throne of grace for mercy. So perfectly has Christ identified Himself with us, that He even now feels our sufferings.

The Flesh and the Spirit—"For they that are after the flesh do mind the things of the flesh; but they that are after the Spirit, the things of the Spirit." Note that this depends on the preceding statement, "that the righteousness of the law might be fulfilled in us, who walk not after the flesh, but after the Spirit." The things of the Spirit are the commandments of God, because the law is spiritual. The flesh serves the law of sin (see the preceding chapter, and Galatians 5:19-21, where the works of the flesh are described). But Christ came in the same flesh, to show the power of the Spirit over the flesh. "They that are in the flesh cannot please God. But ye are not in the flesh, but in the Spirit, if so be that the Spirit of Christ dwell in you."

Now no one will claim that the flesh of a man is any different after his conversion from what it was before. Least of all will the converted man himself say so; for he has continual evidence of its perversity. But if he is really converted, and the Spirit of Christ dwells in him, he is no more in the power of the flesh. Even so Christ came in the same sinful flesh, yet He was without sin, because He was always led by the Spirit.

The Enmity—"The carnal mind is enmity against God; for it is not subject to the law of God, neither indeed can be." The flesh never becomes converted. It is enmity against God; and that enmity consists in opposition to His law. Therefore, whoever opposes the law of God is fighting against Him. But Christ is our Peace, and He came preaching peace. "You, that were sometime alienated and enemies in your mind by wicked works, yet now hath He reconciled in the body of His flesh through death, to present you holy and unblamable and unreprovable in His sight." Colossians 1:21, 22. In His own flesh He abolishes the enmity, so that all who are crucified with Him are at peace with God; that is, they are subject to His law, which is in their hearts.

"Life and Peace"—"To be carnally minded is death; but to be spiritually minded is life and peace." To be spiritually minded is to have a mind controlled by the law of God, "for we know that the law is spiritual." "Great peace have they which love Thy law." Psalm 119:165. "Being justified [made righteous] by faith, we have peace with God through our Lord Jesus Christ." The carnal mind is enmity against God. Therefore, to be carnally minded is death. But Christ "hath abolished death, and hath brought life and immortality to light through the gospel." 2 Timothy 1:10. He has abolished death by destroying the power of sin in all who believe in Him; for death has no power except through sin. "The sting of death is sin." 1 Corinthians 15:56. So that even now we may joyfully say, "Thanks be to God, which giveth us the victory through our Lord Jesus Christ."

The eighth chapter of Romans is full of the glorious things that God has promised to them that love Him. Freedom, the Spirit of life in Christ, sons of God, heirs of God and with Christ, glory and victory, are the words that outline the chapter.

Sons of God—Romans 8:9-17

9 But ye are not in the flesh, but in the Spirit, if so be that the Spirit of God dwell in you. Now if any man have not the Spirit of Christ, he is none of His. 10 And if Christ be in you, the body is dead because of sin; but the Spirit is life because of righteousness. 11 But if the Spirit of Him that raised up Jesus from the dead dwell in you, He that raised up Christ from the dead shall also quicken your mortal bodies by His Spirit that dwelleth in you. 12 Therefore, brethren, we are debtors, not to the flesh, to live after the flesh. 13 For if ye live after the flesh, ye shall die; but if ye through the Spirit do mortify the deeds of the body, ye shall live. 14 For as many as are led by the Spirit of God, they are the sons of God. 15 For ye have not received the spirit of bondage again to fear; but ye have received the Spirit of adoption, whereby we cry, Abba, Father. 16 The Spirit itself beareth witness with our Spirit, that we are the children of God; 17 and if children, then heirs; heirs of God, and joint-heirs with Christ; if so be that we suffer with Him, that we may be also glorified together.

Opposing Forces—The flesh and the Spirit are in opposition. These are always contrary the one to the other. The Spirit never yields to the flesh, and the flesh never gets converted. The flesh will be of the nature of sin until our bodies are changed at the coming of the Lord. The Spirit strives with the sinful man, but he yields to the flesh, and so is the servant of sin. Romans 6:12-20.

Such a man is not led by the Spirit, although the Spirit has by no means forsaken him. The flesh is just the same in a converted man that it is in a sinner, but the difference is that now it has no power, since the man yields to the Spirit, which controls the flesh. Although the man's flesh is precisely the same that it was before he was converted, he is said to be not "in the flesh," but "in the Spirit," since he through the Spirit mortifies the deeds of the body.

Life in Death—"And if Christ be in you, the body is dead because of sin; but the Spirit is life because of righteousness." Here we have the two individuals of which the apostle speaks in 2 Corinthians 4:7-16. "For we which live are alway delivered unto death for Jesus' sake, that the life also of Jesus might be made manifest in our mortal flesh." Then he says that "though our outward man perish, yet the inward man is renewed day by day." Though our body should fail and be worn out, yet the inward man, Christ Jesus, is ever new. And He is our real life. "Ye are dead, and your life is hid with Christ in God." Colossians 3:3.

This is why we are not to fear them that can kill only the body, and after that have no more that they can do. Though the body be burned at the stake, wicked men cannot touch the eternal life which we have in Christ, who cannot be destroyed. No man can take his life from him.

The Surety of the Resurrection—"But if the Spirit of Him that raised up Jesus from the dead dwell in you, He that raised up Christ from the dead shall also quicken your mortal bodies by His Spirit that dwelleth in you." Jesus said of the water that He gave, which was the Holy Spirit, that it should be in us a well of water springing up unto eternal life. John 4:14; compare John 7:37-39. That is, the spiritual life which we now live in the flesh by the Spirit is the surety of the spiritual body to be bestowed at the resurrection when we will have the life of Christ made manifested in immortal bodies.

Not Debtors to the Flesh—"Therefore, brethren, we are debtors, not to the flesh, to live after the flesh." We are indeed debtors, but we do not owe anything to the flesh. It has done nothing for us, and can do nothing. All the work that the flesh can do avails nothing, for its works are sin and therefore death. But we are debtors to the Lord Jesus Christ, "who gave

Himself for us." Consequently, everything must be yielded to His life. "For if ye live after the flesh, ye shall die; but if ye through the Spirit do mortify the deeds of the body, ye shall live."

Sons of God—Those who yield to the strivings of the Spirit, and continue so to yield, are led by the Spirit; and they are the sons of God. They are taken into the same relation to the Father that the only begotten Son occupies. "Behold, what manner of love the Father hath bestowed upon us, that we should be called the sons of God; therefore the world knoweth us not, because it knew Him not. Beloved, now are we the sons of God, and it doth not yet appear what we shall be; but we know that, when He shall appear, we shall be like Him; for we shall see Him as He is." If we are led by the Spirit of God, we are now just as much the sons of God as we can ever be.

We Are Sons Now—There is a notion held by some people that no man is born of God until the resurrection. But this is settled by the fact that we are now sons of God. "But," says one, "we are not yet manifested as sons." True, and neither was Christ when He was on earth. There were but very few that knew Him to be the Christ, the Son of the living God. And they knew it only by revelation from God. The world knows us not, because it knew Him not. To say that believers are not sons of God now because there is nothing in their appearance to indicate it, is to bring the same charge against Jesus Christ. But Jesus was just as truly the Son of God when He lay in the manger in Bethlehem, as He is now when sitting at the right hand of God.

The Spirit's Witness—"The Spirit itself beareth witness with our Spirit, that we are the children of God." How does the Spirit witness? This is answered in Hebrews 10:14-17. The apostle says that by one offering He hath perfected them that are sanctified, and then says that the Holy Spirit is a witness to this fact when He says, "This is the covenant that I will make with them after those days, saith the Lord; I will put My laws into their hearts, and in their minds will I write them; and their sins and iniquities will I remember no more." That is to say, the Spirit's witness is the word. We know that we are children of God, because the Spirit assures us of that fact in the Bible. The witness of the Spirit is not a certain ecstatic feeling, but a tangible statement. We are not children of God because we *feel* that we are, neither do we know that we are sons because of any feeling, but because the Lord *tells* us so. He who believes has the word abiding in him, and that is how "he that believeth on the Son of God hath the witness in Himself." 1 John 5:10.

No Fear—"For ye have not received the spirit of bondage again to fear; but ye have received the Spirit of adoption, whereby we cry, Abba, Father." "For God hath not given us the spirit of fear; but of power, and of love, and of a sound mind." 2 Timothy 1:7. "God is love; and he that dwelleth in love dwelleth in God, and God in him. Herein is our love made perfect, that we may have boldness in the day of judgment; because as He is, so are we in this world. There is no fear in love; but perfect love casteth out fear; because fear hath torment. He that feareth is not made perfect in love." 1 John 4:16-18.

Christ gave Himself to deliver them who through fear of death were all their life subject to bondage. Hebrews 2:15. He who knows and loves the Lord cannot be afraid of Him; and he who is not afraid of the Lord has no need to be afraid of any other person or thing. One of the greatest blessings of the gospel is the deliverance from fear, whether real or imaginary. "I sought the Lord, and He heard me, and delivered me from all my fears." Psalm 34:4.

Heirs of God—What a wonderful inheritance that is! It does not merely say that we are heirs of what God *has*, but that we are heirs of God *Himself*. Having Him we have everything, as a matter of course; but the blessedness consists in having Him. "The Lord is the portion of mine inheritance and of my cup." Psalm 16:5. This is the fact; it is a thing to be meditated upon rather than talked about.

Joint-heirs With Christ—If we are sons of God, we stand on the same footing that Jesus Christ does. He Himself said that the Father loves us even as He loves Him. John 17:23. This is proved by the fact that His life was given for ours. Therefore the Father has nothing for His only begotten Son that He has not for us. Not only so, but since we are joint-heirs with Jesus Christ, it follows that He cannot enter upon His inheritance before we do. To be sure, He is sitting at the right hand of God. But God in His great love for us "hath quickened us together with Christ, and hath raised us up together, and made us sit together in heavenly places." Ephesians 2:4-6. The glory which Christ has He shares with us. John 17:22. It means something to be a joint-heir with Jesus Christ! No wonder the apostle exclaims, "Behold, what manner of love the Father hath bestowed upon us, that we should be called the sons of God."

Suffering With Him—"If so be that we suffer with Him, that we may be also glorified together." "For in that He Himself hath suffered being tempted, He is able to succor them that are tempted." Hebrews 2:18. Suffering with Christ means, therefore, enduring temptation with Him. The suffering is that which comes in the struggle against sin. Self-inflicted suffering amounts to nothing. It is not in any honor to the satisfying of the flesh. Colossians 2:23. Christ did not torture Himself in order to gain the approval of the Father. But when we suffer with Christ, then we are made perfect in Him. The strength by which He resisted the temptations of the enemy is the strength by which we are to overcome. His life in us gains the victory. Revelation 3:21; 14:12.

In the preceding verses of the eighth chapter of Romans we have seen how we are adopted into the family of God as sons, and made joint-heirs with Jesus Christ. The Holy Spirit establishes the bond of relationship. It is the "Spirit of adoption," the Spirit proceeding from the Father as the representative of the Son, that proves that we are accepted as brethren of Jesus Christ. Those who are led by the Spirit must be even as Christ was in the world, and are therefore assured of an equal share in the inheritance with Christ. For "the Spirit itself beareth witness with our spirit, that we are the children of God."

Glorified Together—Romans 8:17-25

17 And if children, then heirs; heirs of God, and joint-heirs with Christ; if so be that we suffer with Him, that we may be also glorified together. 18 For I reckon that the sufferings of this present time are not worthy to be compared with the glory which shall be revealed in us. 19 For the earnest expectation of the creature waiteth for the manifestation of the sons of God. 20 For the creature was made subject to vanity, not willingly, but by reason of Him who hath subjected the same in hope, 21 because the creature itself also shall be delivered from the bondage of corruption into the glorious liberty of the children of God. 22 For we know that the whole creation groaneth and travaileth in pain together until now. 23 And not only they, but ourselves also, which have the first-fruits of the Spirit, even we ourselves groan within ourselves, waiting for the adoption, to wit, the redemption of our body. 24 For we are saved by hope; but hope that is seen is not hope; for what a man seeth, why doth he yet hope for? 25 But if we hope for that we see not, then do we with patience wait for it.

Why Suffering?—Christ's life on earth was one of suffering. He was "a man of sorrows, and acquainted with grief." He "suffered, being tempted," but His sufferings were not all in the mind alone. He knew physical pain; "Himself took our infirmities, and bare our diseases." Matthew 8:17. He suffered hunger in the wilderness; and His works of love were done at the expense of much bodily pain and weariness. The sufferings which He endured at the hands of the rough soldiers in connection with His mock trial, and His crucifixion, were simply a continuation in another form of what He had endured throughout His whole life on earth.

Glory Following Suffering—In all the prophets, the Spirit of Christ was witnessing and testifying of "the sufferings of Christ, and the glory that should follow." 1 Peter 1:11. When Christ, after His resurrection, talked with the two disciples on the way to Emmaus, He said, "Ought not Christ to have suffered these things, and to enter into His glory? And beginning at Moses and all the prophets, He expounded unto them in all the Scriptures the things concerning Himself." Luke 24:26, 27. We know that the first part of those prophecies was fulfilled, and therefore must know that the rest are as sure. As surely as Christ suffered, so surely will the glory follow.

Suffering Together—Our suffering is to be "with Him." We are not to suffer alone. But we could not suffer eighteen hundred years ago, before we were born. Therefore it follows that Christ still suffers. Otherwise we could not suffer with Him. Read what is said of His connection with ancient Israel: "In all their affliction He was afflicted." Isaiah 63:9. So in Matthew 25:35-40 we learn that Christ suffers or experiences relief whenever His disciples suffer or are relieved. He is the head of the body.

Now if when one member suffers all the members suffer with it (1 Corinthians 12:26), how much more must that be true of the Head! So we read of Christ that even now, as High Priest, He is "touched with the feeling our infirmities." Hebrews 4:15. A high priest must be one "who can have compassion on the ignorant, and on them that are out of the way; for that He Himself also is compassed with infirmity." Hebrews 5:1, 2. So we learn that Christ has never divested Himself of the human nature which He took upon Himself, but that He is still identified with suffering, sinful men. It is a glorious truth, to be recognized and confessed, that "Jesus Christ is come in the flesh." 1 John 4:2.

Glorified Together—"If so be that we suffer with Him, that we may be also glorified together." Christ does not have anything that is not for us equally with Him. His prayer was, "Father, I will that they also, whom Thou hast given Me, be with Me where I am." John 17:24. And He says, "To him that overcometh will I grant to sit with Me in My throne." Revelation 3:21. Whatever He has, we have, and we have it when He has it, since we are joint-heirs with Him.

There Is Glory Now—The above statement may at first sight seem to be untrue. It is the common idea that Christ is glorified long before those who are fellow-heirs with Him. One text is sufficient to settle this matter: "The elders which are among you I exhort, who am also an elder, and a witness of the sufferings of Christ, and also a partaker of the glory that shall be revealed." 1 Peter 5:1. Peter declared himself to be a partaker of the glory.

This was because He believed the saying of Christ, in His prayer for His disciples, "The glory which Thou gavest Me I have given them." John 17:22. If Christ has glory now, His disciples share it also. Again we have the words of the apostle Peter. Speaking of Christ, he says, "Whom having not seen, ye love; in whom, though now ye see Him not, yet believing, ye rejoice with joy unspeakable and full of glory." 1 Peter 1:8.

Grace and Glory Where Unexpected—The apostle John tells us that although we are now the sons of God the world knows us not, because it knew not Christ. There was nothing in the appearance of Christ on earth to indicate that He was the Son of God. Flesh and blood did not reveal that fact to anybody. To all appearance He was but an ordinary man. Yet all the time He had glory.

We read that when He turned the water into wine He "manifested forth His glory." John 2:11. His glory was manifested in the form of grace. "The Word was made flesh, and dwelt among us (and we beheld His glory, the glory as of the only begotten of the Father), full of grace and truth." John 1:14. The grace with which God strengthens His people is "according to the riches of His glory." Ephesians 3:16. Whoever is in Christ is chosen "to the praise of the glory of His grace." Ephesians 1:6. Grace is glory, but glory veiled so that mortal eyes may not be dazzled by it.

Glory Yet to Be Revealed—"The sufferings of this present time are not worthy to be compared with the glory which shall be revealed in us." The glory is for us to possess now, but it will be revealed only at the coming of Christ. It is then that His glory will be revealed (1 Peter 4:13), and then our trials will "be found unto praise and honor and glory."

Christ's glory has not yet been revealed, except to the chosen three on the mount of transfiguration. At that time the glory that Christ already possessed was allowed to shine forth. He appeared then as He will appear when He comes. But to the mass of mankind there is no more evidence now that Jesus is the Son of God than there was when He was before Pilate's judgment seat.

Those however who see it by faith and who are not ashamed to share His sufferings, also share His hidden glory; and when He shall appear in His glory, "then shall the righteous shine forth as the sun in the kingdom of their Father." Matthew 13:43. That will be "the manifestation of the sons of God." Then for the first time Christ will be manifested to the world as the Son of God, and those who are His will be manifested with Him.

The Hope of Creation—The word "creature" in verses 19-21 means the creation; this may be seen from verse 22 where we read of the whole creation as groaning, waiting to be delivered from that to which it has been made subject. When man sinned, the earth was cursed on his account. See Genesis 3:17. The earth had done no sin, but it was made to share the fall of man, to whom it had been given. A perfect earth was not the dwelling-place for sinful man. But it was made subject to vanity in hope. God made the earth perfect. "He created it not in vain, He formed it to be inhabited." Isaiah 45:18. And He "worketh all things after the counsel of His own will." Ephesians 1:11. Therefore the earth is sure to be glorified as it was in the beginning. "The creation itself also shall be delivered from the bondage of corruption into the liberty of the glory of the children of God."

Adoption and Redemption—Both the earth and we are "waiting for the adoption, to wit, the redemption of our body." The earth waits for it, because it cannot be relieved of its curse until we are set forth as sons of God, and therefore lawful heirs. The Holy Spirit is the pledge of this heirship. The Spirit seals us as heirs, "unto the day of redemption." Ephesians 4:30.

It is to us a witness that we are children of God, but the witness is not accepted by the world. They know not the children of God. But when that glory which He has given us is revealed, and our bodies are redeemed from destruction and made to shine like His glorious body, then there will be no doubt in the minds of any. Then even Satan himself will be obliged to acknowledge that we are God's children, and therefore rightful heirs of the glorified earth.

Hope and Patience—Hope, in the Bible sense, means something more than mere desire. It is certainty, because the ground of the Christian's hope is the promise of God, which is backed by His oath. Hebrews 6:16–19. There is nothing that our eyes can see to indicate that we are the sons of God. We cannot see our own glory, and that is why we are charged not to seek it here. We cannot see Christ, yet we know that He is the Son of God. That is the assurance that we are also sons of God. If there were any uncertainty, then we could not wait with patience. We should be uneasy, and should worry. But, although the natural eye cannot see any indication that we are owned as God's children, faith and hope assure us of it, and so we with patience wait for that which is unseen.

Something Worth Knowing—Romans 8:26-28

26 Likewise the Spirit also helpeth our infirmities; for we know not what we should pray for as we ought; but the Spirit itself maketh intercession for us with groaning which cannot be uttered. 27 And He that searcheth the hearts knoweth what is the mind of the Spirit, because He maketh intercession for the saints according to the will of God.

28 And we know that all things work together for good to them that love God, to them who are called according to His purpose.

"Praying in the Spirit"—The heart is deceitful above all things, and none can know it except God. Jeremiah 17:9, 10. That in itself is sufficient reason why we do not know what we should pray for.

Moreover, we do not know the things that God has to give us; and even if we did, our lips could not describe them, for "eye hath not seen, nor ear heard, neither have entered into the heart of man, the things which God hath prepared for them that love Him. But God hath revealed them unto us by His Spirit; for the Spirit searcheth all things, yea, the deep things of God. For what man knoweth the things of a man, save the spirit of man which is in Him? even so the things of God knoweth no man, but the Spirit of God. Now we have received, not the spirit of the world, but the Spirit which is of God; that we might know the things that are freely given to us of God." 1 Corinthians 2:9-12.

God desires to give to us "exceeding abundantly above all that we ask or think." Ephesians 3:20. Of course a petition for such things cannot be put into words. The next clause however says that it is "according to the power that worketh in us;" and the sixteenth verse tells us that the power that works in us is the Spirit. Thus we find the same thing that we read in the eighth of Romans and the second of 1 Corinthians.

"The Spirit searcheth all things, yea, the deep things of God." Therefore the Spirit knows just what the Lord has for us. The deepest thoughts are too great for language, and so the Spirit makes intercession for us with groanings that cannot be uttered. But, although there is no articulate speech "He that searcheth the hearts knoweth what is the mind of the Spirit, because He maketh intercession for the saints according to the will of God." The Lord knows that the Spirit asks for just the things that He has to bestow. He makes intercession for the saints according to the will of God. And we know that whatever is asked according to God's will is granted. 1 John 5:14, 15.

Now note how this statement in regard to prayer fits in with what goes before in the eighth of Romans. God has given us His Spirit to be in us, to lead us, and to direct our lives. The possession of the Spirit of God proves that we are the sons of God. Being sons, we can come to Him to ask for things to supply our need, with all the confidence of a child to a parent. But while we have all confidence, our thoughts are as the earth is below the heaven. Isaiah 55:8, 9.

Not only are our thoughts feeble, but our language is still more so. We cannot give proper expression even to the little that we do realize. But if we are the sons of God, we have in us His own representative, who helps our infirmity and who is able to take of the things of God to give to us. What wonderful confidence this should give us in praying to God; and especially should it give confidence to those who are particularly infirm in regard to language! It makes no difference if one has a very limited vocabulary, if he stammers, or even if he is dumb; if he prays in the Spirit, he is sure to receive all that he needs, and more than he can ask or think.

With these facts before us, how much more forcible becomes the exhortation of the apostle, "Praying always with all prayer and supplication in the Spirit, and watching thereunto with all perseverance and supplication for all saints." Ephesians 6:18.

All Things Work for Good—"And we know that all things work together for good to them that love God." Without this knowledge we could not have that confidence in prayer that we ought to have and that is indicated in the preceding verses. Whoever knows the Lord must love Him, for He is love. And the Spirit reveals Him to us. Whoever knows that "God so loved the world, that He gave His only begotten Son, that whosoever believeth in Him should not perish, but have everlasting life," cannot fail to love Him. And then all things work together for good to Him.

Take notice that the text does not say that all things shall work together for good to them that love God, but that they do so work now in this present time. Everything as it comes is good to those who love and trust the Lord. Many people lose the blessing of this assurance by reading it as though it were for the future. They try to be resigned to troubles that come by thinking that by and by some good will come from them; but in that case they do not get the good that God gives them.

Note further that the text does not say that we know how all things work together for good to them that love God. People in trouble often sigh piously and say, "Well, I suppose that it is all for good, but I can't see how." Of course not; and they have no business to see how. It is God that makes them work good, because He alone has the power.

Therefore it is not necessary for us to know anything about how it is done. The fact is knowledge enough for us. God can overrule all the plans of the devil, and can make the wrath of man to praise Him. Our part is to believe. There is no trust in the Lord if we must see how He does everything. Those who must be able to see how the Lord works, show that they cannot trust Him out of sight, and thus they give Him a bad name to the world.

Called of God—God has called everybody to come to Him. "The Spirit and the bride say, Come. And let him that heareth say, Come. And let him that is athirst come. And whosoever will, let him take the water of life freely." Revelation 22:17. God is no respecter of persons; He desires that all men shall be saved, and so He calls them all.

Not only does He call us, but He draws us. No man can come to Him without being drawn, and so Christ is lifted up to draw all to God. He tasted death for every man (Hebrews 2:9), and through Him all men have access to God. He has destroyed in His own body the enmity,—the wall that separates men from God,—so that nothing can keep any man from God unless that man builds up again the barrier.

The Lord draws us, but does not employ force. He calls, but does not drive. It remains therefore for us to make our "calling and election sure" by *yielding to the influence that God throws round us.* He says, "Follow Me," and we must make the calling effectual by following Him.

Purpose of the Calling—God calls us "in the grace of Christ." Galatians 1:6. "He hath chosen us in Him before the foundation of the world, that we should be holy and without blame before Him in love." Ephesians 1:4. Still further, we read that He hath "called us with an holy calling, not according to our works, but according to His own purpose and grace, which was given us in Christ Jesus before the world began." 2 Timothy 1:9. In our text in Romans we learned that those who love God are the "called according to His purpose." His purpose is that we should be holy and without blame before Him in love. If we *yield* to His purpose, He will see that it is carried out.

God designed man for a companion for Himself. But there is no true companionship where there is restraint. Therefore, in order that man might associate with Him on terms of intimacy, He made the will of man as free as His own. God cannot work against His own purpose; and therefore He not only will not, but He cannot, force the will of man. All men are as absolutely free to choose as is God Himself; and when they choose to yield to the call of God, His purpose of grace is wrought out in them by the power by which He is able to make all things work together for good.

We have learned about our relation to God through the Spirit, and of the help which the Spirit gives us in prayer, as well as of the assurance that "all things work together for good to them that love God, to them that are called according to His purpose." The grounds for that assurance are infinitely strengthened in the verses that follow.

The Unspeakable Gift—Romans 8:29-32

29 For whom He did foreknow, He also did predestinate to be conformed to the image of His Son, that He might be the first-born among many brethren. 30 Moreover, whom He did predestinate, them He also called; and whom He called, them He also justified; and whom He justified, them He also glorified. 31 What shall we then say to these things? If God be for us, who can be against us? 32 He that spared not His own Son, but delivered Him up for us all, how shall He not with Him also freely give us all things?

Foreknowledge versus Foreordination—The word "predestinate" is the same as "foreordain." Volumes of speculation have been written about these terms, but a few words are sufficient to set forth the facts. With respect to these, as well as the other attributes of God, it is sufficient for us to know the fact. With the explanation we have nothing to do.

It is plainly set forth in the Scriptures that God knows all things. Not only does He know the things that are past, but He sees the future as well. "Known unto God are all His works from the beginning of the world." Acts 15:18. "O Lord, Thou hast searched me, and known me. Thou knowest my downsitting and mine uprising; Thou understandest my thought afar off." Psalm 139:1, 2. Thus God can tell what people even yet unborn will do and say.

This does not make God *responsible* for the evil that they do. Some have foolishly thought it necessary to apologize for the Lord and to relieve Him of the charge that if He is omniscient He is responsible for the evil if He does not prevent it, by saying that He could know if He wished, but that he chooses not to know many things. Such a "defense" of God is both foolish and wicked. It assumes that God would be responsible for the evil if He knew it beforehand and did not prevent it, and that in order not to be in a position to prevent it, He deliberately shuts His eyes from it. Thus their "defense" really puts the responsibility for all evil upon God. Not only so, but it limits Him. It makes Him like a man.

God knows all things, not by study and research as man learns the little he knows, but because He is God. He inhabits eternity. Isaiah 57:15. We cannot understand how this can be any more than we can understand eternity. We must accept the fact and be not only content, but glad, that God is greater than we. All time, past, present, and future, is the same to Him. It is always "now" with God.

The fact that God knew the evil that men would do, even before the foundation of the world, does not make Him responsible for it, any more than the fact that a man can see by means of a telescope what a man is doing ten miles distant makes Him responsible for that other one's actions. God has from the beginning set before people warnings against sin, and has provided them with all the necessary means for avoiding it; but He cannot interfere with man's right and freedom of choice without depriving him of his manhood and making him the same as a stick.

Freedom to do right implies freedom to do wrong. If a man were made so that he could not do wrong, he would have no freedom at all, not even to do right. He would be less than the brutes. There is no virtue in forced obedience, nor would there be any virtue in doing that which is right if it were impossible to do wrong. Moreover, there could be no pleasure or satisfaction in the professed friendship of two persons if one associated with the other just because he could not avoid it. The joy of the Lord in the companionship of His people is that they of their own free will choose Him above all others. And that which is the joy of the Lord is the joy of His people.

The very ones who rail against God for not preventing the ills that He foresees since He is all-powerful, would be the very first to charge Him with cruelty if He did arbitrarily interfere with their freedom and make them do that which they do not choose. Such a course would make everybody unhappy and discontented. The wisest thing for us to do is to stop trying to fathom the ways of the Almighty, and accept the fact that whatever He does is right. "As for God, His way is perfect." Psalm 18:30.

What About Predestination?—The text shows that "whom He did foreknow, He also did predestinate to be conformed to the image of His Son, that He might be the first-born among many brethren." God's thoughts toward men are thoughts of peace, and not of evil. Jeremiah 29:11. He ordains peace for us. Isaiah 26:12. We read nothing about men being foreordained to destruction; the only thing that God has predestinated is that men should be conformed to the image of His Son.

But it is only *in Christ* that we become conformed to His image. It is *in Him* that we come "unto the measure of the stature of the fulness of Christ." Ephesians 4:13. Therefore it is that men are foreordained or predestinated only in Christ. The whole story is told in the following passage of Scripture:

"Blessed be the God and Father of our Lord Jesus Christ, who hath blessed us with all spiritual blessings in heavenly places in Christ: according as He hath chosen us in Him before the foundation of the world, that we should be holy and without blame before Him in love: having predestinated us unto the adoption of children by Jesus Christ to Himself, according to the good pleasure of His will, to the praise of the glory of His grace, wherein He hath made us accepted in the beloved." Ephesians 1:3-6.

Everything is in Christ. We receive all spiritual blessings in Him; we are chosen in Him unto holiness; in Him we are predestinated unto the adoption of children; in Him we are accepted; and in Him we have redemption through His blood. "God hath not appointed us to wrath, but to obtain salvation by our Lord Jesus Christ." 1 Thessalonians 5:9.

That is God's purpose and foreordination concerning man. Still further, "whom He did foreknow, He also did predestinate to be conformed to the image of His Son." Whom did He foreknow? There can be no limit; He must have foreknown all. If there were any exception, then God would not be infinite in knowledge. If He foreknows one person, then He foreknows every person. There has not been a person born into the world whose birth God did not foreknow. "Neither is there any creature that is not manifest in His sight; but all things are naked and opened unto the eyes of Him with whom we have to do."

Therefore, since every person has been known to God even before the foundation of the world, and those whom He foreknew He predestinated to be conformed to the image of His Son, it follows that God has purposed salvation for *every soul that has ever come into the world*. His love embraces all, without respect of persons.

"Then everybody will be saved, no matter what he does," some one will say. Not by any means. Remember that the purpose of God is in Christ. It is only in Him that we are predestinated. And we are free to choose for ourselves whether we will accept Him or not. Man's will has been forever set free, and God Himself will not presume to interfere with it. He holds sacred the choice and will of each individual. He will not carry out His own purpose contrary to man's will. His will is to give man whatever man decides will best please Him.

So He sets before man life and death, good and evil, and tells him to choose which he will have. God knows what is best, and has chosen and prepared that for man. He has gone so far as to fix it beyond all possibility of failure, that man shall have that good thing if he *chooses* it. But the wonderful kindness and courteousness of the great God is seen in this, that He defers in everything to man's wishes. If man, in his turn, will but defer to God's wishes, there will be the most delightful and loving companionship between them.

Called, Justified, Glorified—"Moreover, whom He did predestinate, them He also called; and whom He called, them He also justified; and whom He justified, them be also glorified." This is completed action. We need not stumble over it, if we will but remember that everything is in

Christ. In Christ we have already been blessed with all spiritual blessings. All men are called to that which God has prepared for them, but none are "the called according to His purpose" unless they have made their calling and election sure by submitting to His will. Such ones are predestinated to be saved. Nothing in the universe can hinder the salvation of any soul that accepts and trusts the Lord Jesus Christ.

And all such are justified. The death of Christ reconciles us to God. "He is the propitiation for our sins; and not for ours only, but also for the sins of the whole world." 1 John 2:2. His death has secured pardon and life for all. Nothing can keep them from salvation except their own perverse will. Men must take themselves out of the hand of God, in order to be lost.

Much more, then, those who accept the sacrifice, are justified. "God commendeth His love toward us, in that, while we were yet sinners, Christ died for us. Much more then, being now justified by His blood, we shall be saved from wrath through Him. For if, when we were enemies, we were reconciled to God by the death of His Son; much more being reconciled, we shall be saved by His life."

"And whom He justified, them He also glorified." Have we not read in the prayer of Christ for His disciples, not only for those who were with Him in the garden, but also for all them that should believe on Him through their word and therefore for us, "The glory which Thou gavest Me, I have given them"? Peter said that he was a partaker of the glory that shall be revealed. God has left nothing undone. Everything that Christ has we have if we accept Him. All that remains is that it should be revealed. "The earnest expectation of the creature waiteth for the manifestation of the sons of God." When God asks concerning His people, "What could have been done more to my vineyard, that I have not done in it?" who shall presume to say that there is something that He has overlooked?

All Things Are Ours—But we have anticipated the apostle. Hear him: "He that spared not His own Son, but delivered Him up for us all, how shall He not with Him also freely give us all things?"

"How shall He not?" That is, How can He avoid giving us all things? In giving Christ for and to us, God could not do otherwise than give us all things, "for in Him were all things created, in the heavens and upon the earth, things visible and things invisible, whether thrones or dominions or principalities or powers; all things have been created through Him, and unto Him; and He is before all things, and in Him all things consist." Colossians 1:16, 17.

"Therefore let no man glory in men. For all things are yours; whether Paul, or Apollos, or Cephas, or the world, or life, or death, or things present, or things to come; all are yours; and ye are Christ's; and Christ is God's." 1 Corinthians 3:21-23. This, then, answers the question, "Who can be against us?" Everything is for us. "All things are for your sakes." 2 Corinthians 4:15.

A general once telegraphed to the seat of government, "We have met the enemy, and they are ours." This is what every child of God is privileged to say. "Thanks be to God, which giveth us the victory through our Lord Jesus Christ." 1 Corinthians 15:57.

"This is the victory that hath overcome the world, even our faith." 1 John 5:4. This is what makes us know that all things work together for good to them that love God. No matter how dark and forbidding the things may seem, if we are in Christ, they are for us, and not against us.

We come now to the close of the eighth chapter of Romans. It is the Pisgah of the epistle, for from it the eye of faith sees the promised land a certainty. Perhaps at this point a very brief summary of the ground already passed over may be profitable. The following is perhaps about as briefly as it can be put.

In the first chapter we have the theme of the epistle put in a few words, the gospel of Christ, the power of God unto salvation. It is to both Jew and Gentile, and has been made known to all through the works of God. The condition of men who have refused to learn of God is then described.

Chapter 2 shows us that at heart all are the same; that all are to be judged by one and the same standard; and that knowledge and high profession do not in themselves recommend any one to God. Obedience to God's law is the only mark of an Israelite indeed and an heir of God.

Chapter 3 emphasizes the preceding points, and especially that there are no obedient ones. "By the deeds of the law there shall no flesh be justified in His sight, for by the law is the knowledge of sin." But there is nevertheless hope for all, because the righteousness of the law is put within and upon all who believe in Christ, so that a man is made a doer of the law by faith. One God justifies both Jews and Gentiles alike through faith. Faith is not a substitute for obedience to the law, but insures the doing of it.

In chapter 4 we have Abraham set forth as an illustration of righteousness gained by faith. We learn also that faith in Christ's death and resurrection is the only way by which to inherit the promise to the fathers, which promise embraced nothing less than the possession of the earth made new. The blessing of Abraham is the blessing that comes by the cross of Christ. And since the promise to Israel was only the repetition of the promise to Abraham, we learn that Israel consists of those in every nation who gain the victory over sin through the cross of Christ.

Abounding love and grace, and salvation through the life of Christ, may serve as the barest outline of chapter 5.

New creatures in Christ may serve to bring to the mind of the faithful reader the main thought of chapter 6. It sets forth death, burial, resurrection, and life with Christ.

In chapter 7 we learn how close is the union between Christ and believers. They are married to Him, so that they are "members of His body, of His flesh, and of His bones." The struggles by which freedom is secured from the first husband—the body of sin,—are vividly portrayed.

The eighth chapter, the crown of the book, describes the blessings of the free-born Son of God. The hope of future immortality is the actual possession, through the Spirit, of the present life and glory of Christ. Those who are in Christ are predestined to eternal glory. And thus we are brought to:—

The Shout of Triumph; a Glorious Persuasion— Romans 8:31-39

31 What shall we then say to these things? If God be for us, who can be against us? 32 He that spared not His own Son, but delivered Him up for us all, how shall He not with Him also freely give us all things? 33 Who shall lay anything to the charge of God's elect? It is God that justifieth. 34 Who is he that condemneth? It is Christ that died, yea, rather, that is risen again, who is even at the right hand of God, who also maketh intercession for us. 35 Who shall separate us from the love of Christ? shall tribulation, or distress, or persecution, or famine, or nakedness, or peril, or sword? 36 As it is written, For Thy sake we are killed all the day long; we are accounted as sheep for the slaughter. 37 Nay, in all these things we are more than conquerors through Him that loved us. 38 For I am persuaded, that neither death, nor life, nor angels, nor principalities, nor powers, nor things present, nor things to come, 39 nor height, nor depth, nor any other creature, shall be able to separate us from the love of God which is in Christ Jesus our Lord.

Everything for Us—The apostle has asked, "If God be for us, who can be against us?" The answer must be, "No one." God is greater than all, and none can pluck anything out of His hand. If He who has power to make all things work together for good is for us, then it is certain that everything must be for us.

But the question often arises in the minds of people, "Is God really for us?" People often wickedly charge Him with being against them; and even professed Christians sometimes think that God is working against them. When troubles come, they imagine that God is fighting against them. Now that question is forever settled by one fact, and that is, that God is He who gives Himself for us, and who justifies.

Who shall lay anything to the charge of God's own chosen? Shall God, who justifies them? Impossible. Well, God is the only one in the universe who has the right to lay anything to the charge of any; and since He justifies instead of condemning, we must be free. We are free if we believe it. Whom does He justify? "The ungodly." That leaves no doubt but that He justifies us.

And what about Christ? Will He condemn us? How can He, when He gave Himself for us? But He gave Himself for us, according to the will of God. Galatians 1:4. "God sent not His Son into the world to condemn the world; but that the world through Him might be saved." John 3:17. He is risen again for our justification, and He is at the right hand of God for us. He interposes Himself between us and the death that we have deserved. Then there is now no condemnation to them that are in Christ Jesus.

"But," says one, "Satan comes to me and makes me feel that I am such a sinner that God is angry with me, and that there is no hope for me." Well, why do you listen to him? You know his character. "He is a liar and the father of it." What have you to do with him? Let him accuse all he will; he is not the judge. God is the judge, *and He justifies*. Satan's sole object is to deceive men, and allure them into sin, making them believe that it is right. Be sure, then, that he never tells an unforgiven man that he is a sinner. God does that by His Spirit, in order that the guilty man may accept the pardon that He freely gives.

The case then stands thus: When God tells a man that he is a sinner, it is in order that the man may receive His pardon. If God says that a man is a sinner, then he is a sinner, and ought to acknowledge it, but "the blood of Jesus Christ His Son cleanseth us from all sin." And this is true, no matter who tells us that we are sinners. Suppose that Satan tells us that we are sinners; we do not need to parley with him, or to stop a moment to discuss the question; we can let the accusation go, and comfort ourselves with the assurance that the blood of Christ cleanses us from all sin.

God doesn't condemn even when He convicts of sin; and nobody else has any business to condemn. If they do condemn, their condemnation does not amount to anything. Therefore there is no condemnation to those who trust the Lord. Even Satan's accusations may serve as encouragements to us; for we may be sure that he will never tell a man that he is a sinner, so long as that man is in his power. Since God is for us, everything is for us.

Everlasting Love—"The Lord hath appeared of old unto me, saying, Yea, I have loved thee with an everlasting love; therefore with loving-kindness have I drawn thee." Jeremiah 31:3. Since this is so, "Who shall separate us from the love of Christ?" His love is everlasting, and knows no change. And His love is for us; therefore nothing can separate us from it. Our own deliberate choice can reject it, but even then His love continues the same; only we have in that case removed ourselves from it. "If we believe not, yet He abideth faithful; He cannot deny Himself." 2 Timothy 2:13.

Shall tribulation, or distress, or persecution, or famine, or nakedness, or peril, or sword, separate us from the love of Christ? Impossible, since it was in those very things that His love for us was manifested. Death itself cannot separate us from His love, since He so loved us that He gave Himself to die for us. Death is the pledge of His love. Sin, that separates us from God, does not separate us from His love, for "God commendeth His love toward us, in that, while we were yet sinners, Christ died for us." "Him who knew no sin be made to be sin on our behalf; that we might become the righteousness of God in Him." 2 Corinthians 5:21.

"In all these things we are more than conquerors through Him that loved us." It must be so, since everything is for us. Since Christ suffered hunger, and distress, and peril, and even death itself, in order that He might deliver us, all those things are for us. It was through death that He gained the victory for us; therefore even in death we gain an overwhelming victory. Those whom Satan persecutes even to death, gain the greatest victory over him. That which seems to be a victory for Satan, is his most crushing defeat.

Behold what a wonderful provision God has made for our salvation! It is easy enough to see that if Satan did not trouble us at all, we should be saved. If our enemy would leave us entirely alone, we should have no trouble. So on that side we are safe. But he will not leave us alone. He goes about as a roaring lion, seeking whom he may devour. Very well, God has so ordered it that even his attempts to destroy us help us along. Death is the sum of all the ills that Satan can bring upon us, and even in that we are more than conquerors through Him that loved us. "Thanks be to God, which giveth us the victory through our Lord Jesus Christ."

A Good Persuasion—"For thus saith the Lord God, the Holy One of Israel: In returning and rest shall ye be saved; in quietness and in confidence shall be your strength." Isaiah 30:15. "For we are made partakers of Christ, if we hold the beginning of our confidence steadfast unto the end." Hebrews 3:14. Our faith is the victory. God alone is our strength and salvation.

Therefore our strength consists in confidence in Him. "Trust ye in the Lord forever; for in the Lord Jehovah is everlasting strength." Isaiah 27:5.

The apostle Paul had been "in stripes above measure, in prisons more frequent, in deaths oft." He says: "Of the Jews five times received I forty stripes save one. Thrice was I beaten with rods, once was I stoned, thrice I suffered shipwreck, a night and a day have I been in the deep; in journeyings often, in perils of waters, in perils of robbers, in perils by mine own countrymen, in perils by the heathen, in perils in the city, in perils in the wilderness, in perils in the sea, in perils among false brethren; in weariness and painfulness, in watchings often, in hunger and thirst, in fastings often, in cold and nakedness." 2 Corinthians 11:24-27. Surely he is one who can speak with the authority of great experience. Hear, then, what he says:—

"Neither death, nor life, nor angels, nor principalities, nor powers, nor things present, nor things to come, nor height, nor depth, nor any other creature, shall be able to separate us from the love of God which is in Christ Jesus our Lord."

No Fear for the Future—Only to those who wilfully reject the love of God is there "a fearful looking for of judgment." Christ says to us, "Be not therefore anxious for the morrow." He does not desire that we should have our minds filled with fear and anxious forebodings. Some people can never be at rest, even under the most delightful circumstances, because they are afraid that something terrible will happen by and by. Now it makes no difference what may come, since neither things present nor things to come can separate us from the love of God in Christ Jesus our Lord. We are assured that things to come, as well as things present, are ours. 1 Corinthians 3:22. Therefore *in Christ* we may sing:

> "Let good or ill befall,
>   It must be good for me,—
> Secure of having Thee in all,
>   Of having all in Thee."

Chapter 9

Who Are True Israelites?

Paul's Love for His Brethren—
Romans 9:1-18

1 I say the truth in Christ, I lie not, my conscience also bearing me witness in the Holy Ghost, 2 that I have great heaviness and continual sorrow in my heart. 3 For I could wish that myself were accursed from Christ for my brethren, my kinsmen according to the flesh; 4 who are Israelites; to whom pertaineth the adoption, and the glory, and the covenants, and the giving of the law, and the service of God, and the promises; 5 whose are the fathers, and of whom as concerning the flesh Christ came, who is over all, God blessed forever. Amen.

6 Not as though the word of God hath taken none effect. For they are not all Israel, which are of Israel; 7 neither, because they are the seed of Abraham, are they all children; but, in Isaac shall thy seed be called. 8 That is, they which are the children of the flesh, these are not the children of God; but the children of the promise are counted for the seed.

9 For this is the word of promise, At this time will I come, and Sarah shall have a son. 10 And not only this; but when Rebecca also had conceived by one, even by our father Isaac; 11 (for the children being not yet born, neither having done any good or evil, that the purpose of God according to election might stand, not of works, but of Him that calleth); 12 it was said unto her, The elder shall serve the younger. 13 As it is written, Jacob have I loved, but Esau have I hated.

14 What shall we say then? Is there unrighteousness with God? God forbid. 15 For He saith to Moses, I will have mercy on whom I will have mercy, and I will have compassion on whom I will have

compassion. 16 So then it is not of him that willeth, nor of him that runneth, but of God that showeth mercy. 17 For the Scripture saith unto Pharaoh, Even for this same purpose have I raised thee up, that I might show My power in thee, and that My name might be declared throughout all the earth. 18 Therefore hath He mercy on whom He will have mercy, and whom He will be hardeneth.

This is a long portion of Scripture for study, but if it is diligently questioned, to see exactly what it says, it will not be found so difficult as it is usually thought.

Both Jews and Greeks—Although Paul was "the apostle of the Gentiles," he did not forget his "kinsmen according to the flesh." Wherever he went he sought out the Jews first, and preached to them. To the elders of Ephesus he said, "I kept back nothing that was profitable unto you, but have showed you, and have taught you publicly, and from house to house, testifying both to the Jews, and also to the Greeks, repentance toward God, and faith toward our Lord Jesus Christ." Acts 20:20, 21. Paul's solicitude for all classes, even for those who were personally strangers to him, shows, more than anything else, his likeness to the Lord Jesus Christ.

Israel's Advantage—"What advantage then hath the Jew?" "Much every way; chiefly, because that unto them were committed the oracles of God." Romans 3:1, 2. So here we read a wondrous list of things that pertain to Israel: the adoption, and the glory, and the covenants, and the giving of the law, and the service of God, and the promises. A terrible thing it is indeed to prove unfaithful amid such inestimable privileges!

"Salvation Is of the Jews"—Thus said Jesus to the woman of Samaria at the well. John 4:22. "Of whom as concerning the flesh Christ came." The Bible was written by Jews, and a young Jewess was the mother of our Lord. As man, Christ was a Jew, of the tribe of Judah. When we read that "we are saved by His life," we know that it is by His life as a Jew. There is no divine gift and blessing for man that was not "to the Jew first," and for the knowledge of which we are not indebted to the Jews.

Nothing From the Gentiles—The apostle Paul says of the "Gentiles in the flesh," that they are "aliens from the commonwealth of Israel, and strangers from the covenants of promise, having no hope, and without God in the world." Ephesians 2:11, 12. The covenants, the promises, even Christ Himself, all belong to the Jews, and not to the Gentiles. Therefore whoever is saved must be saved as a Jew. "God at the first did visit the Gentiles to take out of them a people for His name." Acts 15:14.

Accursed From Christ—It makes no difference whether we use the word "accursed," or "anathema," or "separated." All mean the same thing, and express the most deplorable condition. To be without Christ is to be without hope and without God in the world. Ephesians 2:12.

It was in that condition that Paul would have been willing to be placed for his brethren according to the flesh, if it would have done them any good. What does that show? Simply this, that Israel according to the flesh was, and is, in just that condition accursed from Christ, "having no hope, and without God in the world."

But since all the promises of God are in Christ (2 Corinthians 1:20), those who are separate from Christ have no part in the promises; and therefore we learn anew the fact that Israel after the flesh, as a nation of earth, have not and never had any claim upon God above other nations; that God never made any special promises to Israel after the flesh, more than to any other people.

In the wish that Paul expressed, he showed how completely he was given up to the Lord, and how much he shared in His Spirit. Christ gave Himself for men, consenting even to be separated from God, in order that He might reach and save the lost. There is none other name under heaven whereby men can be saved, and consequently Paul's being accursed would not have saved his brethren, as he very well knew.

But he simply showed how desperate was the case of the Jews, and how great was his solicitude. While no human sacrifice can avail, men are privileged to share Christ's sufferings for others. Paul says of himself, "who now rejoice in my sufferings for you, and fill up that which is behind of the afflictions of Christ in my flesh for His body's sake, which is the church." Colossians 1:24.

Circumcision Made Uncircumcision—We have before read the words, "If thou be a breaker of the law, thy circumcision is made uncircumcision." Romans 2:25. This language was addressed to the Jews, who in the same connection were charged with breaking the law. Romans 2:17-24. In verse 31 of this present chapter we also are told that Israel did not attain to the law of righteousness. And the reason is that they did not accept Christ, through whom alone the righteousness of the law can be obtained.

So again we find that Israel, Paul's "kinsmen after the flesh," were not Israelites at all, but Gentiles, separate from Christ, "having no hope, and without God in the world."

No Failure in the Promise—This is a sad state of things. All the promises belong to Israel, and there is nothing from God for any other nation, and yet the very people known as Israel are accursed from Christ. Nevertheless the word of God has not failed, "for they are not all Israel, which are of Israel." The unbelief of some cannot make the faith of God without effect. Romans 3:3. If every literal descendant of Jacob were lost, that would not weaken in the least God's promises to Israel, since the true Israelites are only those who believe the promises.

The Seed of Abraham—"In Isaac shall thy seed be called." Isaac was the child of promise; therefore those who believe the promises of God are the seed of Abraham. To the Jews who were self-satisfied because of their descent, John the Baptist said, "Think not to say within yourselves, We have Abraham to our father; for I say unto you, that God is able of these stones to raise up children unto Abraham." Matthew 3:9. He could do that as easily as He could make man in the beginning from the dust of the earth.

The Flesh and the Promise—"They which are the children of the flesh, these are not the children of God; but the children of the promise are counted for the seed." This text alone should forever set at rest the speculations about the return of the Jews to old Jerusalem, in order that God's promises may be fulfilled. Still more should it put an end to the absurd notion that any nation, as England or America, constitutes Israel, and is heir to those promises of God.

God's Foreknowledge—When the children were not yet born, and had done neither good nor evil, it was said of them, "The elder shall serve the younger." God knows the end from the beginning, and could tell what each one would do. The choice was in accordance with what is said of God, "who hath saved us, and called us with an holy calling, not according to our works, but according to His own purpose and grace, which was given us in Christ Jesus before the world began." 2 Timothy 1:9.

"Esau Have I Hated"—This was not written until many years after the death of both Jacob and Esau. "Was not Esau Jacob's brother? saith the Lord; yet I loved Jacob, and I hated Esau, and laid his mountains and his heritage waste for the dragons of the wilderness." Malachi 1:2, 3. Of his descendants it is said that they shall be called, "The people against whom the Lord hath indignation forever." Verse 4. And why?

"Thus saith the Lord, For three transgressions of Edom, and for four, I will not turn away the punishment thereof; because he did pursue his brother with the sword, and did cast off all pity, and his anger did tear perpetually, and he kept his wrath forever." Amos 1:11. Jacob, on the other hand, while no better by nature than Esau, believed the promises of God, and was by them made partaker of the divine nature and thus an heir of God and a joint heir of Jesus Christ.

No Unrighteousness With God—Mark well verses 14-17 for evidence that there is no arbitrariness in God's choice. It is all of mercy. "He saith to Moses, I will have mercy on whom I will have mercy, and I will have compassion on whom I will have compassion." So it is all of "God that sheweth mercy." The earth is full of the mercy of the Lord (Psalm 119:64), and "his mercy endureth forever."

God's Purpose for Pharaoh—The case of Pharaoh is cited by the apostle as an illustration of the statement that "it is not of him that willeth, nor of him that runneth, but of God that showeth mercy." "For the Scripture saith unto Pharaoh, Even for this purpose have I raised thee up, that I might show My power in thee, and that My name might be declared throughout all the earth."

It is immaterial whether this refers to the bringing of Pharaoh to the throne, or to the preserving of him up to that time. One thing is certain: it does not teach us, as is commonly supposed, that God brought Pharaoh to the throne for the purpose of wreaking his vengeance upon him. It is astonishing that any professed Christian could ever have dishonored God by such a charge against Him.

The purpose of God in raising Pharaoh up, or causing him to stand, was that He might show to him and in him His power, and that his name might be declared throughout all the earth. This purpose was accomplished in the destruction of Pharaoh because of his stubborn resistance. But it would have been accomplished just as well, and much better for Pharaoh if he had listened to the word of God. Pharaoh saw God's power, but would not believe. If he had believed, he would have been saved, because the power of God is salvation to every one that believeth.

Pharaoh had an imperious will. His one great characteristic was steadfastness, pertinacity degenerating into stubbornness. But who can estimate the power for good that Pharaoh would have been if his will had been yielded to the Lord? To yield to the Lord would have meant a great sacrifice, as men count sacrifices, but no greater than that which Moses had made. Moses had given up the same throne, to cast in his lot with God's people.

A wonderful and honorable position was offered to Pharaoh, but he knew not the day of his visitation. It involved humiliation, and he rejected it. As a consequence he lost everything; while Moses, who chose to suffer affliction with the people of God, and to share the reproach of Christ, has a name and a place that will endure throughout eternity. The mercies of God rejected turn into curses. "For the ways of the Lord are right, and the just shall walk in them; but the transgressors shall fall therein." Hosea 14:19.

We have learned that although God did make choice of certain ones, specially named, who afterwards attained great eminence as children of God, the choice was not arbitrary. Jacob was chosen before he was born, but no more than all others are. God has blessed us with all spiritual blessings in Christ, "according as He hath chosen us in Him before the foundation of the world, that we should be holy and without blame before Him in love; having predestinated us unto the adoption of children by Jesus Christ to Himself, according to the good pleasure of His will, to the praise of the glory of His grace, wherein He hath made us accepted in the Beloved." Ephesians 1:4-6.

"So then it is not of him that willeth, nor of him that runneth, but of God that showeth mercy." As proof of this, the apostle cited the case of Pharaoh, who was chosen in Christ just as much as Jacob was, and just as much as we are. He was chosen to the praise of the glory of the grace of God, that he might show forth the excellencies of the Lord; but he obstinately refused to submit. But God will be praised even by the wrath of men, if they are not willing to praise Him voluntarily, and so God's name and power were made known through Pharaoh's stubbornness.

It would have been better if the proud king had yielded himself to the design of God, instead of having that design worked out in spite of him. But the lesson that we are to learn is that every man in every nation under heaven has been chosen, and that this choice is that they should be adopted as sons. In this choice the Jews have no advantage over others, but are on an equality with them, as is further shown by the remainder of the chapter.

"Accepted in the Beloved"—Romans 9:19-33

19 Thou wilt then say unto me, Why doth He yet find fault? For who hath resisted His will? 20 Nay but, O man, who art thou that repliest against God? Shall the thing formed say to him that formed it, Why hast thou made me thus? 21 Hath not the potter power over the clay, of the same lump to make one vessel unto honor, and another unto dishonor? 22 What if God, willing to show His wrath, and to make His power known, endured with much long-suffering the vessels of wrath fitted to destruction; 23 and that He might make known the riches of His glory on the vessels of mercy, which He had afore prepared unto glory, 24 even us, whom He hath called, not of the Jews only, but also of the Gentiles?

25 As He saith also in Osee, I will call them My people, which were not My people, and her beloved, which was not beloved. 26 And it shall come to pass, that in the place where it was said unto them, Ye are not My people; there shall they be called the children of the living God. 27 Esaias also crieth

concerning Israel, Tho the number of the children of Israel be as the sand of the sea, a remnant shall be saved; 28 for He will finish the work, and cut it short in righteousness; because a short work will the Lord make upon the earth. 29 And as Esaias said before, Except the Lord of Sabaoth had left us a seed, we had been as Sodoma, and been made like unto Gomorrha.

30 What shall we say then? That the Gentiles, which followed not after righteousness, have attained to righteousness, even the righteousness which is of faith. 31 But Israel, which followed after the law of righteousness, hath not attained to the law of righteousness. 32 Wherefore? Because they sought it not by faith, but as it were by the works of the law. For they stumbled at that stumbling-stone; 33 as it is written, Behold, I lay in Sion a stumbling-stone and rock of offense; and whosoever believeth on Him shall not be ashamed.

Replying Against God—This is a very common thing, and its commonness has caused most people to lose sight of its wickedness.

The man who begins indignantly to ask, "Why does God do so and so?" or to say, "I can't see the justice in such a course," as though he were especially and personally affronted, makes it impossible for himself to understand even that which a mortal may comprehend of God. It is very foolish and wicked to blame Him because we are not equal to Him in wisdom. The only way to come to the knowledge of the little that may be understood of God is to settle it once for all that He is just and merciful, and that everything He does is for the good of His creatures. Reverence, and not clamorous questioning, becomes a creature in the presence of the infinite God. "Be still, and know that I am God." Psalm 46:10.

The Potter and His Vessels—The one who thinks himself competent to criticize the Lord thinks that he has a sure case against Him in verses 21-24 of this chapter. "Surely," says he, "this text teaches us that God has made some men to be saved, and others to be destroyed."

Most certainly we find nothing of the kind! There is a vast difference between what the text actually says, and what men imagine that it says. The potter has power over the clay, and so the Creator has power over his creatures, of natural and unquestionable right. Consider the figure: the potter has power over the clay to make one vessel to honor and another to dishonor. Very true; but who in the world ever heard of a potter who busied himself making vessels for the sole purpose of destroying them? He makes vessels of different kinds for various purposes, but they are all intended for use, and not for destruction. So God never made anyone for the purpose of destroying him.

God's Long-suffering—The fact that God does not plan the destruction of any one is shown in that He hesitates long before allowing any to suffer the destruction which their own evil deeds have justly earned. He "endured with much long-suffering the vessels of wrath fitted to destruction." They fitted themselves for destruction after their hardness, by treasuring up unto themselves wrath against the day of wrath. Romans 2:5. Note that God endured with much long-suffering these "vessels of wrath." Now we are to "account that the long-suffering of our Lord is salvation." 2 Peter 3:15. He "is long-suffering to usward, not willing that any should perish, but that all should come to repentance." Verse 9. The fact, therefore, that God endured with much long-suffering the vessels of wrath, even after they were fitted to destruction, shows that He longed for their salvation, and would give them every possible chance for it.

"Whom He Hath Called"—God's long-suffering is also for the purpose of making known the riches of His glory "on the vessels of mercy, which He had afore prepared unto glory." And who are these? "Even us, whom He hath called." And who are they who are called? Are they of some particular nation? "Not of the Jews only, but also of the Gentiles." The entire chapter is a vindication of God's choice of men even before their birth, as illustrated in the case of Jacob; and this verse shows that the choosing of Jacob did not mean that God had special privileges for the Jewish nation, but that He bestows His favors impartially on Jews and Gentiles alike, if they will accept them.

God's People—This is still further shown by verses 25, 26: "As He saith also in Osee (Hosea 1:9, 10), I will call them My people, which were not My people; and her beloved, which was not beloved. And it shall come to pass, that in the place where it was said unto them, Ye are not My people; there shall they be called the children of the living God." God visited the Gentiles, to take out of them a people for His name. The apostle Peter described this visit in these words: "God, which knoweth the hearts, bare them witness, giving them the Holy Ghost, even as He did unto us; and put no difference between us and them, purifying their hearts by faith." And further, "We believe that through the grace of the Lord Jesus Christ we shall be saved, even as they." Acts 15:7-11.

And so "there is no difference between the Jew and the Greek; for the same Lord over all is rich unto all that call upon Him." Romans 10:12 (cf. Galatians 3:28, 29).

The Remnant—"Isaiah also crieth concerning Israel, Though the number of the children of Israel be as the sand of the sea, a remnant shall be saved." Therefore "at this present time also there is a remnant according to the election of grace." Romans 11:5. No matter how many there may be who can trace their genealogy to Jacob according to the flesh, it is only they who are willing subjects of the grace of God who will be saved. There is positively no chance for boasting save in the cross of our Lord Jesus Christ.

The Gentiles Ahead—The Jews professed to keep the law, but did not; the Gentiles were not associated with the law, yet they met its requirements. Now, if the reader will recall Romans 2:25-29, he will see that real circumcision consists (and always did consist) in keeping the law. Therefore since the Gentiles by their faith kept the law, and the Jews through their lack of faith did not keep it, it appears that they had changed places; the Gentiles were really "Jews," and the Jews by nature were the same as the heathen.

Missing the Mark—The Jews followed after the law of righteousness, but did not attain to it. Why not? "Because they sought it not by faith, but as it were by the works of the law." How forcefully this sets forth that of which the entire Epistle is a demonstration, namely, that faith does not clear one from its transgression, but that by faith alone can the law be kept!

The Jews are not blamed for following after the law of righteousness, but for not following after it in the right way. It is not by works, but by faith, that the works which the law requires can be attained. That is to say that bad works cannot produce good works; good cannot come of evil. There is no discount upon good works. They are the most necessary things in the world. They are the result of the keeping of the law by faith. But there can not by any possibility be good works without faith; for "whatsoever is not of faith is sin." Romans 14:23.

The Stumbling-Stone—Do not fail to connect the last part of this chapter with the first part. Remember that the beginning presents Israel according to the flesh as accursed from Christ. To them pertained, among other things, the giving of the law, but they came miserably short of it. Why? "For they stumbled at that stumbling-stone." What stumbling-stone? Christ. They were in the very same condition that so many people are today,—they would not believe that the promises of God to Israel were wholly and solely in Christ. They thought, as many professed Christians now do, that God honored them for their own sake, without any regard to Christ. Christ is the stumbling-stone over which all stumble who regard the promises to Israel as made to a certain earthly nation, to the exclusion of all others.

A Sure Foundation—Strange to say, that very stumbling-stone is a stepping-stone, and a sure foundation. That over which some fall, is the means of lifting up and building up others. "The ways of the Lord are right, and the just shall walk in them; but the transgressors shall fall therein."

Hosea 14:9. Christ is a rock of offense to those who disbelieve, but a sure foundation to those who have faith. He is "the Holy One of Israel," "the King of Israel," "the Shepherd of Israel," and at the same time the fold, and the door into the fold. Without Him there could be no such thing as a nation of Israel.

Those who think to claim an inheritance in Israel because of their birth and without respect to Christ, will be ashamed at the last because whosoever comes not in at the door, the same will be proved to be "a thief and a robber." But "whosoever believeth on Him shall not be put to shame," because his faith will show him to be Abraham's seed, and thus an heir of God according to the promise.

Chapter 10

Glad Tidings of Good Things

Let it be remembered that the ninth chapter of Romans sets forth the condition of Israel according to the flesh—they who are called Israel. They are "accursed from Christ." They "followed after the law of righteousness," but did not attain to righteousness, because they sought it not by faith, but by works." The Gentiles, therefore, gained the precedence over them, because they sought righteousness in the right way, namely, by faith.

Thus were fulfilled the words of Christ to the self-righteous Jews: "The publicans and the harlots go into the kingdom of God before you;" and again, "The kingdom of God shall be taken from you, and given to a nation bringing forth the fruits thereof." Matthew 21:31, 43.

But the Lord did not cast off His people because they stumbled at the Stone which He had placed for a foundation. He endured with much long-suffering even the vessels of wrath fitted to destruction. So the apostle continues:

The Glorious Gospel—Romans 10:1-21

1 Brethren, my heart's desire and prayer to God for Israel is, that they might be saved. 2 For I bear them record that they have a zeal of God, but not according to knowledge. 3 For they being ignorant of God's righteousness, and going about to establish their own righteousness, have not submitted themselves unto the righteousness of God. 4 For Christ is the end of the law for righteousness to every one that believeth. 5 For Moses describeth the righteousness which is of the law, That the man which doeth those things shall live by them. 6 But the righteousness which is of faith speaketh on this wise, Say not in thine heart, Who shall ascend into heaven (that is, to bring Christ down from above:) 7 or,

Who shall descend into the deep (that is, to bring up Christ again from the dead.) 8 But what saith it? The word is nigh thee, even in thy mouth, and in thy heart; that is, the word of faith, which we preach; 9 that if thou shalt confess with they mouth the Lord Jesus, and shalt believe in thine heart that God hath raised Him from the dead, thou shalt be saved. 10 For with the heart man believeth unto righteousness; and with the mouth confession is made unto salvation. 11 For the Scripture saith, Whosoever believeth on Him shall not be ashamed. 12 For there is no difference between the Jew and the Greek; for the same Lord over all is rich unto all that call upon Him. 13 For whosoever shall call upon the name of the Lord shall be saved.

14 How then shall they call on Him in whom they have not believed? and how shall they believe in Him of whom they have not heard? and how shall they hear without a preacher? 15 And how shall they preach, except they be sent? as it is written, How beautiful are the feet of them that preach the gospel of peace, and bring glad tidings of good things! 16 But they have not all obeyed the gospel. For Esaias saith, Lord, who hath believed our report? 17 So then faith cometh by hearing, and hearing by the word of God. 18 But I say, Have they not heard? Yes verily, their sound went into all the earth, and their words unto the ends of the world. 19 But I say, Did not Israel know? First Moses saith, I will provoke you to jealousy by them that are no people, and by a foolish nation I will anger you. 20 But Esaias is very bold, and saith, I was found of them that sought Me not; I was made manifest unto them that asked not after Me. 21 But to Israel He saith, All day long I have stretched forth My hands unto a disobedient and gainsaying people.

Zeal without Knowledge—"It is good to be zealously affected always in a good thing." Zeal is very necessary to the accomplishment of anything; but zeal without knowledge is like a wild horse without bit or bridle. There is plenty of activity, but it is of no use. Or it is like the man who displays great zeal and earnestness in reaching a certain place, but who is traveling in the wrong direction. No matter how zealous a man may be, he will never reach a place that is north of him by traveling southward. Ignorance nullifies zeal. "My people are destroyed for lack of knowledge." Hosea 4:6.

Israel's Ignorance—They were "ignorant of God's righteousness." It is a kind of ignorance that did not cease with the generation then living, and which is not confined to any certain people. But that which made it so much worse in this instance was that this ignorance of God's righteousness was coupled with the highest profession of serving Him.

God's Righteousness—The righteousness of God is something besides a name. It is something far different from a form of words, or even the mere statement of a law. It is nothing less than the life and character of God. As there cannot be sweetness apart from something that is sweet, so there is no such thing as abstract righteousness. Righteousness must necessarily be connected with some living being. But God alone is righteous. See Mark 10:18. Therefore wherever righteousness is, there God must be active. Righteousness is the essential characteristic of God.

Form and Fact—The Jews had "the form of knowledge and of the truth in the law;" but they had not the truth itself. The law of God, as written on the tables of stone, or in a book, is as perfect as it could possibly be. But there was just the same difference between that and the real law that there is between a photograph of a man and the man himself. It was but a shadow. There was no life in the written characters, and they could not do anything. They were simply the statement of that which exists only in the life of God.

Empty Righteousness—The Jews very well knew that the words on the stone or in the book could not do anything; and since they were ignorant of the righteousness of which those words were but the description, they went about to establish a righteousness of their own. This they would never have done if they had not been ignorant of God's righteousness. Of that the psalmist says, "Thy righteousness is like the great mountains." Psalm 26:6. They were trying to produce from themselves the essential attribute of God.

Such an effort, no matter how great the zeal, could end only in miserable failure. Saul of Tarsus was "more exceedingly zealous of the traditions" of the fathers than any others of his class, yet when he came to a right understanding, those things that were gain to him he was obliged to count but loss. That is, the more he did to establish his own righteousness, the worse off he became.

Submitting to Righteousness—If the Jews had not been ignorant of God's righteousness, they would not have attempted to establish a righteousness of their own. They tried to make God's righteousness submit to them, whereas they should have submitted to it. God's righteousness is active. It is His own life. Just as the air will rush into any place where there is an opening, so the righteous life of God will fill every heart that is open to receive it. When men try to handle the law of God, they invariably pervert it, and fit it to their own ideas; the only way to have its perfection appear is to submit to it, allowing it to rule. Then it will work itself out in the life. "It is God which worketh in you both to will and to do of His good pleasure." Philippians 2:13.

The End of the Law—"Now the end of the commandment is charity out of a pure heart, and of a good conscience, and of faith unfeigned." 1 Timothy 1:5. Charity is love, and "love is the fulfilling of the law." Romans 13:10. Therefore the end of the law is its perfect fulfillment. That is self-evident. It makes no difference in what sense the word "end" is taken. Suppose it be used in the common sense of "object." It is very plain that the things which it requires shall be done. Or use the word "end" in the ordinary sense of the farthest extent, and we have the same thing. You arrive at the end of a law only when you reach the utmost limit of its requirement.

Christ the End of the Law—We have seen that the end or object of the law is the righteousness which it requires. So it is said that Christ is the end of the law "for righteousness." The law of God is the righteousness of God. See Isaiah 51:6, 7. But this righteousness is the real life of God Himself, and the words of the law are only the shadow of it. That life is found only in Christ, for He alone declares the righteousness of God. Romans 3:24, 25. His life is the law of God, since God was in Him. That which the Jews had only in form, is found in fact only in Christ. In Him the end of the law is found. Does any one say that "the end of the law" means its abolition? Very well; when they find the abolition of Christ, they will have found the abolition of the law, and not before. Only a study of the life of Christ will reveal the righteousness which the law of God requires.

To Whom?—To whom is Christ the end of the law for righteousness? "To every one that believeth." Christ dwells in the heart by faith. Ephesians 3:17. The perfect righteousness of the law is found only in Him. It is in Him in absolute perfection. Therefore since Christ dwells in the heart of the believer, in Him only is the end of the law attained. "This is the work of God, that ye believe on Him whom He hath sent." John 6:29. "With the heart man believeth unto righteousness."

Doing to Live and Living to Do—The righteousness which is of the law, that is, men's own righteousness (see Philippians 3:9), is on the principle of doing something in order to live. The mere statement of the case is sufficient to show its impossibility; for life must necessarily precede action. A dead body does not do something in order that it may live, but it must be given life in order that it may do something. Peter did not tell the dead Dorcas to do some more charitable work, to sew some more garments, in order that she might live, but in the name of Jesus he restored her to life, in order that she might pursue her good works. The man that doeth those things shall live in them, but he must first live before he can do them. Therefore the righteousness which is of the law is but an empty dream. Christ gives life, even the eternal and righteous life of God, which works righteousness in the soul that it has quickened.

Christ the Word—Verses 6-8 of this chapter are a direct quotation from Deuteronomy 30:11-14. Moses had been rehearsing the law to the people, and exhorting them to obedience, and told them that the commandment was not "far off," so that they needed to send some one to bring it to them, "but the word is very nigh unto thee, in thy mouth, and in thy heart, that thou mayest do it." Paul, writing by inspiration of the Spirit, quotes the words of Moses, and shows that they refer to Christ. Christ is the Word, the commandment, which is not "far off," which needs not to be brought down from heaven, nor to be raised from the dead. Let the reader compare these two portions of Scripture very carefully, and he will clearly see that the real commandment of the Lord is nothing less than Christ.

Law and Life—This truth was not necessarily hidden till the New Testament was written. The thoughtful Jew in the days of Moses could clearly understand that only in the life of God could the righteousness of the law be found. Moses said: "I call heaven and earth to record this day against you, that I have set before you life and death, blessing and cursing; therefore choose life, that both thou and thy seed may live; that thou mayest love the Lord thy God, and that thou mayest obey His voice, and that thou mayest cleave unto Him; for He is thy life, and the length of thy days." Deuteronomy 30:19, 20.

In setting the law before the people, Moses set before them the life of God, and that is to be found only in Christ. "I know that His commandment is life everlasting." John 12:50. "And this is life eternal, that they might know Thee the only true God, and Jesus Christ, whom Thou hast sent." John 17:3.

The Word Very Near—Remembering that the word is Christ, we read, "The word is nigh thee, even in thy mouth, and in thy heart; that is, the word of faith, which we preach." Is Christ so near as that? Indeed He is; for He Himself says, "Behold, I stand at the door, and knock." Revelation 3:20. It is not alone to the good that He is near, but He is "not far from every one of us." Acts 17:27. So near is He that "in Him we live, and move, and have our being."

We cannot reach out our hand without finding Him. Christ is near the heart even of wicked men, waiting for them to recognize the fact that already exists, and will in all their ways acknowledge Him; then He will dwell in their hearts "by faith." He will then direct them in all their ways. In nothing is the love of Christ more fully shown than in His dwelling with sinful men, and enduring all their hatefulness, in order that by His patience He may win them from their evil ways.

Belief in the Resurrection—"If thou shalt confess with thy mouth the Lord Jesus, and shalt believe in thine heart that God hath raised Him from the dead, thou shalt be saved." He "was delivered for our offenses, and was raised again for our justification." Romans 4:25. And "He died for all." He tasted death for every man. Therefore He was raised for the justification of every man. To believe in the heart that God hath raised Him from the dead, is to believe that He justifies me. The one who does not believe that Jesus does cleanse him from sin, does not really believe that God has raised Him from the dead; for we cannot believe in the resurrection of Jesus, without believing that for which He was raised. The resurrection of Jesus is much less generally believed than is commonly supposed.

Not Ashamed—The root of the word "believe" indicates a foundation, something upon which one can build. To believe on Jesus is to build upon Him. He is the tried Stone, the sure Foundation, the Rock. Isaiah 28:16. Whosoever builds upon Him will not be obliged to flee in confusion when the rain descends, and the floods come, and the winds blow and beat upon his house; for He is the Rock of Ages.

No Difference—The keynote of the gospel call is "whosoever." "God so loved *the world*, that He gave His only-begotten Son, that whosoever believeth in Him should not perish, but have everlasting life." John 3:16. "Whosoever *will*, let him take the water of life freely." Rev. 22:17. "Whosoever shall call upon the name of the Lord shall be saved." No distinction is made; "for there is no difference between the Jew and the Greek."

Read again the second and third chapters of Romans, and the fourth also. Indeed, the whole book of Romans gives a death-blow to that wicked idea that God is partial, and that He favors some people more than others. The idea that God has special blessings for one nation of earth that He has not for others, no matter whether that one nation be called Jews, Israelites, Anglo-Saxons, Englishmen, or anything else, is a direct denial of the gospel of the grace of God.

The Gospel to All—The thirteenth, fourteenth, and fifteenth verses show the steps necessary for salvation. First, men must call upon the Lord. But in order to call upon Him, they must believe in Him. But they cannot hear without someone being sent. But preachers have been sent, yet all have not believed and obeyed, although they have all heard.

What have they all heard? They have all heard the word of God. In proof of this, the apostle says that faith comes by hearing the word of God, and adds: "Have they not heard? Yes verily, their sound went into all the earth, and their words unto the ends of the world." All in the world have heard, and there is no excuse for unbelief on the part of any. Read again Romans 1:16-20.

Glorious Preachers—The gospel of Christ is "the glorious gospel." It shines its way into the heart. See 2 Corinthians 4:4. So it is fitting that those who preach it should be arrayed in glory. The sun, moon, and stars are the beautiful "preachers" whose words have gone to the ends of the world. They preach the glorious gospel of Christ. They are a continual example of the right way to preach the gospel—they shine forth the glory of God.

So the apostle says to us who have heard and believed the word, "Ye are a chosen generation, a royal priesthood, an holy nation, a peculiar people; that ye should show forth the praises of Him who hath called you out of the darkness into His marvelous light." 1 Peter 2:9. The gospel is the revelation of God to men. "God is light," therefore the proclaiming of the gospel consists in showing forth His light. "Let your light so shine before men, that they may see your good works, and glorify your Father which is in heaven." Matthew 5:16.

NOTES

"Forasmuch as ye know that ye were not redeemed with corruptible things, as silver and gold, from your vain conversation received by tradition from your fathers; but with the precious blood of Christ, as of a lamb without blemish and without spot: Who verily was foreordained before the foundation of the world, but was manifest in these last times for you." 1 Peter 1:18-20.

Chapter 11

All Israel Shall Be Saved

The eleventh chapter of Romans closes up the special discussion of Israel. In each of these three chapters we are plainly shown that the Gentiles, if they believe, have an equal share with the Jews, and that the latter forfeit all the privileges of the people of God through unbelief. Nothing could show more plainly than do these chapters that all men are on a level, and that the promises of God are to all who believe, irrespective of birth or nation.

God Hath Not Cast Away His People—
Romans 11:1-22

1 I say then, Hath God cast away His people? God forbid. For I also am an Israelite, of the seed of Abraham, of the tribe of Benjamin. 2 God hath not cast away His people which He foreknew. Wot ye not what the Scripture saith of Elias? how he maketh intercession to God against Israel, saying, 3 Lord, they have killed Thy prophets, and digged down Thine altars; and I am left alone, and they seek my life.

4 But what saith the answer of God unto him? I have reserved to Myself seven thousand men, who have not bowed the knee to the image of Baal. 5 Even so then at this present time also there is a remnant according to the election of grace. 6 And if by grace, then is it no more of works: otherwise grace is no more grace. But if it be of works, then is it no more grace: otherwise work is no more work. 7 What then? Israel hath not obtained that which He seeketh for; but the election hath obtained it, and the rest were blinded 8 (according as it is written, God

hath given them the spirit of slumber, eyes that they should not see, and ears that they should not hear;) unto this day. 9 And David saith, Let their table be made a snare, and a trap, and a stumblingblock, and a recompence unto them: 10 let their eyes be darkened, that they may not see, and bow down their back alway.

11 I say then, Have they stumbled that they should fall? God forbid: but rather through their fall salvation is come unto the Gentiles, for to provoke them to jealousy. 12 Now if the fall of them be the riches of the world, and the diminishing of them the riches of the Gentiles; how much more their fulness?

13 For I speak to you Gentiles, inasmuch as I am the apostle of the Gentiles, I magnify mine office: 14 if by any means I may provoke to emulation them which are my flesh, and might save some of them. 15 For if the casting away of them be the reconciling of the world, what shall the receiving of them be, but life from the dead? 16 For if the firstfruit be holy, the lump is also holy: and if the root be holy, so are the branches.

17 And if some of the branches be broken off, and thou, being a wild olive tree, were graffed in among them, and with them partakest of the root and fatness of the olive tree; 18 boast not against the branches. But if thou boast, thou bearest not the root, but the root thee. 19 Thou wilt say then, The branches were broken off, that I might be graffed in. 20 Well; because of unbelief they were broken off, and thou standest by faith. Be not highminded, but fear: 21 for if God spared not the natural branches, take heed lest He also spare not thee. 22 Behold therefore the goodness and severity of God: on them which fell, severity; but toward thee, goodness, if thou continue in His goodness: otherwise thou also shalt be cut off.

Not a Castaway—The apostle Paul knew that God had not cast off His people, the lineal descendants of Abraham, and his proof was the fact that he himself was accepted with God. If the Jewish nation had been cast off by the Lord, then there would have been no hope for Paul, because he was "an Hebrew of the Hebrews." The words "God forbid" mislead some people. The idea obtains that Paul was praying that the Lord would not cast off His people, lest he also should be cast away. Instead of "God forbid," read, "by no means." Then all is clear. Thus: "I say then, Hath God cast away His people? By no means." How do you prove that? Why, "I also am an Israelite, of the seed of Abraham, of the tribe of Benjamin."

Who Are Rejected?—Although God had not cast away His people, they were in a bad way. The fact that God had not cast them off, did not prove that they would be saved. Paul intimated that there was danger that even he, after he had preached to others, might be a castaway. 1 Corintians 9:27. The case, however, lay wholly in his own hands. There was no danger that God would cast him away against his will. We have the words of the Lord, "Him that cometh to Me I will in nowise cast out." John 6:37. And all may come; for He says also that "whosoever will" may come. God casts no one off; but if they utterly reject Him, then, since He forces no one, He has no alternative but to leave them to themselves.

"Because I have called, and ye refused; I have stretched out My hand, and no man regarded; but ye have set at naught all My counsel, and would none of My reproof; … therefore shall they eat of the fruit of their own way, and be filled with their own devices. For the turning away of the simple shall slay them, and the prosperity of fools shall destroy them." Proverbs 1:24-32.

God stretches forth His hands to a disobedient and gainsaying people (Romans 10:21), and they have it in their own power to say if they will be saved. God accepts everybody; the only question is, Will they accept Him?

The Remnant—In the illustration from Elijah's time, we learn something further about the matter of acceptance and rejection. It seemed then as though all Israel had departed from the Lord, but there were seven thousand men who had not acknowledged Baal. "Even so at this present moment there is a remnant according to the election of grace." The grace of God appears to all men, and is extended to all. Those who accept the grace are the elect, no matter of what tribe or nation they are. Although the plan of salvation embraces all the world, it is a sad fact that but few of any people or generation will accept it. "Though the number of the children of Israel be as the sand of the sea, a remnant shall be saved."

The Olive Tree—While there are single expressions in the eleventh chapter of Romans that are difficult to understand, the chapter as a whole is very simple. Under the figure of an olive tree, the people of God are represented, and by the figure of grafting, the relation of all men to God is shown. Before going into the particulars of this illustration, we must for a moment consider the Commonwealth of Israel.

In the second chapter of Ephesians we learn that as Gentiles, the Ephesians had been "aliens from the commonwealth of Israel," "having no hope, and without God in the world." That is, those who are not of the commonwealth of Israel are without God; or, those who are without God are aliens from the commonwealth of Israel.

Now Christ is the only manifestation of God to man, and "He came unto His own, and His own received Him not." John 1:11. Therefore the mass of the Jewish nation were without God, just as surely as the heathen were, and consequently were aliens from the commonwealth of Israel. The same chapter of Ephesians tells us that Christ came to reconcile both Jews and Gentiles unto God, showing that both were separate from Him. Still further in the same chapter we learn that the commonwealth of Israel is the "household of God," and is composed of saints, those who are reconciled to God. Only such are not "strangers and foreigners" from Israel.

The Origin of Israel—The name originated that night when Jacob wrestled with the Lord, and finally by his faith obtained the blessing that he sought. He could not gain anything whatever by his physical strength; indeed, one touch by the Lord was sufficient to make him utterly helpless; but it was when, in his utter helplessness, he cast himself in simple faith on the Lord, that he gained the victory, and was named Israel—prince of God. This title was applied to all his descendants, although it strictly belonged only to those who had living faith in God, just as we use the term "Christian" of those who are in "the church," with no thought of asserting that they really know the Lord.

Everyone Has to Be Grafted In—Romans 11:23-26

23 And they also, if they abide not still in unbelief, shall be graffed in: for God is able to graff them in again. 24 For if thou were cut out of the olive tree which is wild by nature, and wert graffed contrary to nature into a good olive tree: how much more shall these, which be the natural branches, be graffed into their own olive tree? 25 For I would not, brethren, that ye should be ignorant of this mystery, lest ye should be wise in your own conceits; that blindness in part is happened to Israel, until the fulness of the Gentiles be come in. 26 And so all Israel shall be saved: as it is written, There shall come out of Sion the Deliverer, and shall turn away ungodliness from Jacob.

A Righteous Nation—Much is said of the unbelief of the children of Israel; but there were times when they as an entire nation had faith to a marked degree. One instance will suffice at present. "By faith the walls of Jericho fell down, after they were compassed about seven days." Hebrews 11:30. Thirteen times the whole host marched round the city, seemingly to no purpose, without a murmur. Such faith showed that they were then a righteous nation, in close union with God; because, "being justified by faith, we have peace with God through our Lord Jesus Christ." Romans 5:1. Then their name truly indicated their character; they were Israelites indeed. They were walking "in the steps of that faith of our father Abraham."

Severed Branches—But they did not keep the faith. "We are made partakers of Christ, if we hold the beginning of our confidence steadfast unto the end." Hebrews 3:14. This they did not do, and so they became "without Christ," "aliens from the commonwealth of Israel." Ephesians 2:12. In Romans 11:17 the apostle asks, What "if some of the branches be broken off?" etc., not meaning, however, to imply that some were not broken off, as we learn from what follows. For he says, "Because of unbelief they were broken off" (verse 20), and again, "God hath concluded them all in unbelief" (verse 32), thus showing that all were broken off. So we find the people who were "beloved for the fathers' sakes" (verse 28) and who had at one time in their history been "children of God by faith in Christ Jesus" (Galatians 3:26) reduced through their unbelief to the level of those who had never known God.

Grafted Branches—All the branches of the olive tree—Israel—were broken off through unbelief. To supply their places God took branches from the wild olive tree—the Gentiles—and grafted them on. This grafting was "contrary to nature" (verse 24), since it was wholly a work of grace. If it had been according to nature, then the branches would have borne natural fruit, and there would be no gain from the grafting, since the natural fruit was bad. See Galatians 5:19-21; Ephesians 2:1, 2. But a miracle was wrought by grace, and the branches that were grafted in partook of the nature of the root. The fruit of the grafted-in branches is no more natural, but that of the Spirit. Galatians 5:22, 23.

A Reunion—We must remember that God did not cast off His people. They fell away through unbelief. "They also, if they abide not still in unbelief, shall be graffed in; for God is able to graff them in again." Verse 23. The Jew has as good a chance as the Gentile. "There is no difference between the Jew and the Greek; for the same Lord over all is rich unto all that call upon Him." Romans 10:12. Christ came "that He might reconcile both unto God in one body by the cross," and "through Him we both have access by one Spirit unto the Father." Ephesians 2:16, 18.

No Change of Plan—Let us not forget that in thus grafting in the Gentiles to take the place of rebellious Israel, there has been no change in God's plan. It was all included in the original promise to Abraham. "Know ye therefore that they which are of faith, the same are the children of Abraham. And the Scripture, foreseeing that God would justify the heathen through faith, preached before the gospel unto Abraham, saying, In thee shall all nations be blessed." Galatians 3:7, 8.

In the beginning God made Adam, the father of the human race. Adam was the son of God (Luke 3:38); therefore all his descendants are by right God's people. He did not cast them off because they sinned. His love embraced the world (John 3:16), and it did not contract in the days of Abraham, Isaac, and Jacob. The only advantage of Israel was that they had the privilege of carrying the glorious gospel to the Gentiles, for whom it was always designed as much as for them.

Visiting the Gentiles—The Gentiles, as well as the descendants of Jacob, were from the beginning intended to become Israel. This was shown at the conference in Jerusalem. Peter told how he had been divinely sent to preach the gospel to them, and that God put no difference between them and the Jews. Then James said: "Simeon hath declared how God at the first did visit the Gentiles, to take out of them a people for His name. And to this agree the words of the prophets; as it is written, After this I will return, and will build again the tabernacle of David, which is fallen down; and I will build again the ruins thereof, and I will set it up; that the residue of men might seek after the Lord, and all the Gentiles, upon whom My name is called, saith the Lord, who doeth all these things. Known unto God are all His works from the beginning of the world." Acts 15:14-18. See also Amos 9:11-15.

From the above we learn that the "tabernacle of David," the house or kingdom of David, is to be restored through the preaching of the gospel to the Gentiles, and that this is according to the mind of the Lord from the beginning of the world. What these scriptures need is not comment, but believing thought.

"The Fulness of the Gentiles"—"Blindness in part is happened to Israel, until the fulness of the Gentiles be come in." Romans 11:25. Until the fulness of the Gentiles "be come" into what place? Into Israel, of course; for it is by the bringing in of the fulness of the Gentiles that "all Israel shall be saved." When will the fulness of the Gentiles "be come" in?

The Lord Himself furnishes the answer: "This gospel of the kingdom shall be preached in all the world for a witness unto all nations; and then shall the end come." Matthew 24:14. God is visiting the Gentiles, "to take out of them a people for His name." By them Israel is to be made full or complete. As soon as this work of preaching the gospel to the Gentiles is finished, then the end will come. There will then be no more preaching to anybody—not to the Gentiles, because they will all have made the final decision; and not to the Jews, because then "all Israel shall be saved." There will then be no more need of the gospel; it will have accomplished its work.

A Great Ingathering of Jews—Romans 11:27-36

27 For this is My covenant unto them, when I shall take away their sins. 28 As concerning the gospel, they are enemies for your sakes: but as touching the election, they are beloved for the fathers' sakes. 29 For the gifts and calling of God are without repentance. 30 For as ye in times past have not believed God, yet have now obtained mercy through their unbelief: 31 even so have these also now not believed, that through your mercy they also may obtain mercy. 32 For God hath concluded them all in unbelief, that He might have mercy upon all. 33 O the depth of the riches both of the wisdom and knowledge of God! how unsearchable are His judgments, and His ways past finding out! 34 For who hath known the mind of the Lord? or who hath been His counselor? 35 Or who hath first given to Him, and it shall be recompensed unto him again? 36 For of Him, and through Him, and to Him, are all things: to whom be glory for ever. Amen.

All Through Christ—Note carefully verses 25-27. When the fulness of the Gentiles shall have been brought in, "all Israel shall be saved." Indeed, it is only by the bringing in of the Gentiles that all Israel will be saved. And this will be a fulfillment of that which is written, "There shall come out of Zion the Deliverer, and shall turn away ungodliness from Jacob." Only through Christ can Israel be saved and gathered; and all who are Christ's are Israel; for "if ye be Christ's then are ye Abraham's seed, and heirs according to the promise." Galatians 3:29.

Taking Away Sin—There shall come out of Zion the Deliverer, who shall turn away ungodliness from Israel. Christ is "the Lamb of God, which taketh away the sin of the world." John 1:29. "He is the propitiation for our sins; and not for ours only, but also for the sins of the whole world." 1 John 2:2. The high priest Caiaphas spoke by the Spirit "that Jesus should die for that nation; and not for that nation only, but that also He should gather together in one the children of God that were scattered abroad." John 11:51, 52.

So Peter, speaking in the temple at Jerusalem, said: "Ye are the children of the prophets, and of the covenant which God made with our fathers, saying unto Abraham, And in thy seed shall all the kindred of the earth be blessed. Unto you first God, having raised up His Son Jesus, sent Him to bless you, in turning away every one of you from His iniquities." Acts 3:25, 26. The blessing of Abraham is the forgiveness of sins through Christ; and people of all nations become Israelites indeed by the taking away of iniquity.

All of Faith—It was through faith that Jacob became Israel. It was through unbelief that his descendants were broken off from the stock of

Israel. It is through faith that the Gentiles are grafted in, and only by faith that they stand; and it is through faith that the Jews may become reunited to the parent stock.

Faith in Christ is the only thing that makes one an Israelite, and only unbelief cuts one off from being an Israelite; this was fully shown by Christ when He marveled at the faith of the centurion, saying; "I have not found so great faith, no, not in Israel. And I say unto you, That many shall come from the east and west, and shall sit down with Abraham, and Isaac, and Jacob, in the kingdom of heaven. But the children of the kingdom shall be cast out into outer darkness." Matthew 8:10-12.

All in Prison—"God hath concluded them all in unbelief, that He might have mercy upon all." The word "conclude" means literally "to shut up," as indicated in the margin. He hath "shut them all up together." So in Galatians 3:22 we read that "the Scripture hath concluded all under sin, that the promise by faith of Jesus Christ might be given to them that believe."

And the next verse speaks of all being "shut up" and guarded by the law. Both Jews and Gentiles "are all under sin." Romans 3:9. All are shut up in prison together, with no hope of escape except by Christ, "the Deliverer," who proclaims "liberty to the captives, and the opening of the prison to them that are bound." Isaiah 61:1. He comes as the deliverer "out of Zion," bringing the freedom of "Jerusalem which is above." Galatians 4:26. All therefore who accept the liberty wherewith Christ makes free, are the children of Jerusalem which is above, heirs of heavenly Canaan, members of the true commonwealth of Israel.

Wonderful Knowledge—"By His knowledge shall My righteous servant justify many; for He shall bear their iniquities," says the Lord. Isaiah 53:11. Thus *by forgiving sins He will build the walls of Jerusalem* (Psalm 51:18), and restore her captive children. "O the depth of the riches both of the wisdom and knowledge of God! how unsearchable are His judgments, and His ways past finding out!"

Let no one, therefore, presume to criticize God's plan, or to reject it because he cannot understand it. "For who hath been His counselor?" "For of Him, and through Him, and to Him, are all things; to whom be glory forever. Amen."

Chapter 12

How Righteousness by Faith Becomes Practical

We have now finished that which might be called the argumentative portion of the Epistle to the Romans. The five chapters which follow are devoted to exhortations to the church. Those in the chapter before us are very simple, but will be much better understood if read in connection with that which immediately precedes. Accordingly, we preface our reading of the twelfth chapter with the last four verses of the eleventh:

> 33 O the depth of the riches both of the wisdom and knowledge of God! how unsearchable are his judgments, and His ways past finding out! 34 For who hath known the mind of the Lord? or who hath been His counselor? 35 or who hath first given to Him, and it shall be recompensed unto him again? 36 For of Him, and through Him, and to Him, are all things; to whom be glory forever. Amen.

Live Peaceably With All Men— Romans 12:1-21

> 1 I beseech you therefore, brethren, by the mercies of God, that ye present your bodies a living sacrifice, holy, acceptable unto God, which is your reasonable service. 2 And be not conformed to this world: but be ye transformed by the renewing of your mind, that ye may prove what is that good, and acceptable, and perfect will of God. 3 For I say, through the grace given unto me, to every man that is among you, not to think of himself more highly than he ought to think; but to think soberly, according as God hath dealt to every man the measure of faith.

4 For as we have many members in one body, and all members have not the same office: 5 so we, being many, are one body in Christ, and every one members one of another. 6 Having then gifts differing according to the grace that is given to us, whether prophecy, let us prophesy according to the proportion of faith; 7 or ministry, let us wait on our ministering: or he that teacheth, on teaching; 8 or he that exhorteth, on exhortation: he that giveth, let him do it with simplicity; he that ruleth, with diligence; he that showeth mercy, with cheerfulness.

9 Let love be without dissimulation. Abhor that which is evil; cleave to that which is good. 10 Be kindly affectioned one to another with brotherly love; in honor preferring one another; 11 not slothful in business; fervent in spirit; serving the Lord: 12 Rejoicing in hope; patient in tribulation; continuing instant in prayer; 13 distributing to the necessity of saints; given to hospitality. 14 Bless them which persecute you: bless, and curse not. 15 Rejoice with them that do rejoice, and weep with them that weep. 16 Be of the same mind one toward another. Mind not high things, but condescend to men of low estate. Be not wise in your own conceits. 17 Recompense to no man evil for evil. Provide things honest in the sight of all men. 18 If it be possible, as much as lieth in you, live peaceably with all men.

19 Dearly beloved, avenge not yourselves, but rather give place unto wrath: for it is written, Vengeance is mine; I will repay, saith the Lord. 20 Therefore if thine enemy hunger, feed him; if he thirst, give him drink; for in so doing thou shalt heap coals of fire on his head. 21 Be not overcome of evil, but overcome evil with good.

A Logical Conclusion—The closing verses of the eleventh chapter set forth the infinite, unsearchable power and wisdom of God. Nobody can add anything to Him. No one can put God under obligations to him. No one can give Him something for which he should receive something in return. "For of Him, and through Him, and to Him are all things." "He giveth to all life, and breath, and all things." "In Him we live, and move, and have our being." Acts 17:25, 28.

This being so, it is but reasonable that all should yield their bodies to Him, for Him to control. He alone has the wisdom and the power to do it properly. The word "reasonable" is, literally, "logical." The logical result of acknowledging God's power and wisdom and love, is to submit to Him. He who does not yield to God, virtually denies His existence.

Exhorting and Comforting—It is interesting to know that the Greek word rendered "beseech" is from the same root as "the Comforter," applied to the Holy Spirit. It is the word used in Matthew 5:4, "Blessed are they that mourn; for they shall be comforted." It occurs also in 1 Thessalonians 4:18, "Comfort one another with these words."

The following passage contains the word several times, as indicated: "Blessed be God, even the Father of our Lord Jesus Christ, the Father of mercies, and the God of all comfort; who comforteth us in all our tribulation, that we may be able to comfort them which are in any trouble, by the comfort wherewith we ourselves are comforted of God. For as the sufferings of Christ abound in us, so our consolation also aboundeth by Christ." 2 Corinthians 1:3-5. The fact that the Greek word for "exhort," or "beseech," is identical with that for "comfort," may give a new force to the exhortations of the Spirit of God.

There is comfort in the thought that God is all-powerful. Therefore there is comfort in all His exhortations and commandments, since He does not expect us to act in our own strength, but in His. When He utters a command, it is but the statement of what He will do in and for us, if we yield to His power. When He reproves, He is simply showing to us our need, which He can abundantly supply. The Spirit convicts of sin, but is always the Comforter.

Power and Mercy—"God hath spoken once; twice have I heard this; that power belongeth unto God. Also unto thee, O Lord, belongeth mercy." Psalm 62:11, 12. "God is love." Therefore His power is love, so that when the apostle cites the power and wisdom of God as the reason why we should yield to Him, he exhorts us by the mercies of God. Never forget that all the manifestation of God's power is but the manifestation of His love, and that love is the power by which He works. Jesus Christ, in whom God's love is revealed (1 John 4:10), is "the power of God, and the wisdom of God" (1 Corinthians 1:24).

True Nonconformity—In England, religious people have often been divided into two classes—Churchmen and Nonconformists. Now every true Christian is a nonconformist, but not in the sense that the word is ordinarily used. "Be not conformed to this world, but be ye transformed by the renewing of your minds." When those who call themselves Nonconformists adopt worldly methods, and engage in worldly schemes, then they dishonor the name. "The friendship of the world is enmity with God."

How to Think of Self—The exhortation to every man is not to think of himself more highly than he ought to think. How highly ought one to think of himself? "Put them in fear, O Lord; that the nations may know themselves to be but men." Psalm 9:20. "Put not your trust in princes, nor in the son of man, in whom there is no help." Psalm 146:3. "Cease ye from man, whose breath is in his nostrils: for wherein is he to be accounted of?" Isaiah 2:22. "Verily every man at his best state is altogether vanity." Psalm 39:5. "The wisdom of this world is foolishness with God." "The Lord knoweth the thoughts of the wise, that they are vain." 1 Corinthians 3:19, 20. "What is your life? It is even a vapor, that appeareth for a little time, and then vanisheth away." James 4:14. "We are all as an unclean thing, and all our righteousnesses are as filthy rags; and we all do fade as a leaf; and our iniquities, like the wind, have taken us away." Isaiah 64:6. "In lowliness of mind let each esteem other better than themselves." Philippians 2:3.

Faith and Humility—Pride is the enemy of faith. The two cannot live together. A man can think soberly and humbly only as the result of the faith that God gives. "Behold, his soul which is lifted up is not upright in him; but the just shall live by His faith." Habakkuk 2:4. The man who has confidence in his own strength and wisdom, will not depend upon another. Trust in the wisdom and power of God comes only when we recognize and acknowledge our own weakness and ignorance.

Faith a Gift of God—That faith which God deals to man is indicated in Revelation 14:12: "Here is the patience of the saints; here are they that keep the commandments of God, and the faith of Jesus." God does not give faith to the saints only, any more than He gives the commandments to them alone; but the saints *keep* the faith, and others do not. The faith which they keep is the faith of Jesus; therefore it is the faith of Jesus that is given to men.

Faith Given to Every Man—Every man is exhorted to think soberly, because God hath dealt to every man the measure of faith. Many people have a notion that they are so constituted that it is impossible for them to believe. That is a grave error. Faith is just as easy, and just as natural, as breathing. It is the common inheritance of all men, and the one thing wherein all are equal. It is as natural for the child of the infidel to believe as it is for the child of the saint. It is only when men build up a barrier of pride about themselves (Psalm 73:6) that they find it difficult to believe. And even then they will believe; for when men disbelieve God, they believe Satan; when they disbelieve the truth, they greedily swallow the most egregious falsehoods.

In What Measure?—We have seen that faith is given to every man. This may be known also by the fact that salvation is given to every man, and placed within his grasp, and salvation is only by faith. If God had not given faith to every man, He could not have brought salvation within the reach of all.

The question is, In what measure has God given every man faith? This is really answered in the fact already learned, that the faith which He gives is the faith of Jesus. The faith of Jesus is given in the gift of Jesus Himself, and Christ is given in His fulness to every man. He tasted death for every man. Hebrews 2:9. "Unto every one of us is given grace according to the measure of the gift of Christ." Ephesians 4:7. Christ is not divided; therefore to every man is given all of Christ and all of His faith. There is but one measure.

The Body and Its Members—"There is one body" (Ephesians 4:4), and that is the church, of which Christ is the head (Ephesians 1:22, 23; Colossians 1:18). "We are members of His body, of His flesh, and of His bones." Ephesians 5:30. There are many members in the body, "so we, being many, are one body in Christ, and every one members one of another."

As in the human body, so in the body of Christ, "all members have not the same office;" yet they are so joined together, and so mutually dependent, that none can boast over the others. "The eye cannot say unto the hand, I have no need of thee; nor again the head to the feet, I have no need of you." 1 Corinthians 12:21. So it is in the true church of Christ; there are no divisions and no boastings, and no member seeks to occupy the place or perform the work of another. No member thinks himself independent of the others, and all have an equal care for one another.

Various Gifts—All members have not the same office, and all have not the same gifts. "There are diversities of gifts, but the same Spirit. ... And there are diversities of operations, but it is the same God which worketh all in all. ... For to one is given by the Spirit the word of wisdom; to another the word of knowledge by the same Spirit; to another faith by the same Spirit; to another the gifts of healing by the same Spirit; to another the working of miracles; to another prophecy; to another discerning of Spirits; to another divers kind of tongues; to another the interpretation of tongues; but all these worketh that one and the selfsame Spirit, dividing to every man severally as he will." 1 Corinthians 12:4-11.

"The Proportion of Faith"—"Having then gifts differing according to the grace that is given to us, whether prophecy, let us prophesy according to the proportion of faith." As we have seen, there is but "one faith" (Ephesians 4:5), and that is "the faith of Jesus." Although there are various gifts, there is but one power behind them all. "All these worketh that one and the selfsame Spirit." Therefore, to prophesy or to exercise any other of the gifts "according to the proportion" or measure of faith, is to do it "as of the ability which God giveth." 1 Peter 4:11. "As every man hath received the gift, even so minister the same one to another, as good stewards of the manifold grace of God."

"In Honor Preferring One Another"—This can be done only when one is able "in lowliness of mind" to esteem others better than himself. Philippians 2:3. And this can be done only when one knows his own worthlessness. The man who "knows the plague of his own heart" cannot think that others are as bad as himself. "Let this mind be in you, which was also in Christ Jesus; who…made Himself of no reputation, and took upon Him the form of a servant."

How to Treat Persecutors—"Bless them which persecute you; bless, and curse not." To curse does not necessarily always mean to use profane language—to swear. To curse means to speak ill. It is the opposite of bless, which means to speak well of. Sometimes men persecute according to law, and sometimes they persecute without any legal warrant; but whether it is "due process of law" or mob violence, no hard words are to be used against those who do it. On the contrary, they are to be spoken well of.

One cannot do this without the Spirit of Christ, who prayed for his betrayers and murderers, and who did not venture to bring railing accusation even against the devil. Jude 9. To hold persecutors up to contempt is not according to God's instruction.

Rejoicing and Weeping—To rejoice with them that rejoice and to weep with them that weep, is not an easy thing for the natural man. Only the grace of God can work such sympathy in men. It is not so difficult to weep with those who are afflicted, but it is often very difficult to rejoice with those who rejoice. For instance, suppose another has received something which we very much desired, and is rejoicing over his gain; it requires much grace to rejoice with him.

Keeping the Peace—We are to live peaceably with all men if it be possible. But what is the limit of possibility? Some will say that they tried to keep peace until "forbearance ceased to be a virtue," and then they paid the troublesome one in his own coin. Many think that this verse exhorts them to hold out as long as they can, and not to take part in any disturbance until they have had great provocation. But this verse says, "as much as lieth in you, live peaceably with all men."

That is, there is to be no trouble so far as we are concerned. We cannot always keep other people from warring, but we can be at peace ourselves. "Thou wilt keep him in perfect peace, whose mind is stayed on Thee; because he trusteth in Thee." Isaiah 26:3. "Being justified by faith, we have peace with God through our Lord Jesus Christ." Romans 5:1. "Let the peace of God rule in your hearts." Colossians 3:15. "And the peace of God, which passeth all understanding, shall keep your hearts and minds through Christ Jesus." Philippines 4:7. He who has this abiding peace of God will never have any trouble with people.

Chapter 13

The Believer and the Civil Government

Owe No Man Anything—Romans 13:1-14

1 Let every soul be subject unto the higher powers. For there is no power but of God: the powers that be are ordained of God. 2 Whosoever therefore resisteth the power, resisteth the ordinance of God: and they that resist shall receive to themselves damnation. 3 For rulers are not a terror to good works, but to the evil. Wilt thou then not be afraid of the power? do that which is good, and thou shalt have praise of the same: 4 for he is the minister of God to thee for good. But if thou do that which is evil, be afraid; for he beareth not the sword in vain: for he is the minister of God, a revenger to execute wrath upon him that doeth evil.

5 Wherefore ye must needs be subject, not only for wrath, but also for conscience sake. 6 For for this cause pay ye tribute also: for they are God's ministers, attending continually upon this very thing. 7 Render therefore to all their dues: tribute to whom tribute is due; custom to whom custom; fear to whom fear; honour to whom honour.

8 Owe no man anything, but to love one another: for he that loveth another hath fulfilled the law. 9 For this, Thou shalt not commit adultery, Thou shalt not kill, Thou shalt not steal, Thou shalt not bear false witness, Thou shalt not covet; and if there be any other commandment, it is briefly comprehended in this saying, namely, Thou shalt love thy neighbour as thyself. 10 Love worketh no ill to his neighbour; therefore love is the fulfilling of the law.

11 And that, knowing the time, that now it is high time to wake out of sleep: for now is our salvation nearer than when we believed. 12 The night is far spent, the day is at hand: let us therefore cast off

the works of darkness, and let us put on the armour of light. 13 Let us walk honestly, as in the day; not in rioting and drunkenness, not in chambering and wantonness, not in strife and envying. 14 But put ye on the Lord Jesus Christ, and make not provision for the flesh, to fulfil the lusts thereof.

We come now to the second of the purely hortatory chapters of Romans. This chapter contains matter that is of the greatest importance, and which is perhaps the least regarded of any chapter in the book.

To Whom Addressed?—In studying this chapter it is necessary to remember that the Epistle is addressed to professed followers of the Lord. "Behold, thou art called a Jew, and restest in the law, and makest thy boast of God, and knowest His will," etc. Romans 2:17, 18. And again, "Know ye not, brethren (for I speak to them that know the law)." etc. Romans 7:1. The last part of the chapter also shows the same thing.

It is a mistake, therefore, to suppose that this chapter was designed to set forth the duties of earthly rulers, or as a treatise on civil government, or on the relation that the state should occupy to the church. Since it is addressed to professed Christians, it is evident that its object is simply to tell them how they ought to behave towards the governments under which they live.

All Power From God—"God hath spoken once; twice have I heard this; that power belongeth unto God." Psalm 62:11. "There is no power but of God." This is absolutely true, without any exception. The Roman power, even in the days of the infamous and brutal Nero, was as much derived from God as was the Jewish power in the days of David. When Pilate told Christ that he had power to crucify Him or to let Him go, Christ replied, "Thou couldest have no power at all against Me, except it were given thee from above." John 19:11. This fact does not, however, prove that the acts of that power were right, or that God sanctioned them.

This will be the more apparent if we take the cases of individuals. All human power comes from God. It is as true of the heathen as of Christians, that "in Him we live, and move, and have our being;" "for we are also His offspring." Acts 17:28. It can as truly be said of every individual as of governments, that they are ordained, or appointed, of God. He has a plan for every one's life.

But that does not make God responsible for all their actions, because they are free to do as they choose, and they rebel against God's plan, and pervert His gifts. The power with which the scoffer blasphemes God is as much from God as is the power with which the Christian serves Him. Yet no one can suppose that God approves of blasphemy. Even so we are not to suppose that He necessarily approves the acts of governments, simply because the powers that be are ordained of Him.

"Ordained"—Let no one entertain the idea that this word necessarily implies the imparting of some spiritual power. It means nothing more than appointed or ordered, which we find in the margin. The Greek word from which it is rendered is found in Acts 28:23, where we read that the Jews in Rome appointed a day for Paul to tell them about the gospel. It could as well be said that they "ordained" a day for him.

God Over All—"The higher powers" are not above the Most High. "Wisdom and might are His; and He changeth the times and the seasons; He removeth kings, and setteth up kings." Daniel 2:20, 21. He set Nebuchadnezzar, king of Babylon, over all the kingdoms of earth (see Jeremiah 27:5-8; Daniel 2:37, 38); but when Nebuchadnezzar arrogated to himself divine power, he was driven out among the beasts, that he might know that "the Most High ruleth in the kingdom of men, and giveth it to whomsoever He will" (Daniel 4:32).

Resisting God—Since there is no power but of God, "he that resisteth the power withstandeth the ordinance of God; and they that withstand shall receive to themselves judgment." This is a warning against rebellion and insurrection. It is God who removes kings as well as sets them up. Therefore whoever presumes to remove a king is assuming God's prerogative. It is as though he knew better than God when the government should be altered. Unless those who rise up against any earthly government can show a direct revelation to them from heaven appointing them to that work, they are setting themselves against God, by seeking to overthrow his order. They are putting themselves ahead of God.

Resisting or Overthrowing—To resist the civil authority is in the same line as seeking to overthrow it. He who opposes a power with force would overthrow it if the contest were continued and he had the power. This the followers of Christ are strictly forbidden to do.

Christ's Example—Christ suffered, "leaving us an example, that ye should follow His steps; who did no sin, neither was guile found in His mouth; who, when He was reviled, reviled not again; when He suffered, He threatened not; but committed Himself to Him that judgeth righteously." 1 Peter 2:21-23. It is worth while to remember that Christ was condemned on a political charge, and for political reasons, yet He made no resistance, although He showed that He had power to do so. See John 18:5-11; Matthew 26:51-53. It may be said that Christ knew that His hour had come. True; but He did not resist at previous times. He continually committed Himself into the hands of the Father. That is an example for His followers. If they are submissive in God's hands, they can suffer no indignity nor oppression that God does not appoint or allow; no injury can be done them before their hour comes. It is easier to profess faith in Christ than to show real faith by following His example.

Another Striking Example—Saul had been anointed king of Israel by command of God; but had afterwards been rejected because of his reckless course. Then David was anointed king in his stead. Saul was jealous of David's preferment, and sought his life. David did not resist, but fled. More than once Saul was within David's power, but David would not lift up a hand against him. If there is any excuse for resisting a ruler, David had it.

In the first place, if he had done so, it would have been only in self-defense; and, in the second place, he had already been anointed king in Saul's stead. Yet when urged even to consent to allow another to kill Saul, David said: "Destroy him not; for who can stretch forth his hand against the Lord's anointed, and be guiltless? ... As the Lord liveth, the Lord shall smite him; or his day shall come to die; or he shall descend into battle, and perish. The Lord forbid that I should stretch forth mine hand against the Lord's anointed." 1 Samuel 26:9-11. And yet Saul was a wicked man, who had cast off allegiance to God, and was not fit to rule.

Subject to God—God's word admonishes us to be subject to the powers that be, but it never countenances disobedience to God. God has never ordained any power to be above Himself. It is the height of folly for us to argue from this chapter that it is the duty of Christians to obey human laws when they conflict with the law of God. God does not grant indulgence to sin; much less does He command us to sin. We are not to be subject to the powers that be instead of to God, but because we are subject to God. "Whatsoever ye do in word or deed, do all in the name of the Lord Jesus." Colossians 3:17.

Subjection and Obedience—Ordinarily subjection implies obedience. When we read that Jesus was subject to His parents, we are sure that He was obedient to them. So when we are exhorted to be subject to the powers that be, the natural conclusion is that we are to be obedient to the laws. But it must never be forgotten that God is above all; that both individual and national power comes from Him; and that He has a right to the undivided service of every soul. We are to obey God all the time, and to be subject to human power as well, but always so that it does not involve disobedience to God.

Can Not Serve Two Masters—"No man can serve two masters. ... Ye cannot serve God and mammon." The reason is that God and mammon are opposite in their demands. Now everybody knows that there have often been human laws that conflicted with God's commandments. There was once a law in America in the days of slavery requiring every man to do all in his power to return fugitive slaves to their masters. But God's word said, "Thou shalt not deliver unto his master the servant which is escaped from his master unto thee." Deuteronomy 23:15. In that case it was impossible to obey the law of the land without disobeying God; and obedience to God made disobedience to the human law absolutely necessary. Men had to make their choice as to whom they would obey.

The Christian cannot hesitate a moment in his choice. The law that contradicts God's law is nothing. "There is no wisdom nor understanding nor counsel against the Lord." Proverbs 21:30.

"Every Ordinance of Man"—Some reader may quote 1 Peter 2:13 as opposed to this. It says, "Submit yourselves to every ordinance of man for the Lord's sake." Others may say that we are to submit to every ordinance except when it is opposed to God's law. No exception, however, is implied, nor is any necessary. Neither does the text teach obedience to human laws that contradict God's law.

The error arises from a misapprehension of the word "ordinance." It is supposed that this word means "law," but a careful reading will show anybody that this supposition is a mistake. Let us read the thirteenth and fourteenth verses of 1 Peter 2 carefully: "Submit yourselves to every ordinance of man for the Lord's sake." Well, what are these ordinances or creations to which we are to be subject? It makes no difference; to all, "whether it be to the king, as supreme; or unto governors, as unto them that are sent by him." It is very clear that the text says nothing whatever about laws, but only about rulers. The exhortation is precisely the same as that in the thirteenth of Romans.

Submissive Yet Disobedient—Let the reader follow on in the chapter last quoted from, and he will see that the submission enjoined does not involve obedience to wicked laws. We are exhorted: "Honor all men. Love the brotherhood. Fear God. Honor the king." We are to be subject to rightful authority, whether the exerciser of that authority be good and gentle, or froward. Then come the words, "For this is thankworthy, if a man for conscience toward God endure grief, suffering wrongfully." 1 Peter 2:17-19.

Now a man could not for conscience toward God endure grief, suffering wrongfully, unless conscience toward God had compelled him to disobey some command laid upon him. This statement, immediately following the exhortation to be submissive, plainly shows that disobedience is contemplated as a probability when those in authority are "froward." This is emphasized by the reference to Christ, who suffered wrongfully, yet made no resistance. "He was oppressed, and He was afflicted, yet He opened not His mouth: He is brought as a lamb to the slaughter, and as a sheep before her shearers is dumb, so He opened not His mouth." Isaiah 53:7.

He was condemned for His loyalty to the truth, which He would not compromise in the least, and yet He was submissive to the authority of the rulers. The apostle says that in this He left us an example, that we should follow in His steps.

Christians and Civil Government—"For our conversation [citizenship] is in heaven; from whence also we wait for the Saviour, the Lord Jesus Christ." Philippians 3:20. Those who through Christ have access by one Spirit unto the Father "are no more strangers and foreigners, but fellow-citizens with the saints, and of the household of God." Ephesians 2:19. Let every man concern himself with the affairs of his own country, and not with those of another. For an American to come to England and presume to lecture Parliament for the way in which it conducts the business of government, or for an Englishman to go to America and distinguish himself by his advice to the authorities, would be the height of impertinence. But if they should begin actively to interfere in the conduct of public affairs, or should stand for office, they would speedily be shown that they had no business there. Let them become naturalized, and then they may speak and act as much as they please; but then they must hold their peace if they return to the country to which they once owned allegiance. No man can be active in the affairs of two governments at the same time.

This applies to the government of heaven as related to earthly governments, as well as to different countries on earth. The one who is a citizen of the heavenly country has no business to meddle with the affairs of earthly governments. He must leave that business to those who acknowledge this earth to be their home. If earthly rulers think to regulate the affairs pertaining to the kingdom of God, they are guilty of gross presumption, to say the least. But if they may not of right presume to regulate the affairs of the kingdom of heaven, much less may the citizens of heaven interfere in the affairs of earthly kingdoms.

Making Earth Heaven—Many Christians and ministers of the gospel seek to justify their dealing in politics by saying that it is their duty to make this earth the kingdom of heaven. In a recent campaign we have heard much about "the regeneration of London," and "making London the city of God." Such language shows a grave misapprehension of what the gospel is. "It is the power of God unto salvation to every one that believeth." Romans 1:16.

Regeneration is accomplished only by the Holy Spirit working upon individual hearts, and cannot be controlled by men. The kingdoms of this world shall become the kingdoms of Christ, but only "the zeal of the Lord of hosts will perform this." Revelation 11:15; Isaiah 9:7. There will be a new earth, in which only righteousness will dwell, but it will be only after the coming of the day of the Lord, in which the elements shall melt, and ungodly men shall be burned up. 2 Peter 3:10-13. It will not be brought about by political action, even though ministers of the gospel be the politicians. The minister of the gospel has but one commission, namely, "Preach the word." In no other way in the world can men be made better. Therefore the minister who turns his attention to politics is denying his calling.

Keeping the Peace—We must needs be subject to earthly governments, for conscience sake; and for this cause also we must pay tribute and perform every duty of that nature that is laid upon us. Taxes may be heavy, and even unjust, but that does not warrant us in rebelling. The apostle James speaks to rich men who oppress the poor, and his language applies as well when they are in public office as when in private life. He says: "Ye have lived in pleasure on the earth, and been wanton; ye have nourished your hearts, as in a day of slaughter. Ye have condemned and killed the just; and he doth not resist you." James 5:5, 6.

Mark this, the just do not resist. Why not? Because of the injunction: "If it be possible, as much as lieth in you, live peaceably with all men. Dearly beloved, avenge not yourselves, but rather give place unto wrath; for it is written, Vengeance is mine; I will repay, saith the Lord." Romans 12:18, 19. As subjects of the King of peace, and citizens of His kingdom, they are bound to live peaceably with all men. Hence they cannot fight even in self-defense. In this, Christ the Prince of peace is their example.

To Whom a Terror—Only the evil workers are afraid of rulers. Well-doers have no fear. This is not because all rulers are good; for we know that many are not. "The broad empire of Rome filled the world," and the one who ruled it when Paul wrote to the Romans was the most vile and cruel of all the monsters who governed it. Nero put men to death for the mere pleasure of killing them. Well might he strike terror to the hearts of men; yet the Christians could be calm, because their trust was in God. "Behold, God is my salvation; I will trust, and not be afraid." Isaiah 12:2.

The Whole Duty of Man—"Owe no man anything, but to love one another; for he that loveth another hath fulfilled the law." "Love worketh no ill to his neighbor; therefore love is the fulfilling of the law." "Love is of God; and every one that loveth is born of God, and knoweth God." 1 John 4:7. "This is the love of God, that we keep His commandments." 1 John 5:3. To fear God and keep His commandments is the whole duty of man. Ecclesiastes 12:13.

Therefore, since he who loves his neighbor from the heart must also love God, and love is the keeping of His commandments, it is evident that the apostle has set forth in this exhortation the whole duty of man. He who heeds this exhortation can never do anything for which earthly governments can justly condemn him, even though he be ignorant of their laws. He who fulfils the law of love will never come in conflict with the powers that be. If they oppress him, they are fighting not against him but against the King whom he serves.

For Christians, Not for the Powers—Some have supposed that verses 8-10 define the limit of civil authority, and show that men may legislate concerning "the second table of the law," but concerning no other portion of the law of God. Two things kept in mind will show the fallacy of this: (1) The epistle is not addressed to rulers, but to individual Christians, as a guide for their private conduct. If the duty of rulers were here laid down, they, and not the brethren, would have been addressed. (2) "The law is spiritual," and consequently none of it is within the power of human legislation. Take the commandment, "Thou shalt not covet;" no human power could enforce that, or tell if it was violated. But that commandment is no more spiritual than the other nine. The language is addressed to the brethren, and the sum of it is this: Live in love, and you will wrong no man, and need have no fear of any rulers.

The End Approaches—The remainder of the chapter is devoted to exhortations that need no comment. Their special force is derived from the fact that "the end of all things is at hand." Therefore we should "be sober, and watch unto prayer." Although living in the night, when darkness covers the earth (Isaiah 60:2), Christians are children of the light and of the day, leaving off works of darkness.

Clothed with Christ—Those who put on the Lord Jesus Christ will not themselves be seen. Christ alone will appear. To make provision for the lusts of the flesh is most unnecessary, since the flesh ever seeks to have its lusts gratified. The Christian has need rather to take heed that it does not assert its own power, and assume control. Only in Christ can the flesh be subdued. He who is crucified with Christ, can say, "I live; yet not I, but Christ liveth in me; and the life which I now live in the flesh I live by the faith of the Son of God, who loved me, and gave Himself for me." Galatians 2:20. And in that case he will conduct himself towards rulers and private persons just as Christ did, "because as He is, so are we in this world."

Chapter 14

God Is the Only Judge

Since the fourteenth chapter consists wholly of practical instruction in Christian living, and has no direct dependence upon the exhortations that have preceded it, we need not now take time to review the previous chapters, but will proceed at once with the text. Let it not be forgotten that this chapter, as well as those which precede, is addressed to the church, and not to those who do not profess to serve the Lord. In the sixth verse it is plainly shown that all who are spoken of in this chapter are those who acknowledge God as their Lord. The chapter therefore tells how we should regard one another as:

Servants of One Common Master—Romans 14:1-13

1 Him that is weak in the faith receive ye, but not to doubtful disputations. 2 For one believeth that he may eat all things: another, who is weak, eateth herbs. 3 Let not him that eateth despise him that eateth not; and let not him which eateth not judge him that eateth: for God hath received him. 4 Who art thou that judgest another man's servant? to his own master he standeth or falleth. Yea, he shall be holden up: for God is able to make him stand.
5 One man esteemeth one day above another: another esteemeth every day alike. Let every man be fully persuaded in his own mind. 6 He that regardeth the day, regardeth it unto the Lord: and he that regardeth not the day, to the Lord he doth not regard it. He that eateth, eateth to the Lord, for he giveth God thanks; and he that eateth not, to the Lord he eateth not, and giveth God thanks. 7 For none of us liveth to himself, and no man dieth to himself. 8 For whether we live, we live unto the Lord; and whether

we die, we die unto the Lord: whether we live therefore, or die, we are the Lord's. 9 For to this end Christ both died, and rose, and revived, that He might be Lord both of the dead and living.

10 But why dost thou judge thy brother? or why dost thou set at naught thy brother? for we shall all stand before the judgment seat of Christ. 11 For it is written, As I live, saith the Lord, every knee shall bow to Me, and every tongue shall confess to God. 12 So then every one of us shall give account of himself to God. 13 Let us not therefore judge one another any more: but judge this rather, that no man put a stumbling-block or an occasion to fall in his brother's way.

The School of Christ—The church of Christ is not composed of perfect men, but of those who are seeking perfection. He is the perfect One, and He sends out the invitation: "Come unto Me, all ye that labor and are heavy laden, and I will give you rest. Take My yoke upon you, and learn of Me." Matthew 11:28, 29. Having called all to come to Him, he says, "Him that cometh to Me I will in no wise cast out." John 6:37. As one has said, "God reaches for the hand of faith in man to direct it to lay fast hold upon the divinity of Christ, that man may attain to perfection of character."

The faith may be very weak, but God does not reject him on that account. Paul thanked God that the faith of the Thessalonian brethren grew exceedingly (2 Thessalonians 1:3), which shows that they did not have perfect faith at the first. It is true that God is so good that every person ought to trust Him fully; but just because He is so good, He is very patient and forbearing with those who are not well acquainted with Him, and He does not turn away from them because they are doubtful. It is this very goodness and forbearance of God that develops perfect faith.

The Pupils Not Masters—It is not for the pupils to say who shall attend school. It is true that in this world there are schools that are exclusive, in which only a certain set of pupils are allowed. If one inferior in wealth and standing in society should seek to enter, there would be at once an uproar. The students themselves would make so strong a protest against the entrance of the newcomer, that the masters would feel obliged not to receive him. But such schools are not the schools of Christ. "There is no respect of persons with God." He invites the poor and needy, and the weak. It is He, and not the pupils, that decides who shall be admitted.

He says, "Whosoever will, let him take the water of life freely," and He asks all who hear to extend the invitation. The only qualification necessary for entering the school of Christ is willingness to learn of Him. If any man is willing to do His will, God will receive him and teach him. John 7:17. Whoever sets up any other standard, sets himself above God. No man has any right to reject one whom God receives.

Master and Servant—Christ said to His disciples: "Be not ye called Rabbi; for one is your Master; and all ye are brethren." "Neither be ye called masters; for one is your Master, even Christ." Matthew 23:8, 10. It is the master who sets the task for each pupil or servant. It is to the master that the servant looks for his reward. Therefore it is the master alone who has the right to give orders, and to pronounce judgment if there is failure. "Who art thou that judgest another man's servant?" If you have not the power to reward his success, you have not the right to judge his failures.

"God Is the Judge"—"He putteth down one, and setteth up another." Psalm 75:7. "For the Lord is our judge, the Lord is our lawgiver, the Lord is our king; He will save us." Isaiah 33:22. "There is one Lawgiver, who is able to save and to destroy; who art thou that judgest another?" James 4:12. The power to save and to destroy determines the right to judge. To condemn when one has not the power to carry the judgment into effect, is but a farce. Such an one makes himself ridiculous, to say the least.

The Spirit of the Papacy—The apostle Paul describes the apostasy as the revelation of "that man of sin," "the son of perdition; who opposeth and exalteth himself above all that is called God, or that is worshiped; so that he as God sitteth in the temple of God, showing himself that he is God," or, "setting himself forth as God." 2 Thessalonians 2:3, 4. In Daniel 7:25 the same power is described as speaking great words against the Most High, and thinking to change times and laws.

To set one's self up against or above the law of God, is the strongest possible opposition to God, and the most presumptuous usurpation of His power. The end of the power that thus exalts itself is this: to be consumed by the Spirit of Christ, and destroyed by the brightness of His coming. 2 Thessalonians 2:8.

Now read in James 4:11: "He that speaketh evil of his brother, and judgeth his brother, speaketh evil of the law, and judgeth the law; but if thou judge the law, thou art not a doer of the law, but a judge." That tells us that whoever speaks evil of his brother, or judges or sets at naught his brother, is speaking against the law of God, and sitting in judgment upon it. In other words, he is putting himself in the place and doing the work of "that man of sin." What else can result, but that he receive the reward of the man of sin? Surely there is enough in this thought to give us all pause.

We have learned that the members of the church of Christ are not judges one of another, but fellow-servants of one common Lord. We are not taught that it is a matter of indifference whether or not we keep the commandments of God—quite the contrary, since we are all to appear before the judgment seat of Christ, and be judged by them—but we are taught that in those things concerning which the law of God does not speak particularly, one man's ways are as good as another's. We learned even further that even one who may be faulty with respect to an express commandment, is not to be dealt with harshly, and condemned. Such a course cannot help one, and, besides, we have no right to do so, since we are but servants.

Living for Others—Romans 14:14-23

14 I know, and am persuaded by the Lord Jesus, that there is nothing unclean of itself: but to him that esteemeth any thing to be unclean, to him it is unclean. 15 But if thy brother be grieved with thy meat, now walkest thou not charitably. Destroy not him with thy meat, for whom Christ died. 16 Let not then your good be evil spoken of: 17 for the kingdom of God is not meat and drink; but righteousness, and peace, and joy in the Holy Ghost. 18 For he that in these things serveth Christ is acceptable to God, and approved of men.

19 Let us therefore follow after the things which make for peace, and things wherewith one may edify another. 20 For meat destroy not the work of God. All things indeed are pure; but it is evil for that man who eateth with offense. 21 It is good neither to eat flesh, nor to drink wine, nor any thing whereby thy brother stumbleth, or is offended, or is made weak. 22 Hast thou faith? Have it to thyself before God. Happy is he that condemneth not himself in that thing which he alloweth. 23 And he that doubteth is damned if he eat, because he eateth not of faith: for whatsoever is not of faith is sin.

Many errors arise from careless reading of the Bible, and from hasty conclusions from detached statements, as from wilful perversion of the word. Possibly many more are the result of lack of proper thought than of deliberate willfulness. Let us therefore always take heed how we read.

Clean and Unclean—If we consider well the subject under consideration, we shall not wrest this scripture from its connection. The thing presented from the beginning of the chapter is the case of a man with so little real knowledge of Christ that he thinks righteousness is to be obtained by the eating of certain kinds of food, or by not eating certain things. The idea clearly conveyed by the entire chapter is that it is by faith, and not by eating and drinking, that we are saved.

A little consideration of the question of clean and unclean food will help us much. There is a strange idea prevalent, to the effect that things that were at one time unfit for food are perfectly wholesome now. Many people seem to think that even unclean beasts are made clean by the gospel. They forget that Christ purifies men, not beasts and reptiles.

There were plants that were poisonous in the days of Moses, and those same plants are poisonous now. The very people who seem to think that the gospel makes everything fit to eat, would be as much disgusted at the thought of eating cats, dogs, caterpillars, spiders, flies, etc., as any Jew would have been in the days of Moses. Instead of finding that a knowledge of Christ reconciles one to such a diet, we find, on the contrary, that it is only the most degraded savages who make use of them for food, and such a diet is both a sign and cause of degradation. Enlightenment brings carefulness in the selection of food.

Now there is no one who can imagine the apostle Paul or any other person of good sense and refinement eating everything that he could possibly find on earth. Although most people think themselves wiser than God in the matter of eating and drinking, there are, as there always have been, certain things universally held to be unfit for food. Therefore when the apostle says that nothing is unclean of itself, he evidently confines his remark to those things which God has provided for man's eating. There are people whose conscience is so poorly instructed that they fear to eat even of things which God has given to be eaten; just as there are some who forbid the eating of "food which God hath created to be received with thanksgiving." 1 Timothy 4:3.

So when the apostle says, "One believeth that he may eat all things," it is evident that the "all things" does not include filth. The idea evidently is that one believes that he may eat everything that is fit to be eaten. But another, having for instance the thought that some of those things may have been devoted to an idol, fears to eat of them lest he should thereby become an idolater. The eighth chapter of 1 Corinthians makes this whole subject plain, as it runs parallel with the fourteenth of Romans.

This throws light also upon the subject of days. Since the apostle evidently confines his remarks concerning food to that which it is allowable to eat, it is more clear that those days which may be considered as all alike are those days only which God has not sanctified to Himself.

The Nature of the Kingdom—"For the kingdom of God is not meat and drink; but righteousness, and peace, and joy in the Holy Ghost." Over that kingdom Christ has been set as King, for God has said, "Yet have I set my king upon My holy hill of Zion." Psalm 2:6. Now read further the words of the Father to the Son, whom He has appointed heir of all things: "Thy throne, O God, is forever and ever: a scepter of righteousness is the scepter of Thy kingdom. Thou hast loved righteousness, and hated iniquity; therefore God, even Thy God, hath anointed Thee with the oil of gladness above Thy fellows." Hebrews 1:8, 9.

A scepter is the symbol of power. Christ's scepter is a scepter of righteousness; therefore the power of His kingdom is righteousness. He rules by righteousness. His life on earth was a perfect manifestation of righteousness, so that He rules His kingdom by the power of His life. All those who own His life are subjects of His kingdom. No other thing but the life of Christ is the badge of citizenship in the kingdom of Christ.

But with what was Christ anointed King? The text last read says that it was with "the oil of gladness." Then gladness, or joy, is a necessary part of the kingdom of Christ. It is a kingdom of joy, as well as of righteousness. Therefore it is that every subject of that kingdom must be filled with joy. "A gloomy Christian" is as much a contradiction of terms as "a cold sun." The sun is for the purpose of shedding the warmth of which it is composed; so the Christian is for the purpose of diffusing the peace and joy which is a part of his nature. The Christian is not joyful simply because he thinks that he ought to be, but because he has been translated into the kingdom of joy.

"He that in these things serveth Christ is acceptable to God, and approved of men. Let us therefore follow after the things which make for peace, and things wherewith one may edify another." He who in what things serves Christ? Why, he who serves Christ in righteousness, and peace, and joy. Or, as some translations have it, "He that thus serves Christ."

God accepts such service, and men approve. Not only do Christians approve such service, but unbelievers are constrained to approve. The enemies of Daniel were forced to bear witness to the uprightness of his life, when they said that they could find nothing against him except in the law of his God. But that very statement was an approval of the law of his God, obedience to which made him the faithful man that he was.

Unselfishness—Peace is a characteristic of the kingdom. Therefore those who are in the kingdom must follow the things which make for peace. But selfishness never causes peace. On the contrary, selfishness is always the cause of war, and inevitably produces war if it is persisted in. Therefore the subject of the kingdom must always be ready to sacrifice his own desires and ideas in behalf of others. The unselfish person will give up his own ways whenever they interfere with the peace of another.

But do not forget that the kingdom of God is righteousness as well as peace. Righteousness is obedience to the law of God; for "all unrighteousness is sin" (1 John 5:17), and "sin is the transgression of the law" (1 John 3:4). Therefore, although by the laws of the kingdom one must necessarily give up his own wishes in order not to interfere with the feelings of others, by those same laws he is precluded from giving up any of the commandments of God.

Obedience to the law of God is that which makes for peace, for we read: "Great peace have they which love Thy law." Psalm 199:165. "O that thou hadst hearkened to My commandments! Then had thy peace been as a river, and thy righteousness as the waves of the sea." Isaiah 48:18. Therefore he who is so "charitable" as to give up any portion of the law of God because some people are displeased with it, is not following the things which make for peace. On the contrary, he is rebelling against the kingdom of Christ.

This again shows us that the Sabbath of the Lord is not under consideration, as one of the things which are to be held as matters of mere personal opinion. The Christian has no option with regard to that. He must keep it. It is not one of the days which the subject of the kingdom may disregard if he wishes. It is one of the things that are obligatory.

But there are things which one has the right to do if he wishes, but which he is not obliged to do. For instance, a man has the right to eat his food with the fingers, if he wishes to; but if that annoys his companion, the law of Christ requires him not to do so. And thus it appears that the law of Christ alone, will, if carefully heeded, make a man perfectly courteous. The true Christian is a gentleman in the best sense of that word.

There are many things that are allowable, which some people with faith that is weak, because it is uninstructed, think to be wrong. Christian courtesy, as laid down in the fourteenth chapter of Romans, requires that the better-instructed person should regard the scruples of his weaker brother. To roughly ignore those scruples, although they may be destitute of reason, is not the way to help that brother into a wider liberty. On the contrary, it is the way to discourage him. "It is good neither to eat flesh, not to drink wine, nor anything whereby thy brother stumbleth, or is offended, or is made weak."

Thus it becomes evident that the fourteenth chapter of Romans is simply a lesson in Christian courtesy and helpfulness instead of teaching that the Sabbath, or anything else that pertains to the commandments of God, may be disregarded at pleasure. Consideration is to be shown for "him that is weak in the faith;" but the one who is offended by the keeping of the commandments of God, has no faith at all.

The Limitations of Conscience—"Hast thou faith? Have it to thyself before God." Faith and conscience pertain to single individuals. No man can have faith for another. No man can have faith enough to serve for two. The teaching of the Roman Church is that certain ones have had more faith than they needed, and have been more righteous than was necessary, so that they can divide with other people; but the Bible teaches that it is impossible for any man to have more faith than will serve to save himself. Therefore, no matter how well one man's faith may be instructed, no other man can be judged by it.

We hear a great deal in these days about the public conscience. We are often told that the conscience of one man is outraged by the course of another. But it is with conscience as with faith,—no man can have enough for two. The man who thinks that his conscience will serve for himself and for somebody else, has mistaken selfish obstinacy for conscience. It is this mistaken idea of conscience that has led to all the horrible persecutions that have ever been perpetrated in the name of religion.

Let Christians all understand that conscience is between themselves and God alone. They are not at liberty to impose even their freedom of conscience upon another; but by the laws of the kingdom of Christ, they are obliged even to refrain at times from exercising their own freedom, out of consideration for others. That is to say, the man who can walk fast, is to help along his weak brother, who is going the same way, but more slowly. But he is not to turn around to please somebody who is walking the other way.

Chapter 15

"Praise the Lord, All You Gentiles!"

The fourteenth chapter of Romans presented to us our duty towards those who are weak in the faith, and who have excessively conscientious scruples with regard to things that are in themselves of no consequence. We are not judges of one another, but must all appear before [Christ's] judgment seat. If we have more knowledge than our brother, we are not arbitrarily to bring him to our standard, any more than he is to bring us down to his. Our greater knowledge rather throws upon us the responsibility of exercising the greater charity and patience.

The sum of it all is contained in these verses: "For meat destroy not the work of God. All things indeed are pure; but it is evil for that man who eateth with offense. It is good neither to eat flesh, nor drink wine, nor any thing whereby thy brother stumbleth, or is offended, or is made weak. Hast thou faith? Have it to thyself before God."

The Duty of Helping One Another—Romans 15:1-7

1 We then that are strong ought to bear the infirmities of the weak, and not to please ourselves. 2 Let every one of us please his neighbor for his good to edification. 3 For even Christ pleased not Himself; but, as it is written, The reproaches of them that reproached Thee fell on Me. 4 For whatsoever things were written aforetime were written for our learning, that we through patience and comfort of the Scriptures might have hope. 5 Now the God of patience and consolation grant you to be likeminded one toward another according to Christ Jesus: 6 that ye may with one mind and one mouth glorify God, even the Father of our Lord Jesus Christ. 7 Wherefore receive ye one another, as Christ also received us, to the glory of God.

Receiving One Another—The verses composing this chapter supplement the instruction given in chapter fourteen, and are a continuation of that. Thus, that chapter opens with the exhortation, "Him that is weak in the faith receive ye." The last verse of our present study is, "Wherefore receive ye one another."

How are we to receive one another? The answer is, "As Christ also received us." This again emphasizes the statement that the apostle had not the slightest intention in any way of depreciating any one of the Ten Commandments when in the fourteenth chapter he said: "One man esteemeth one day above another: another esteemeth every day alike. Let every man be fully persuaded in his own mind."

Christ did not in the slightest degree make any concessions in the commandments in order to accommodate those whom He would receive. He said, "Think not that I came to destroy the law, or the prophets." Matthew 5:17. Again, "If ye keep My commandments, ye shall abide in My love; even as I have kept My Father's commandments, and abide in His love." John 15:10.

Christ's commandments and those of the Father are the same, because he says, "I and My Father are one." John 10:30. When a young man wished to follow him, He said to him, "Keep the commandments." Matthew 19:17. Therefore it is evident that in making concessions for the sake of peace and harmony, no concession is to be made in respect to keeping the commandments of God.

How to Please Others—This is still further shown by the exhortation, "Let every one of us please his neighbor for his good to edification." We are never exhorted to aid a brother to sin, in order to please him. Neither are we exhorted to close our eyes to a brother's sin, and allow him to go on in it without warning him, lest we displease him. There is no kindness in that. The exhortation is, "Thou shalt not hate thy brother in thine heart; thou shalt in anywise rebuke thy neighbor, and not suffer sin upon him." Leviticus 19:17. The mother who would be so fearful of displeasing her child that she would not stop it from putting its hand into the blaze, would be exhibiting cruelty instead of kindness. We are to please our neighbors, but only for their good, not to lead them astray.

Bearing Others' Weaknesses—Going back to the first verse, we find this lesson still more strongly emphasized: "We then that are strong ought to bear the infirmities of the weak, and not to please ourselves." "For even Christ pleased not Himself." Compare this with Galatians 6:1, 2: "Brethren, if a man be overtaken in a fault, ye which are spiritual, restore such on one in the spirit of meekness; considering thyself, lest thou also be tempted. Bear ye one another's burdens, and so fulfill the law of Christ." In bearing the infirmities of the weak, we are fulfilling the law of Christ. But to bear another's burdens does not mean to teach him that he can safely ignore any of the commandments. To keep the commandments of God is not a burden; for "His commandments are not grievous." 1 John 5:3.

How Christ Bears Our Burdens—Christ bears our burdens, not by taking away the law of God, but by taking away our sins, and enabling us to keep the law. "For what the law could not do, in that it was weak through the flesh, God sending His own Son in the likeness of sinful flesh, and for sin, condemned sin in the flesh; that the righteousness of the law might be fulfilled in us." Romans 8:3, 4.

He Says "Come"—One blessed thing in the service of the Lord is that He does not say, "Go," but, "Come." He does not send us away to labor by ourselves, but calls us to follow Him. He does not ask anything of us that He does not Himself do. When He says that we ought to bear the infirmities of them that are weak, we should take it as an encouragement, instead of a task laid upon us, since it reminds us of what He does for us. He is the mighty One, for we read, "I have laid help upon One that is mighty; I have exalted One chosen out of the people." Psalm 89:19. "Surely He hath borne our griefs, and carried our sorrows." "All we like sheep have gone astray; we have turned every one to his own way; and the Lord hath laid on Him the iniquity of us all." Isaiah 53:4, 6.

Why the Task Is Easy—This is what makes it easy to bear one another's burdens. If we know that Christ bears our burdens, it will become a pleasure for us to bear the burdens of others. The trouble is that too often we forget that Christ is the Burden-bearer, and, being over powered with the weight of our own infirmities, we have still less patience with those of others. But when we know that Christ is indeed the Burden-bearer, we cast our own care upon him; and then when we make the burden of another our own, he bears that too.

"The God of All Comfort"—God is "the God of patience and consolation." He is "the Father of mercies, and the God of all comfort; who comforteth us in all our tribulation, that we may be able to comfort them which are in any trouble, by the comfort wherewith we ourselves are comforted of God." 2 Corinthians 1:3, 4. He takes upon Himself all the reproaches that fall upon men. "The reproaches of them that reproached thee fell on Me." Of the children of Israel it is said, "In all their affliction He was afflicted." Isaiah 63:9. The words of Christ are, "Thou hast known My reproach, and My shame, and My dishonor." "Reproach hath broken My heart." Psalm 69:19, 20. Yet in all this there was no impatience, no murmuring. Therefore, as He has already borne the burdens of the world in the flesh, He is fully able to bear ours in our flesh, without complaining; so that we may be "strengthened with all might, according to His glorious power, unto all patience and long-suffering with joyfulness." Colossians 1:11.

The Gospel According to Moses—It is this lesson that is taught us throughout all the Scriptures: "For whatsoever things were written aforetime were written for our learning, that we through patience and comfort of the Scriptures might have hope." In the book of Job this is made manifest. "Ye have heard of the patience of Job, and have seen the end of the Lord; that the Lord is very pitiful, and of tender mercy." James 5:11. In the writings of Moses it is as clearly set forth. Christ says: "Had ye believed Moses, ye would have believed Me; for he wrote of Me. But if ye believe not the writings, how shall ye believe My words?" John 5:46, 47. If the gospel according to Moses is neglected, it will be of no use to read the gospel according to John, because the gospel cannot be divided. The gospel of Christ, like Himself, is one.

How to Receive One Another—Finally, "Receive ye one another, as Christ also received us, to the glory of God." Whom does Christ receive? "This man receiveth *sinners*." How many will He receive? "Come unto Me, *all ye* that labor and are heavy laden, and I will give you rest."

How will he receive them? "All day long have I stretched forth My hands unto a disobedient and gainsaying people." And if they come, what assurance have they? "Him that cometh to Me I will in no wise cast out." Let us learn of Him; and remember that, wherever you may open the Scriptures, they are they which testify of Him.

Standing on the Threshold—Our study of the book of Romans, while there have been many articles, has not been exhaustive. Indeed, it is impossible to have an exhaustive study of the Bible; for no matter how thoroughly we study any portion of it, we shall still find ourselves but upon the threshold. The more we study the Bible, the more will our best study seem to be only preliminary to further study that will be seen to be necessary. But although we cannot expect ever to exhaust the truth, so that we can say that we have it all, we may be sure that as far as we have gone we have only the truth. And this assurance arises not from any wisdom that we have, but solely from adhering closely to the word of God, and not allowing the alloy of human ideas to mingle with its pure gold.

"All Joy and Peace in Believing"—Romans 15:8-14

8 Now I say that Jesus Christ was a minister of the circumcision for the truth of God, to confirm the promises made to the fathers: 9 and that the Gentiles might glorify God for His mercy; as it is written,

For this cause I will confess to Thee among the Gentiles, and sing unto Thy name. 10 And again He saith, Rejoice, ye Gentiles, with His people. 11 And again, Praise the Lord, all ye Gentiles; and laud Him, all ye people. 12 And again, Esaias saith, There shall be a root out of Jesse, and He that shall rise to reign over the Gentiles; in Him shall the Gentiles trust. 13 Now the God of hope fill you with all joy and peace in believing, that ye may abound in hope, through the power of the Holy Ghost. 14 And I myself also am persuaded of you, my brethren, that ye also are full of goodness, filled with all knowledge, able also to admonish one another.

"A Minister of the Circumcision"—Jesus Christ was a minister of the circumcision. Bear this in mind. Shall we learn from it that He saves only the Jews? By no means, but we must learn from it that "salvation is of the Jews." John 4:22. "Jesus Christ our Lord" was "made of the seed of David according to the flesh." Romans 1:3. He is the "root of Jesse," which stands "for an ensign of the people," to which the Gentiles seek. Isaiah 11:10; Romans 15:12. The Gentiles who find salvation must find it in Israel. None can find it anywhere else.

"The Commonwealth of Israel"—In writing to the brethren at Ephesus, Paul refers to the time before they were converted as the time when they were "Gentiles in the flesh," and says, "At that time ye were without Christ, being aliens from the commonwealth of Israel, and strangers from the covenants of promise, having no hope, and without God in the world." Ephesians 2:11, 12.

That is, outside of Israel there is no hope for mankind. They who are "aliens from the commonwealth of Israel" are "without Christ," and "without God in the world." In Christ Jesus we are brought to God. But being brought to God we are "no more strangers and foreigners, but fellow-citizens with the saints, and of the household of God." Verses 18, 19. Therefore we have two things most clearly and positively taught, namely, That none are saved unless they are of the house of Israel; and, That none are of the house of Israel except those who are in Christ.

Confirming the Promises—"Jesus Christ was a minister of the circumcision for the truth of God, to confirm the promises made unto the fathers." That shows that all the promises of God to the fathers were made in Christ. "For all the promises of God in Him are yea, and in Him Amen." 2 Corinthians 1:20. "To Abraham and his seed were the promises made. He saith not, And to seeds, as of many; but as of one, And to thy seed, which is Christ." Galatians 3:16. There was therefore never any promise made to the fathers which was not to be obtained only through Christ, and therefore through the righteousness which is by Him.

Christ Not Divided—Jesus Christ is declared to be a minister of the circumcision. Suppose now we hold that the promises to the fathers mean the natural descendants of Abraham, Isaac, and Jacob; we should then be shut up to the conclusion that only those natural descendants—those who are circumcised—can be saved. Or, at least, we should be driven to the conclusion that Christ does something for them that He does not do for the rest of mankind.

But Christ is not divided. All that He does for one man He does for every man. All that He does for any He does through His cross; and He is crucified but once. "God so loved the world, that He gave his only begotten Son, that whosoever believeth in Him should not perish, but have everlasting life."

Therefore since Christ is the minister of the circumcision to confirm the promises made unto the fathers, it is evident that those promises included all mankind. "There is no difference between the Jew and the Greek; for the same Lord over all is rich unto all that call upon Him" Romans 10:12. "Is He the God of the Jews only? Is He not also of the Gentiles? Yes, of the Gentiles also; seeing it is one God, which shall justify the circumcision by faith, and uncircumcision through faith." Romans 3:29, 30.

The "Tabernacle of David"—At the time when the apostles and elders were assembled in Jerusalem, Peter told how he had been used by the Lord to carry the gospel to the Gentiles. Said he, "God, which knoweth the hearts, bare them witness, giving them the Holy Ghost, even as He did unto us; and put no difference between us and them, purifying their hearts by faith." Acts 15:8, 9.

Then James added, "Simeon hath declared how God at the first did visit the Gentiles, to take out of them a people for His name. And to this agree the words of the prophets; as it is written, After this I will return, and will build again the tabernacle of David, which is fallen down; and I will build again the ruins thereof, and I will set it up; that the residue of men might seek after the Lord, and all the Gentiles, upon whom My name is called, saith the Lord, who doeth all these things. Known unto God are all His works from the beginning of the world." Acts 15:14-18.

That is, the house of David is to be built up only by the preaching of the gospel to the Gentiles, and the taking from them of a people for God. And this was the purpose of God from the beginning, as the prophets witness, that through His name whosoever believeth in Him shall receive remission of sins." Acts 10:43.

"The Blessing of Abraham"—Again we read that "Christ hath redeemed us from the curse of the law, being made a curse for us; ... that the blessing of Abraham might come on the Gentiles through Jesus Christ; that we might receive the promise of the Spirit through faith." Galatians 3:13, 14. The curse that Christ was made for us, was the cross, as is stated in the words omitted from the text just quoted.

Therefore we learn that the promises to the fathers were assured only by the cross of Christ. But Christ tasted death for every man. Hebrews 2:9. He was "lifted up, that whosoever believeth in Him should not perish, but have eternal life." John 3:14, 15. Therefore the promises made to the fathers were simply the promises of the gospel, which is "to every creature." By the cross, Christ confirms the promises made to the fathers, in order "that the Gentiles might glorify God for His mercy."

"One Fold, and One Shepherd"—In the tenth chapter of John we find some of the most beautiful, tender, and encouraging words of the Lord Jesus. He is the Good Shepherd. He is the gate by which the sheep enter into the fold. He gives His life to save them. Then He says, "And other sheep I have, which are not of this fold; them also I must bring, and they shall hear My voice; and there shall be one fold, and one Shepherd." Verse 16. Therefore when His work is completed, there will be but one fold, and He will be the Shepherd. Let us see who will compose that flock.

The Lost Sheep—In the fifteenth chapter of Luke, that wonderful bouquet of blessed illustrations of the love and mercy of the Saviour, Jesus represents His work as that of the shepherd going to seek the lost and wandering sheep. Now who are the sheep that He is seeking? He himself gives the answer: "I am not sent but unto the lost sheep of the house of Israel." Matthew 15:24. This is emphatic. Therefore it is evident that all the sheep whom He finds, and whom He brings back to the fold, will be Israel. And so it is just as evident that the "one fold" will be the fold of Israel. There will be no other fold, since it is to be "one fold." And He will be the Shepherd. Today, as well as in the days of old, we may pray, "Give ear, O Shepherd of Israel, thou that leadest Joseph like a flock; thou that dwellest between the cherubim, shine forth." Psalm 80:1.

The Characteristic of the Sheep—Those who are following Christ are His sheep. But He has "other sheep." There are many who are not now following Him, who are His sheep. They are lost and wandering, and He is seeking them.

What determines who are His sheep? Hear Him tell: "The sheep hear His voice." "Other sheep I have, which are not of this fold; them also I must bring, and they shall hear My voice." "Ye believe not, because ye are not of My sheep, as I said unto you. My sheep hear My voice." John 10:3, 16, 26, 27. When He speaks, those who are His sheep will hear His voice, and come to Him. The word of the Lord is the test as to who are His sheep. Every one therefore who hears and obeys the word of the Lord is of the family of Israel; and those who reject or neglect the word, are eternally lost. "If ye be Christ's, then are ye Abraham's seed, and heirs according to the promise." Galatians 3:29.

"One Faith"—We may now stop to see how this that the apostle has said connects with what he has said in the fourteenth chapter, about Christ's being the minister of the circumcision, to confirm the promises made to the fathers, in order that the Gentiles might glorify God.

"Him that is weak in the faith receive ye, but not to doubtful disputations." Mark this: They who are to be received "as Christ also received us to the glory of God," are those who have the faith. Now there is but "one faith," as there is but "one Lord." Ephesians 4:5. And faith comes by hearing the word of God. Romans 10:17.

Since there is to be but one fold, and Christ, the one Shepherd, is not divided, there must be no division in the fold. Disputings, which come from human wisdom and human ideas, are to be left out, and the word of God alone followed. That allows of no disputing, since it tells ever one and the same thing. This is the rule: "Wherefore laying aside all malice, and all guile, and hypocrisies, and envies, and all evil speakings, as newborn babes, desire the sincere milk of the word, that ye may grow thereby; if so be ye have tasted that the Lord is gracious." 1 Peter 1:1-3.

Faith, Hope, Joy, and Peace—"Now the God of hope fill you with all joy and peace in believing, that ye may abound in hope, through the power of the Holy Ghost." Here we have faith and hope, joy and peace. The God of hope is to fill us with all joy and peace in believing, and this is to be by the power of the Holy Ghost. This connects the present instruction with that of the fourteenth chapter, where we are told that "the kingdom of God is not meat and drink; but righteousness, and peace, and joy in the Holy Ghost."

Paul's Successful Gospel Outreach—
Romans 15:15-33

15 Nevertheless, brethren, I have written the more boldly unto you in some sort, as putting you in mind, because of the grace that is given to me of God, 16 that I should be the minister of Jesus Christ to the Gentiles, ministering the gospel of God, that the offering up of the Gentiles might be acceptable, being sanctified by the Holy Ghost.

17 I have therefore whereof I may glory through Jesus Christ in those things which pertain to God. 18 For I will not dare to speak of any of those things which Christ hath not wrought by me, to make the Gentiles obedient, by word and deed. 19 Through mighty signs and wonders, by the power of the Spirit of God; so that from Jerusalem, and round about unto Illyricum, I have fully preached the gospel of Christ.

20 Yea, so have I strived to preach the gospel, not where Christ was named, lest I should build upon another man's foundation: 21 But as it is written, To whom He was not spoken of, they shall see: and they that have not heard shall understand. 22 For which cause also I have been much hindered from coming to you. 23 But now having no more place in these parts, and having a great desire these many years to come unto you; 24 whensoever I take my journey into Spain, I will come to you: for I trust to see you in my journey, and to be brought on my way thitherward by you, if first I be somewhat filled with your company.

25 But now I go unto Jerusalem to minister unto the saints. 26 For it hath pleased them of Macedonia and Achaia to make a certain contribution for the poor saints which are at Jerusalem. 27 It hath pleased them verily; and their debtors they are. For if the Gentiles have been made partakers of their spiritual things, their duty is also to minister unto them in carnal things. 28 When therefore I have performed this, and have sealed to them this fruit, I will come by you into Spain. 29 And I am sure that, when I come unto you, I shall come in the fulness of the blessing of the gospel of Christ.

30 Now I beseech you, brethren, for the Lord Jesus Christ's sake, and for the love of the Spirit, that ye strive together with me in your prayers to God for me; 31 that I may be delivered from them that do not believe in Judaea; and that my service which I have for Jerusalem may be accepted of the saints; 32 that I may come unto you with joy by the will of God, and may with you be refreshed. 33 Now the God of peace be with you all. Amen.

The Gospel Commission—When Jesus was about to leave this world, He told His disciples that they should first receive power by the Holy Spirit, and then, said He, "Ye shall be witnesses unto me both in Jerusalem, and in all Judea, and in Samaria, and unto the uttermost part of the earth." Acts 1:8. "To the Jew first, and also to the Greek," but to all alike, and the same gospel to all. So Paul declared that his work as a minister of the gospel consisted in "testifying both to the Jews, and also to the Greeks, repentance toward

God, and faith toward our Lord Jesus Christ." Acts 20:21. So in our text he tells us that as "the minister of Jesus Christ to the Gentiles, ministering the gospel of God," he had "through mighty signs and wonders, by the power of the Spirit of God" "fully preached the gospel of Christ" "from Jerusalem and round about unto Illyricum."

Partaking the Same Spiritual Things—The apostle, speaking of his desire to visit the Romans, said that he hoped to see them when he took his journey into Spain. "But now," said he, "I go unto Jerusalem to minister unto the saints. For it hath pleased them of Macedonia and Achaia to make a certain contribution for the poor saints which are at Jerusalem. It hath pleased them verily; and their debtors they are. For if the Gentiles have been made partakers of their spiritual things, their duty is also to minister unto them in carnal things."

A very simple statement, but it shows that the Gentiles received nothing spiritual except that which came from the Jews. The spiritual things of which the Gentiles had been made partakers came from the Jews, and were ministered to them by Jews. Both partook of the same spiritual meat, and therefore the Gentiles showed their gratitude by ministering to the temporal necessities of the Jews. So here again we see but one fold and one Shepherd.

The God of Israel—Many times in the Bible God is declared to be the God of Israel. Peter, full of the Holy Spirit, immediately after the healing of the lame man, said to the people, "The God of Abraham, and of Isaac, and of Jacob, the God of our fathers, hath glorified his Son Jesus." Acts 3:13. Even in this age, therefore, God is identified as the God of Abraham, Isaac, and Jacob,—the God of Israel.

God desires to be known and remembered, and so we read His words, "Speak thou also unto the children of Israel, saying, Verily My Sabbaths ye shall keep; for it is a sign between Me and you throughout your generations, for a perpetual covenant. It is a sign between Me and the children of Israel forever; for in six days the Lord made heaven and earth, and on the seventh day He rested, and was refreshed." Exodus 31:13, 16, 17. God is the God of Israel. True, He is the God of the Gentiles also, but only as they accept Him, and become Israel through the righteousness by faith. But Israel must keep the Sabbath. It is the sign of their connection with God.

Chapter 16

Personal Greetings

Two-thirds of the last chapter of Romans consists of greetings:
"Greet Priscilla and Aquila my helpers in Christ Jesus." "Likewise greet the church that is in their house." "Greet Mary, who bestowed much labor on us." "Salute Andronicus and Junia, my kinsmen." "Greet Amplias my beloved in the Lord." "Salute Urbane, our helper in Christ, and Stachys my beloved." "Salute Trypena and Tryphosa, who labor in the Lord." "Salute Philologus, and Julia, Nercus, and his sister, and Olympas, and all the saints which are with them."

And so the list runs, including both men and women impartially. Let one but read that blessed list, realizing that it shows not only the largeness and heartiness of Paul's sympathy, but also the special care which the Holy Spirit has for each individual member of the household of faith, singling them out by name, and there will be no questioning as to why such things were written.

A Significant Omission—But one thing is very significant, and that is the fact that there is no mention of Peter, who is claimed to have been "the first Bishop of Rome." We may sometimes learn as much by what the Bible does not say as by what it does say. From what is not said in this place we may learn that so far from being Bishop of Rome, Peter was not in Rome at all when Paul wrote, and that if he was ever in Rome it was after the Epistle to the Romans was written, and long after the church was established and flourishing there.

It is most certain that in saluting the members of the church by name Paul would not have omitted the name of the chief person in it, whose hospitality he had once shared in Jerusalem for fifteen days. Of course there is abundance of the most positive evidence that neither the church of Christ nor the church of Rome was founded upon Peter; but if there were no other, this testimony of the sixteenth chapter of Romans would be sufficient to settle the matter.

In Conclusion—Romans 16:24-27

24 The grace of our Lord Jesus Christ be with you all. Amen. 25 Now to Him that is of power to stablish you according to my gospel, and the preaching of Jesus Christ, according to the revelation of the mystery, which was kept secret since the world began, 26 but now is made manifest, and by the scriptures of the prophets, according to the commandment of the everlasting God, made known to all nations for the obedience of faith: 27 to God only wise, be glory through Jesus Christ for ever. Amen.

What a Magnificent Conclusion! It reaches from eternity to eternity. The gospel of God is the thing of the ages. It was kept secret in the mind of God from times eternal. Christ "was foreordained before the foundation of the world." 1 Peter 1:19, 20. But now the mystery is "made manifest." Not simply is it made manifest by the preaching of the apostles, but "according to the commandment of the everlasting God," "by the scriptures of the prophets" it is "made known to all nations, for the obedience of faith."

The gospel plan originated in the mind of God in the eternity of the past. Patriarchs, prophets and apostles have worked in unison in making it manifest; and "in the ages to come" it will be both the science and the song of the redeemed "of all nations, and kindreds, and people, and tongues," who shall gather with Abraham, Isaac and Jacob in the kingdom of God, and will say, "Unto Him that loved us, and washed us from our sins in His own blood, and hath made us kings and priests unto God and His Father, to Him be glory and dominion for ever and ever. Amen."

Appendix A

Notes from Chapters

The following supplemental references have been included in this new edition of Waggoner's great Bible study on the Book of Romans to provide the reader with cross reference materials for additional study. These ancillary readings provide evidence that the Holy Spirit inspired E.J. Waggoner with a message that was consistent throughout not only his work, but also was supported in the work of A.T. Jones and Ellen G. White. The "most precious message" of Christ and His righteousness contained in these studies is the "third angel's message in verity" that "God commanded to be given to the world" (see Ellen G. White, *Review and Herald*, April 1, 1890; *Ellen G. White 1888 Materials*, pp. 1336–1338).

1. From page 47 : However, in that day, as in all other days, it is not upon *men themselves* that God's wrath is visited; but upon the *sins* of men, and upon men only as they are *identified with their sins*. "For the wrath of God is revealed from heaven," not against all ungodly men, not against all unrighteous men, but "against all ungodliness and unrighteousness of men." (Romans 1:18). And only as the man *clings to his ungodliness*, only as he *holds down* the truth in unrighteousness, shall it be that the wrath of God will be revealed from heaven against him: and even then not against *him* primarily, but against the *sin to which he clings*, and will not leave. And as he has thus made his choice, *clinging fast* to his choice, he must take the consequences of his choice, when his choice shall have reached its ultimate. So it is written, and I read it again, "The wrath of God is revealed from heaven against all ungodliness and unrighteousness of men, who hold the truth [who hold down, who press back the truth] in unrighteousness." ...

Yet, as already stated, the wrath of God is not *primarily against them*, but *against the thing which they love*; against the t*hing which they cling to*, and *will not be separated from*. And at last, in that great day when the judgment is set, and on the right and on the left are all the people who have ever lived, those on the left will depart "into everlasting fire, prepared"—not for them, but "for the devil and his angels." The Lord has done His utmost that they might never see it. He gave His Son to save them, that they might never know it. It was not prepared for *them*. He does not desire that they should be lost; but they have to go there because there is the company which they have chosen; that is the place with which they have connected themselves, and from which they would not be separated. Therefore, He says, "depart from Me, ye cursed, into everlasting fire, prepared for the devil and his angels."

Not prepared for *you*. God in that day,—the Lord Jesus Christ in that hour,—when that word shall be spoken, will be just as sorrowful as He was in the hour of the cross. He will be just as sorry that these have to go into that place [the lake of fire], which was not prepared for *them*, as He was in the hour of the cross. It is not His pleasure that any should be there. They are there because of that sin to which they have inseparably joined themselves. And that being their irrevocable choice, they simply have the opportunity now of receiving indeed, and to the full, that which they have chosen. They always had their choice; they made their choice; they stuck to their choice: and when they receive the consequences of their choice, indeed there is no room for complaint. God has done all that He could do, but they would not have it.

So, though it is a fact that the Lord does not desire any of this to come upon any man, yet, as "God is a consuming fire," that is the way that He must come. Being a consuming fire, and coming as He is, He comes in flaming fire to visit upon wickedness that which is due; and whoever is joined with the wickedness has to go the same way. (A.T. Jones, *Review and Herald*, January 24, 1899).

2. From page 56 : Faith justifies. Faith makes righteous. If the people had had Abraham's faith, they would have had the righteousness that he had. At Sinai the law, which was "spoken because of transgression," would have been in their *hearts*. They would not have needed to be awakened by its thunders to a sense of their condition. …

The apostle when speaking of Hagar and Sarah says: "These women are two covenants." These two covenants exist today. The two covenants are not matters of time, but of condition [of the heart]. Let no man flatter himself that he cannot be bound under the old covenant, thinking that its time is past. … So the covenant from Sinai holds all who adhere to it in bondage "under the law," while the covenant from above gives freedom, not freedom from *obedience* to the law, but freedom from *disobedience* to it. (E.J. Waggoner, *The Glad Tidings*, p. 100, 2016 CFI edition).

3. From page 62 : In the depths of heathenism, men who have had no knowledge of the written law of God, who have never even heard the name of Christ, have been kind to His servants, protecting them at the risk of their own lives. Their acts show the working of a divine power. The Holy Spirit has implanted the grace of Christ in the heart of the savage, quickening his sympathies contrary to his nature, contrary to his education. The "Light which lighteth every man that cometh into the world" (John 1:9), is shining in his soul; and this light, if heeded, will guide his feet to the kingdom of God. (Ellen G. White, *Christ's Object Lessons*, p. 385).

4. From page 65 : Every question of truth and error in the long-standing controversy has now been made plain. The results of rebellion, the fruits of setting aside the divine statutes, have been laid open to the view of all created intelligences. The working out of Satan's rule in contrast with the government of God has been presented to the whole universe. Satan's own works have condemned him. God's wisdom, His justice, and His goodness stand fully vindicated. It is seen that all His dealings in the great controversy have been conducted with respect to the eternal good of His people and the good of all the worlds that He has created. "All Thy works shall praise Thee, O Lord; and Thy saints shall bless Thee." Psalm 145:10. The history of sin will stand to all eternity as a witness that with the existence of God's law is bound up the happiness of all the beings He has created. With all the facts of the great controversy in view, the whole universe, both loyal and rebellious, with one accord declare: "Just and true are Thy ways, Thou King of saints."

Before the universe has been clearly presented the great sacrifice made by the Father and the Son in man's behalf. (Ellen G. White, *The Great Controversy*, pp. 670, 671).

5. From page 66 : Since the best efforts of a sinful have not the least effect toward producing righteousness, it is evident that the only way it can come to him is as a gift. (E.J. Waggoner, *Christ and His Righteousness*, p. 68, 1999 edition).

6. From page 68 : The impossibility of good deeds proceeding from a sinful heart is thus forcibly illustrated by the Saviour, "For every tree is known by his own fruit. For of thorns men do not gather figs, nor of a bramble-bush gather they grapes. A good man out of the good treasure of his heart bringeth forth that which is good; and an evil man out of the evil treasure of his heart bringeth forth that which is evil; for of the abundance of the heart his mouth speaketh." Luke 6:44, 45. That is to say, a man cannot do good until he first becomes good. Therefore, deeds done by a sinful person have no effect whatever to make him righteous, but, on the contrary, coming from an evil heart, they are evil and so add to the sum of his sinfulness. Only evil can come from an evil heart, and multiplied evil cannot make one good deed; therefore, it is useless for an evil person to think to become righteous by his own efforts. He must first be made righteous before he can do the good that is required of him and which he wants to do.

The case, then, stands thus:

1) The law of God is perfect righteousness, and perfect conformity to it is demanded of everyone who shall enter the kingdom of heaven.
2) But the law has not a particle of righteousness to bestow upon any man, for all are sinners and are unable to comply with its requirements.

No matter how diligently nor how zealously a man works, nothing that he can do will meet the full measure of the law's demands. It is too high for him to attain to; he cannot obtain righteousness by the law. "By the deeds of the law there shall no flesh be justified [made righteous] in His sight." What a deplorable condition! We must have the righteousness of the law or we cannot enter heaven, and yet the law has no righteousness for one of us. It will not yield to our most persistent and energetic efforts the smallest portion of that holiness without which no man can see the Lord. (Ibid., p. 62).

Since the best efforts of a sinful man have not the least effect toward producing righteousness, it is evident that the only way it can come to him is as a gift. That righteousness is a gift is plainly stated by Paul in Rom. 5:17: "For if by one man's offense death reigned by one; much more they which receive abundance of grace and of the gift of righteousness shall reign in life by One, Jesus Christ." It is because righteousness is a gift that eternal life, which is the reward of righteousness, is the gift of God, through Jesus Christ our Lord. (Ibid., p. 68).

The convicted sinner tries again and again to obtain righteousness from the law, but it resists all his advances. It cannot be bribed by any amount of penance or professedly good deeds. But here stands Christ, "full of grace" as well as of truth, calling the sinner to Him. At last the sinner, weary of the vain struggle to get righteousness from the law, listens to the voice of Christ and flees to His outstretched arms. Hiding in Christ, he is covered with His righteousness, and now behold! he has obtained, through faith in Christ, that for which he has been vainly striving. He has the righteousness which the law requires, and it is the genuine article, because he obtained it from the Source of Righteousness, from the very place whence the law came. And the law witnesses to the genuineness of this righteousness. It says that so long as the man retains that, it will go into court and defend him against all accusers. It will witness to the fact that he is a righteous man. With the righteousness which is "through the faith of Christ, the righteousness which is of God by faith" (Phil. 3:9), Paul was sure that he would stand secure in the day of Christ.(Ibid., pp. 70, 71).

Surely if He wishes to pardon the injury done Himself, He has the right; and more because He vindicates the integrity of His law, by submitting in His own Person to the penalty which was due the sinner. (Ibid., p. 71).

7. From page 69 : Well, there we have seen the heathen idea openly, broadly, and rawly, just as it is. Now let us see what this same thing is, as it stands before the world, professing to be justified by faith. And that is as it is manifested in the papacy. For the papacy is the very incarnation of Satan and this mind of self. For he "opposeth and exalteth himself above all that is called God or that is worshipped." And all this under the name and form of Christianity; all this as a counterfeit of the truth. ...

I want you to see what the Roman Catholic idea of justification by faith is, because I have had to meet it among professed Seventh-day Adventists the past four years right straight through. These very things, these very expressions that are in this Catholic book, as to what justification by faith is and how to obtain it, are just such expressions as professed Seventh-day Adventists have made to me as to what justification by faith is.

I want to know how you and I carry a message to this world, warning them against the worship of the beast, when we hold in our very profession the doctrines of the beast. Can it be done? [Congregation: "No."] And so I call your attention to this tonight so you may see just what it is, and so that, if possible, knowing what it is to start with, knowing that it is papal, knowing that it is the beast, you will let it go because it is that, even if you are not ready to believe in justification by faith, indeed, even if you cannot see that, as some are unable to, as God gives it. Now, if we find out that it is papal, I hope those who have held that, or expressed it at any rate, whatever they have held, will be willing to let it go any way. (A.T. Jones, *1893 General Conference Bulletin*, [February 14, 1893], p. 261 original pagination).

8. From page 71 : "Do you mean to teach universal salvation?" someone may ask. We mean to teach just what the Word of God teaches,—that "the grace of God hath appeared, bringing salvation to all men." Titus 2:11, R.V. God has wrought out salvation for every man, *and has given it to him*; but the majority spurn it, and throw it away. The judgment will reveal the fact that full and complete salvation was given to every man, and that the lost have deliberately thrown away their birthright possession. (*The Glad Tidings*, pp. 13, 14).

9. From page 74: The covenant (that is, the promise of God to give men the whole earth made new after having made them free from the curse) was "previously ratified by God." Christ is the Surety of the new covenant, even the everlasting covenant. "For all the promises of God find their Yes in Him. That is why we utter the Amen through Him, to the glory of God." 2 Corinthians 1:20. In Him we have obtained the inheritance (1 Peter 1:3, 4), for the Holy Spirit is the firstfruits of the inheritance, and the possession of the Holy Spirit is Christ Himself dwelling in the heart by faith. God blessed Abraham, saying, "In thy seed shall all the kindreds of the earth be blessed," and this is fulfilled in Christ, whom God has sent to bless us in turning us away from our iniquities. Acts 3:25, 26, KJV.

It was the oath of God that ratified the covenant made to Abraham. That promise and that oath to Abraham become our ground of hope, our strong consolation. They are "sure and steadfast" (Hebrews 6:19), because the oath sets forth Christ as the pledge, the surety, and "He always lives" (Hebrews 9:25). He upholds all things by His word of power. Hebrews 1:3. "In Him all things hold together." Colossians 1:17. Therefore "when God desired to show more convincingly to the heirs of the promise the unchangeable character of His purpose, He interposed with an oath." Hebrews 6:17. This is our consolation and hope in fleeing for refuge from sin. *He pledged His own existence, and with it the entire universe, for our salvation.* Surely a firm foundation for our hope is laid in His excellent Word!

Do not forget as we proceed that the covenant and the promise are the same thing, and that it conveys land, even the whole earth made new, to Abraham and his children. Remember also that since only righteousness will dwell in the new heavens and the new earth, the promise includes the making righteous of all who believe. This is done in Christ, in whom the promise is confirmed. Now, "no one annuls even a man's will, or adds to it, once it has been ratified." How much more must this be the case with God's "will"!

Therefore, since perfect and everlasting righteousness was assured by the "will" made with Abraham, which was also confirmed in Christ, by the oath of God, it is impossible that the law which was spoken four hundred and thirty years later could introduce any new feature. The inheritance was given to Abraham by promise. But if after four hundred and thirty years it should develop that now the inheritance must be gained in some other way, then the promise would be of no effect, and the "will" or covenant would be made void. But that would involve the overthrow of God's government and the ending of His existence. For He pledged His own existence to give Abraham and his seed the inheritance and the righteousness necessary for it. "For the promise, that he should be the heir of the world, was not to Abraham, or to his seed, through the law, but through the righteousness of faith." Romans 4:13, KJV. The gospel was as full and complete in the days of Abraham as it has ever been or ever will be. No addition to it or change in its provisions or conditions could possibly be made after God's oath to Abraham. Nothing can be taken away from it as it thus existed, and not one thing can ever be required from any man more than what was required of Abraham. (*The Glad Tidings*, pp. 71-73).

10. From page 75 : See Note 5, p. 217.

11. From page 83 : So, then, they who are of faith are keepers of the law; for they who are of faith are blessed, and those who do the commandments are blessed. By faith they do the commandments. Since the gospel is contrary to human nature, we become doers of the law not by doing but by believing. If we *worked* for righteousness, we would be exercising only our own sinful human nature, and so would get no nearer to righteousness, but farther from it. But by *believing* the "exceeding great and precious promises," we become "partakers of the divine nature" (2 Peter 1:4, KJV), and then all our works are wrought in God. "The Gentiles, which followed not after righteousness, have attained to righteousness, even the righteousness which is of faith. But Israel, which followed after the law of righteousness, hath not attained to the law of righteousness. Wherefore? Because they sought it not by faith, but as it were by the works of the law. For they stumbled at that stumbling stone; as it is written, Behold, I lay in Sion a stumbling stone and rock of offense: and whosoever believeth on Him shall not be ashamed." Romans 9:30-33, KJV.

No one can read Galatians 3:10 carefully and thoughtfully without seeing that the curse is transgression of the law. Disobedience to God's law is itself the curse; for "sin came into the world through one man and death through sin." Romans 5:12. Sin has death wrapped up in it. Without sin death would be impossible, for "the sting of death is sin." 1 Corinthians 15:56. "For all who rely on works of the law are under a curse." Why? Because the law is a curse? Not by any means: "The law is holy, and the commandment is holy and just and good." Romans 7:12. Why, then, are all who rely on works of the law under a curse? Because it is written, "Cursed be everyone who does not abide by all things written in the book of the law, and do them."

Mark it well: They are not cursed because they *do* the law, but because they do *not* do it. So, then, we see that relying on works of the law does not mean that one is doing the law. No! "The carnal mind is enmity against God: for it is not subject to the law of God, neither indeed can be." Romans 8:7, KJV. *All* are under the curse, and he who thinks to get out by his own works, remains there. Since the "curse" consists in not continuing in all things that are written in the law, therefore the "blessing" means perfect conformity to the law. (*The Glad Tidings*, pp. 56, 57).

12. From page 86 : Look to Abraham, brought up a heathen, and see what God did for him and what He promised to him, confirming it with an oath by Himself, for your sake. You think that it would make no difference with the Lord if you were lost, because you are so obscure and insignificant. Why, your worthiness or unworthiness has nothing whatever to do with the matter. The Lord says, "I, even I, am He that blotteth out thy transgressions for Mine own sake, and will not remember thy sins." Isaiah 43:25. For His own sake? Yes, certainly; because of His great love wherewith He loved us, He has placed Himself under bonds to do it. He swore by Himself to save all that come to Him through Jesus Christ. and "He abideth faithful; He cannot deny Himself." 2 Timothy 2:13.

Think of it; God swore by Himself! That is, He pledged Himself, and His own existence, to our salvation in Jesus Christ. He put Himself in pawn. His life for ours, if we are lost while trusting Him. His honour is at stake. It is not a question of whether or not you are insignificant and of little or no worth. He Himself says that we are "less than nothing." Isaiah 40:17. He says that "we have sold ourselves for naught," (Isaiah 52:3) which shows our true value; but we are redeemed without money, even by the precious blood of Christ. The blood of Christ is the life of Christ; and the life of Christ bestowed upon us makes us partakers of His worth. The only question is, Can God afford to break or forget His oath? And the answer is that we have "two immutable things, in which it was impossible for God to lie." Hebrews 6:18. (E.J. Waggoner, *The Everlasting Covenant*, pp. 87, 88, 2002 edition).

Note also again that the covenant made with Abraham, and confirmed in Christ by God's oath, is that which gives us our hope in Christ. It was confirmed by the oath, in order that we might have strong consolation in fleeing for refuge to lay hold on the hope set before us. The sum of the covenant was righteousness by faith in Jesus crucified, as shown by the words of Peter: "Ye are the children of the prophets, and of the covenant which God made with our fathers, saying unto Abraham, And in thy seed shall all the kindreds of the earth be blessed. Unto you first God, having raised up His Son Jesus, sent Him to bless you, in turning away every one of you from his iniquities." Acts 3:25, 26. (Ibid., p. 212).

It was the oath of God that ratified the covenant made to Abraham. That promise and that oath to Abraham become our ground of hope, our strong consolation. They are "sure and steadfast" (Hebrews 6:19), because the oath sets forth Christ as the pledge, the surety, and "He always lives" (Hebrews 9:25). He upholds all things by His word of power. Hebrews 1:3. "In Him all things hold together." Colossians 1:17. Therefore "when God desired to show more convincingly to the heirs of the promise the unchangeable character of His purpose, He interposed with an oath." Hebrews 6:17. This is our consolation and hope in fleeing for refuge from sin. He pledged His own existence, and with it the entire universe, for our salvation. Surely a firm foundation for our hope is laid in His excellent Word!

Do not forget as we proceed that the covenant and the promise are the same thing, and that it conveys land, even the whole earth made new, to Abraham and his children. Remember also that since only righteousness will dwell in the new heavens and the new earth, the promise includes the making righteous of all who believe. This is done in Christ, in whom the promise is confirmed. Now, "no one annuls even a man's will, or adds to it, once it has been ratified." How much more must this be the case with God's "will"! Therefore, since perfect and everlasting righteousness was assured by the "will" made with Abraham, which was also confirmed in Christ, by the oath of God, it is impossible that the law which was spoken four hundred and thirty years later could introduce any new feature. The inheritance was given to Abraham by promise. But if after four hundred and thirty years it should develop that now the inheritance must be gained in some other way, then the promise would be of no effect, and the "will" or covenant would be made void. But that would involve the overthrow of God's government and the ending of His existence. For He pledged His own existence to give Abraham and his seed the inheritance and the righteousness necessary for it. "For the promise, that he should be the heir of the world, was not to Abraham, or to his seed, through the law, but through the righteousness of faith." Romans 4:13, KJV. The gospel was as full and complete in the days of Abraham as it has ever been or ever will be. No addition to it or change in its provisions or conditions could possibly be made after God's oath to Abraham. Nothing can be taken away from it as it thus existed, and not one thing can ever be required from any man more than what was required of Abraham. (*The Glad Tidings*, pp. 72, 73).

13. From page 90 : And "whatever does not proceed from faith [believing with the heart] is sin." Romans 14:23. Therefore, all the efforts of men to keep the law of God by their own power, no matter how earnest and sincere they may be, can never result in anything but imperfection—sin.

When the question came up in Jerusalem, Peter said to those who would have been justified by their own works instead of by faith in Christ, "Now therefore why tempt ye God, to put a yoke upon the neck of the disciples, which neither our fathers nor we were able to bear?" Acts 15:10, KJV.

This yoke was a yoke of bondage, as is shown by Paul's words that the "false brethren" slipped in "to spy out our freedom which we have in

Christ Jesus, that they might bring us into bondage." Galatians 2:4. Christ gives freedom from sin. His life is "the perfect law of liberty." "Through the law comes knowledge of sin" (Romans 3:20), but not freedom from sin. "The law is holy, and the commandment is holy and just and good" (Romans 7:12) because it gives the knowledge of sin by condemning it. It is a signpost which points out the way, but it does not carry us. It can tell us that we are out of the way, but Jesus Christ alone can make us walk in it, for He is the way. Sin is bondage. Only those who keep the commandments of God are at liberty (Psalm 119:45); and the commandments can be kept only by faith in Christ (Romans 8:3, 4).

Therefore whoever induces people to trust in the law for righteousness without Christ simply puts a yoke upon them and fastens them in bondage. When a man convicted by the law is cast into prison, he cannot be delivered from his chains by the law which holds him there. But that is no fault of the law. Just because it is a good law, it cannot say that a guilty man is innocent. (Ibid., p. 32).

14. From page 90 : The earth fresh and new from the hand of God, perfect in every respect, was given to man for a possession. Genesis 1:27, 28, 31. Man sinned and brought the curse upon himself. Christ has taken the whole curse, both of man and of all creation, upon Himself. He redeems the earth from the curse, that it may be the everlasting possession that God originally designed it to be; and He also redeems man from the curse, that he may be fitted for the possession of such an inheritance. This is the sum of the gospel. "The free gift of God is eternal life in Jesus Christ our Lord." Romans 6:23. This gift of eternal life is included in the promise of the inheritance, for God promised the land to Abraham and to his seed for "an everlasting possession." Genesis 17:8. It is an inheritance of righteousness, because the promise that Abraham should be heir of the world was through the righteousness of faith. Righteousness, eternal life, and a place in which to live eternally—these are all in the promise, and they are all that could possibly be desired or given. To redeem man, but to give him no place in which to live, would be an incomplete work. The two actions are parts of one whole. The power by which we are redeemed is the power of creation, by which the heavens and the earth are made new. When all is accomplished, "there shall be no more curse." Revelation 22:3, KJV. (Ibid., pp. 70, 71).

15. From page 104 : It follows, then, that as the issue of one misdeed was condemnation for all men, so the issue of one just act is acquittal and life for all men. For as through the disobedience of the one man the many were made sinners, so through the obedience of the One Man the many were will be made righteous. Romans 5:18, The New English Bible (Oxford University Press, 1970).

16. From page 104 : "Christ redeemed us from the curse of the law." Some who superficially read this rush off frantically exclaiming, "We don't need to keep the law, because Christ has redeemed us from the curse of it," as though the text said that Christ redeemed us from the curse of obedience. Such read the Scriptures to no profit. The curse, as we have seen, is disobedience: "Cursed be everyone who does not abide by all things written in the book of the law, and do them." Therefore Christ has redeemed us from disobedience to the law. God sent forth His Son "in the likeness of sinful flesh and for sin, ... in order that the just requirement of the law might be fulfilled in us." Romans 8:3, 4.

Someone may lightly say, "Then we are all right; whatever we do is right so far as the law is concerned, since we are redeemed." It is true that all are redeemed, but not all have accepted redemption. Many say of Christ, "We will not have this Man to reign over us," and thrust the blessing of God from them. But redemption is for all. All have been purchased with the precious blood—the life—of Christ, and all may be, if they will, free from sin and death. By that blood we are redeemed from "the futile ways inherited from your fathers." 1 Peter 1:18. (*The Glad Tidings*, pp. 60, 61).

17. From page 104 : The blessing has come upon all men. For "as by the offense of one judgment came upon all men to condemnation; even so by the righteousness of One the free gift came upon all men unto justification of life." Romans 5:18, KJV. God, who is no respecter of persons, "has blessed us in Christ with every spiritual blessing in the heavenly places." Ephesians 1:3. The gift is ours to keep. *If anyone has not this blessing, it is because he has not recognized the gift, or has deliberately thrown it away.*

"Christ redeemed us from the curse of the law," from sin and death. This He did by "being made a curse for us," and so we are freed from all necessity of sinning. Sin can have no dominion over us if we accept Christ in truth and without reserve. This was just as much a present truth in the days of Abraham, Moses, David, and Isaiah, as it is today. (Ibid., p. 66).

18. From page 105 : It is true that God will by no means clear the guilty; He could not do that and still be a just God. But He does something which is far better: He removes the guilt, so that the one formerly guilty does not need to be cleared—he is justified, and counted as though he never had sinned. (*Christ and His Righteousness*, p. 72).

19. From page 106 : Discussions may be entered into by mortals strenuously advocating creature merit, and each man striving for the supremacy, but they simply do not know that all the time, in principle and character, they are misrepresenting the truth as it is in Jesus. They are in a fog of bewilderment. They need the divine love of God which is represented by gold tried in the fire; they need the white raiment of Christ's pure character; and they need the heavenly eyesalve that they might discern with astonishment the utter worthlessness of creature merit to earn the wages of eternal life. ...

I ask, How can I present this matter as it is? The Lord Jesus imparts all the powers, all the grace, all the penitence, all the inclination, all the pardon of sins, in presenting *His* righteousness for man to grasp by living faith—which is also the gift of God. If you would gather together everything that is good and holy and noble and lovely in man and then present the subject to the angels of God as acting a part in the salvation of the human soul or in merit, the proposition would be rejected as treason. Standing in the presence of their Creator and looking upon the unsurpassed glory which enshrouds His person, they are looking upon the Lamb of God given from the foundation of the world to a life of humiliation, to be rejected of sinful men, to be despised, to be crucified. Who can measure the infinity of the sacrifice!

Christ for our sakes became poor, that we through His poverty might be made rich. And any works that man can render to God will be far less than nothingness. My requests are made acceptable only because they are laid upon Christ's righteousness. The idea of doing anything to merit the grace of pardon is fallacy from beginning to end. "Lord, in my hand no price I bring, simply to Thy cross I cling." (Ellen G. White, *Faith and Works*, pp. 23, 24).

20. From page 113 : Now is your will submitted to God for Him to use as He pleases and you have no objection to raise at all; you have no thought or inclination to use it your way; you want Him to do His way, and that is all you care for? Is that so? Is your will there?

Are any here in whom it is not so? You just go and tell the Lord all about it. Tell Him, "Lord, I submit everything to Thee; everything goes; nothing stays; I do not retain a single thing; all is gone; everything, will and all—to Thee, that Thou mayest use it both to will and to do." Brethren, we every one need to do just that, here, each day. The Lord wants to come in here in just the way that will let Him in.

But as long as I reserve some of my will, I will go my way in spite of myself, I cannot have God use me fully. He cannot come in fully, Christ cannot come in fully, unless there is a full submission to Him. Let there be some dying here. Let there be some actual dying to self. That is what it means; it means death: and of course people never struggle to die. They struggle to stay alive, if there are any struggles.

Bear in mind that it is not enough to "want" to die. Go ahead and die; that is what the Lord wants. Says one, How shall I do that? He tells how: "Reckon ye also yourselves to be dead indeed." Dead indeed. Brother Durland read to us here yesterday, "He that is dead is freed from sin." It is so. "Reckon ye also yourselves to be dead indeed unto sin," and God will furnish the fact. The point is, brethren, we need to get acquainted with the Lord. The trouble is, people are not personally acquainted with the Lord and do not know how these things are with Him. (A.T. Jones, *1893 General Conference Bulletin*, [February 20, 1893], p. 299, original pagination).

21. From page 117 : What do we learn from this?—That they who know the righteousness of God are those in whose heart is His law, and therefore that the law of God is the righteousness of God.

This may be proved again, as follows:—"All unrighteousness is sin." 1 John 5:17. "Whosoever commiteth sin transgresseth also the law; for sin is the transgression of the law." 1 John 3:4. Sin is the transgression of the law, and it is also unrighteousness; therefore sin and unrighteousness are identical. But if unrighteousness is transgression of the law, righteousness must be obedience to the law. Or, to put the proposition into mathematical form:—

Unrighteousness = sin. John 5:17.

Transgression of the law = sin. 1 John 3:4.

Therefore, as two things that are equal to the same thing are equal to each other, we have:—

Unrighteousness = transgression of the law.

which is a negative equation. The same thing, stated in positive terms, would be:—

Righteousness = obedience to the law.

Now what law is it obedience to which is righteousness and disobedience to which is sin? It is that law which says, "Thou shalt not covet;" for the Apostle Paul tells us that this law convinced him of sin. Romans 7:7. The law of Ten Commandments, then, is the measure of the righteousness of God. Since it is the law of God and is righteousness, it must be the righteousness of God. There is, indeed no other righteousness.

Since the law is the righteousness of God—a transcript of His character—it is easy to see that to fear God and keep His commandments is the whole duty of man. Ecclesiastes 12:13. (*Christ and His Righteousness*, pp. 55, 56).

22. From page 117 : Who are under the curse? "All who rely on works of the law." Note that it does not say that those who do the law are under the curse, for that would be a contradiction of Revelation 22:14, KJV: "Blessed are they that do His commandments that they may have right to the tree of life, and may enter in through the gates into the city." "Blessed are those whose way is blameless, who walk in the law of the Lord!" Psalm 119:1. (*The Glad Tidings*, pp. 55, 56).

So we see that the just, or righteous, man is the man who *obeys* the law, and to be justified is to be made a *keeper* of the law. Right doing is the end to be obtained, and the law of God is the standard. "The law worketh wrath," because "all have sinned," and "the wrath of God cometh on the children of disobedience." How shall we become doers of the law and thus escape wrath, or the curse? The answer is, "He who through *faith* is righteous shall live." By faith, not by works, we become doers of the law! "With the heart man believeth *unto righteousness*." Romans 10:10, KJV. That no man is justified by the law in the sight of God is evident. How? From this, that "the just shall live by faith." If righteousness came by works, then it would not be by faith; "if it is by grace, it is no longer on the basis of works; otherwise grace would no longer be grace." Romans 11:6. "To him that worketh is the reward not reckoned of grace, but of debt. But to him that worketh not, but believeth on Him that justifieth the ungodly, his faith is counted for righteousness." Romans 4:4, 5, KJV.

There is no exception, no halfway working. It is not said that some of the just shall live by faith, or that they shall live by faith and works; but simply, "the just shall live by faith." And that proves righteousness comes not by their own works. All of the just are *made* just and *kept* just by faith alone. This is because the law is so holy. It is greater than can be done by man; only divine power can accomplish it; so by faith we receive the Lord Jesus, and He lives the perfect law in us. (Ibid., pp. 58, 59).

23. From page 125 : See Note 20, page 227.

24. From page 130 : "And the Lord descended in the cloud, and stood with him there, and proclaimed the name of the Lord. And the Lord passed by before him, and proclaimed, The Lord, The Lord God, merciful and gracious, long-suffering, and abundant in goodness and truth, keeping mercy for thousands, forgiving iniquity and transgression and sin, and that will by no means clear the guilty." Exodus 34:5-7.

This is God's name. It is the character in which He reveals Himself to man, the light in which He wishes men to regard Him. But what of the declaration that He "will by no means clear the guilty"? That is perfectly in keeping with His longsuffering, abundant goodness and His passing by the transgression of His people. It is true that God will by no means clear the guilty. He could not do that and still be a just God. But He does something which is far better. He removes the guilt, so that the one formerly guilty does not need to be cleared—he is justified and counted as though he never had sinned. (*Christ and His Righteousness*, p. 72).

"Hereby perceive we the love of God, because He laid down His life for us: and we ought to lay down our lives for the brethren. ... Beloved, let us love one another: for love is of God; and every one that loveth is born of God, and knoweth God. He that loveth not knoweth not God; for God is love." 1 John 3:16; 4:7, 8.

www.ingramcontent.com/pod-product-compliance
Lightning Source LLC
Chambersburg PA
CBHW020420010526
44118CB00010B/343